A
HISTORY
OF
DANGEROUS
ASSUMPTIONS

Published in the UK by Unicorn
an imprint of the Unicorn Publishing Group LLP, 2021
5 Newburgh Street
London W1F 7RG

www.unicornpublishing.org

Every effort has been made to trace copyright holders and to obtain
their permission for the use of copyrighted material. The publisher
apologises for any errors or omissions and would be grateful to be
notified of any corrections that should be incorporated in future
reprints or editions of this book.

10 9 8 7 6 5 4 3 2 1

ISBN 978-1-913491-89-5

Typesetting by Vivian@Bookscribe

Printed in Malta by Gutenberg Press Ltd

FROM THE WOODEN HORSE OF TROY TO
THE DAWN OF THE TWENTY-FIRST CENTURY

A
HISTORY
OF
DANGEROUS
ASSUMPTIONS

OVER 200 INTRIGUING AND ILLUMINATING
CASES LINKED BY THE MYSTERIOUS
MISCHIEF OF ASSUMPTION

JOHN MOLESWORTH

UNICORN

CONTENTS

Why I have compiled this history ------------------------------ 10

PART ONE: CHRONOLOGICAL

Assumption in Ancient Greece ------------------------------ 13
The Garden of Eden ------------------------------------ 16
Hubris in the Book of Proverbs --------------------------- 16
The Wooden Horse of Troy, *c.* 1180 BC --------------------- 16
Xerxes the Great, 480 BC --------------------------------- 18
Sun Tzu, Fifth Century BC -------------------------------- 19
Plato's *Dialogues*, from 399 BC -------------------------- 20
A Flat Earth? -- 20
Ambiguity of the Oracles --------------------------------- 21
Hannibal's Crossing of the Alps, 218 BC ------------------- 22
The Birth of Christianity --------------------------------- 23
Pliny the Younger --------------------------------------- 26
Weakness of the Later Roman Empire: the Emperor Valerian,
    AD 253–268 --------------------------------------- 27
The Invention of Chess ----------------------------------- 28
Ockham's Razor --- 29
The Middle Ages -- 29
An Architect of the Renaissance and his Enemies, 1462 ------- 31
Richard III and Henry VII: history written by the victor ------- 33
Shakespearean Tragedy ----------------------------------- 33
The Scottish Play: *Macbeth*, 1606 ----------------------- 33
Miguel de Cervantes: *Don Quixote*, 1605, 1615 ------------- 34
Sir Francis Bacon, 1561–1626 ---------------------------- 36
Sir Thomas Browne, *Pseudodoxia Epidemica*, 1646 --------- 37
René Descartes, 1644 ------------------------------------ 37

Baruch Spinoza, 1677 --------------------------------------- 38

John Milton: *Paradise Lost*, 1667 ----------------------------- 39

Pierre Bayle, 1647–1706 ------------------------------------- 39

Louis XIV: the Decision of 16 November 1700 ------------------ 42

The Loss of Gibraltar, 1704 ---------------------------------- 44

The Path to Moscow I: Charles XII of Sweden, 1708–09 ----------- 45

The Quebec Expedition, 1711 --------------------------------- 50

The Elusive Northwest Passage -------------------------------- 53

Louis XV's 'Deerpark' --------------------------------------- 56

Charles VII, Holy Roman Emperor, 1742 ----------------------- 56

Collapse of a Vast Assumption, 1755 -------------------------- 57

Voltaire, Defender of Free Speech, 1758 ----------------------- 58

Parliament and the North American Colonies, 1763–1783 --------- 59

Jean-Jacques Rousseau, 1712–1783 ---------------------------- 60

J.W. von Goethe: *The Sorrows of Young Werther*, 1774 ------------- 62

Edward Gibbon, 1776 --------------------------------------- 62

Louis XVI: the Flight to Varennes, 21 June 1791 ---------------- 64

Joseph Haydn: *Mass in Troubled Times*, 1798 ------------------- 65

Jane Austen: *Northanger Abbey*, 1799 ------------------------- 66

J.W. von Goethe: *Faust, Part One*, 1808 ---------------------- 70

The Path to Moscow II: Napoleon Bonaparte, 1812 --------------- 70

Jane Austen: *Emma*, 1815 ----------------------------------- 73

Thomas Carlyle and the Historian's Illusion, 1830 --------------- 77

Dr David Strauss: Biblical Prophecy and Exegesis, 1835 ----------- 77

Legend and Myth -- 80

Lord John Russell, an Assumption in Himself, 1838 -------------- 81

The First Anglo-Afghan War, 1839–1842 ----------------------- 82

Marxism, 1848 --- 83

Mazeppa, 1852 -- 83

Lady Dedlock's Fatal Assumption, 1852 ----------------------- 85

Pioneer Alpine Mountaineering, 1854 ------------------------- 86

Alexander Bain: *The Emotions of the Will*, 1859 --------------------- 87

Charles Darwin: *On the Origin of Species*, 1859 -------------------- 87

John Stuart Mill: *On Liberty*, 1859 ----------------------------- 88

Charles Dickens: *Great Expectations*, 1860 ----------------------- 90

The Battle of Bull Run, June 1861 ------------------------------ 92

Professor Tyndall, 1861 --------------------------------------- 93

Abraham Lincoln Provoked by his Generals, 1862–3 -------------- 94

The Matterhorn Illusion, 1864 --------------------------------- 96

Discovery of the Alpine Winter, 1864 -------------------------- 97

The Staplehurst Accident, 1865 -------------------------------- 98

Victorian Banking, 1866 ------------------------------------- 100

Mr Casaubon in *Middlemarch*, 1871 --------------------------- 100

The Menheniot Accident, 1873 --------------------------------- 101

The Battle of the Little Bighorn, 1876 ------------------------ 102

The Tay Bridge Disaster, 28 December 1879 -------------------- 102

Dr Arthur Conan Doyle and the Science of Deduction, from 1881 -- 105

Paradoxical Words of Oscar Wilde ---------------------------- 111

The Public Moods of the Later Nineteenth Century--------------- 112

Diary of a German Prince, 1898 ------------------------------- 113

A Book about Assumptions, 1902 ------------------------------ 113

Pioneer Alpine Skiing, 1902 --------------------------------- 113

Ski Racing before the First World War ------------------------ 114

Military Hubris of the Russian Empire, 1905------------------- 115

Pioneer Mountaineering on Ski, 1908, 1912 -------------------- 117

A Tribute to Sherlock Holmes? ------------------------------- 121

Assumptions in the Sherlock Holmes Stories ------------------- 121

The Question of Female Suffrage, 1899–1914------------------- 122

The Shift in National Moods, 1914 --------------------------- 124

The Sinking of the *Titanic*, April 1912 --------------------- 125

John Buchan: *The Thirty-Nine Steps*, 1914 ------------------- 126

An Agent of the Kaiser, 1914 -------------------------------- 127

A Reasonable Assumption, August 1914 ----------------------- 128

The Schlieffen-Moltke Plan, 1914 ----------------------------- 129

'Over by Christmas', 1914 ------------------------------------ 133

Working Assumptions in War, 1916 ---------------------------- 133

How the United States Entered the War, 1917 ----------------- 134

Sir Arnold Bax: *November Woods*, 1917 ---------------------- 134

The Armistice, 1918 and the Treaty of Peace, 1919 ----------- 135

The Abermule Disaster, 1921---------------------------------- 138

Good Advice, 1923--- 140

Invention of the Modern Slalom Race, 1924 ------------------ 140

Sir George Jumps to a Conclusion, 1925 --------------------- 141

The Murder of Roger Ackroyd, 1926 ------------------------ 142

G.K. Chesterton, 1927--------------------------------------- 142

Dr Herbert Sumsion, 1928------------------------------------ 145

The 'Cambridge Five'-- 146

The Mirage of Boa Vista, 1933 ------------------------------ 146

An Abdication and an Assumption, 1936 --------------------- 148

Winston Churchill in the Thirties -------------------------- 149

Persuasion Methods of Adolf Hitler ------------------------- 151

The Propaganda of Dr Goebbels ----------------------------- 151

Hitler's 'Foot in the Door': Winter 1933 ------------------- 154

The Burning of the Reichstag, 27 February 1933 ------------- 161

Churchill, a Voice in the Wilderness ----------------------- 162

A Fortnight at a Time with Churchill, 1936–39 -------------- 163

Assumptions of Neville Chamberlain, 1938–40 --------------- 164

A Battleship Sunk in Scapa Flow, 1939 ---------------------- 166

Scharnhorst and *Gneisenau:* the Channel Dash, 1942 ------ 167

The Path to Moscow III: what did Hitler learn from Charles XII

and Bonaparte? --- 169

Hubris of the Japanese in the Pacific Theatre: Battle of the

Coral Sea, 1942 -- 172

The Battle of Midway, 1942 --------------------------------- 174

The Fall of Singapore, 1942 -------------------------------- 175

Another Angle on Hubris: C.S. Lewis, 1943 --------------------- 176

D-Day, 1944 --- 176

'Over by Christmas': Arnhem, September 1944 ----------------- 180

The Twilight of Dr Goebbels, 1945 --------------------------- 182

A Double View of German History --------------------------- 183

Churchill's Speech at Zürich, 1946 --------------------------- 184

A Collection of Generalisations, 1949 ------------------------- 185

Assumption with a Capital 'A': the Blessed Virgin Mary, 1950 ------ 186

'Home by Christmas': General MacArthur, 1950 ----------------- 186

The Path to the Treaty of Rome, 1957 ------------------------ 187

The Cuban Crisis, 1962 ------------------------------------ 188

The Image of President Kennedy, 1961–63 --------------------- 189

Robert Fogel, a Pioneer of Data-led History, 1964 --------------- 189

A School Prize --- 191

The *Torrey Canyon*, 18 March 1967: the first super-tanker disaster --- 191

The United Kingdom Joins the European Project, 1973–75 --------- 193

Chesapeake Bay Collision, 1978 ----------------------------- 194

The Hitler Diaries, 1983 ----------------------------------- 195

The Reith Lectures, 1985: too much politics? ------------------- 196

After the Treaty of Rome, 1957–1997 ------------------------ 198

Marine Safety, 1996 -------------------------------------- 198

Daniel Kahneman: *Thinking, Fast and Slow*, 2011 --------------- 199

Miscellany of assumptions encountered in the last two decades

Useful Advice --- 205

Issues in Ambridge -- 205

Fatal Assumption Within a Family ---------------------------- 205

Party Wall Problem --------------------------------------- 206

'When They Didn't Call Back…' ------------------------------- 206

Marriage and Relationship ------------------------------------ 207

Homeopathy -- 207

Health Screening --- 208

Sad Moment on a Northern Fellside -------------------------- 208

An Avalanche in Scotland ----------------------------------- 209

An Illusion of Rising Ground ------------------------------- 211

An Illusion in Skiing -------------------------------------- 212

The Qualified Pilot Assumption ----------------------------- 212

The Kittyhawk Exchange ------------------------------------ 212

Patriotism --- 213

The European Union -- 214

Richard III and the Mystery of the Two Princes ------------- 216

Are 'Working Assumptions' Dangerous? ---------------------- 217

Guilty Until Proved Innocent – Bishop George Bell ---------- 217

Assumptions in the Boeing 737 MAX Disasters, 2018–19 ------- 218

PART TWO: NON-CHRONOLOGICAL

1. Assumptions from Misleading Language -------------------- 222

2. Hubris in Large Organisations -------------------------- 224

3. Free speech in Universities ---------------------------- 226

4. The Vocabulary of Assumption -------------------------- 230

To summarise --- 235

Sources and Further Reading ------------------------------ 237

WHY I HAVE COMPILED
THIS HISTORY

From Hannibal's crossing of the Alps, to Bonaparte's march on Moscow; from the hubris of Icarus and Phaeton, to the toppling towers of the Tay Bridge; from the maddening phantoms of a Northwest Passage, to the sinking of the Titanic; from the Schlieffen Plan, to the delusions of D-Day; from Jean-Jacques Rousseau to Sherlock Holmes, this book aspires to demonstrate throughout history the danger of assumptions; to recognise their mysterious mischief; and, perhaps, to offer some kind of solution.

When an individual makes an assumption that turns out be false, it would seem there has been a gap in their thinking, a lack of evidence, an unwarranted confidence that something was the case. It seems that we make assumptions quickly and unconsciously. They are the opposite of 'calculation'.

The phrase 'jumping to conclusions'– one of the most vivid synonyms of 'assumption', and there are many – implies both the speed and the gap.

An assumption may remain a private thought, or appear on a page or screen. It can be heard as speech. I knew a submarine commander, the late Jolyon Waterfield, who described spoken assumption as 'opening your mouth before engaging brain'.

DIFFERENT TYPES Accurate assumptions are a regular and useful mechanism of human thought, but are not the subject of this book. Nor, for the most part, are the legions of 'working assumptions', consciously made, though these can be treacherous if left too long to their own devices.

What I am interested in are the false assumptions, that, sooner or later, are found out. In more dramatic cases they may be 'exploded'. False assumptions can be troublesome, undermining, embarrassing, the list is endless; at their worst they can be dangerous almost without limit.

THIS BOOK The stories, crises and incidents that I have compiled are presented in fairly ruthless chronological order, which can make for striking contrast, such as Bonaparte's fatal Russian expedition followed by the misunderstandings of life in a Surrey village.

This book is an experiment in finding out if the subject is worthwhile. It does not attempt to be dogmatic, or encyclopaedic. Indeed, there is an embarrassing dearth of examples from the thousand years of the Middle Ages. Inevitably the selection of examples often reflects my own interests: literature, mountains... And you, Reader, may sometimes reasonably question whether an assumption was really involved, as the unconscious working of the mind must often remain a mystery.

At first, I *assumed* that someone, somewhere must have already written about this problem. Well, there are those noble minds who over the centuries have enquired into the operations of the mind and established themselves as foes of assumption. But of a historical survey of the subject I have found no trace.

Much of the book had been completed, when I discovered Daniel Kahneman's *Thinking, Fast and Slow,* published in 2011. The insights and discoveries of this eminent psychologist take their place as an essential and valuable moment in this history.

I am compiler rather than author, so most of this book consists of the knowledge and opinions of historians, philosophers, novelists, journalists, essayists and many other wielders of the pen or tappers of the keyboard. My text is mostly formed from such multiple sources and expressed in my own words. If I presume to offer my own opinion, I make that clear.

PART ONE
CHRONOLOGICAL

ASSUMPTION IN ANCIENT GREECE To the Greeks the term *hubris* evolved to mean an insolent pride and presumption towards the gods, a wrongful action against the divine order. The bearer, and victim, of hubris – rich or powerful or over-successful – experienced an excessive self-confidence and a delusion of god-like grandeur. He, or she, might easily succumb to the mixed motives of fawning advisors. Later, this might develop into suspicion and mistrust of others.

Hubris is important in this history because it is a general assumption of greater status than is merited, but it's also a perilous state of mind that is vulnerable to the making of further assumptions – and in situations where the stakes can be particularly high.

The sudden reversal of fortune – the turning point – that sooner or later follows hubris was termed *peripeteia* (Gk. *peri* around, *peteia* falling), when Fate catches up, and things come crashing down around you.

The final downfall of the victim of hubris was made manifest by the righteous indignation of the goddess of retribution, *Nemesis* (Gk. *nemo* give what is due, in other words 'had it coming to them'). The indignation was felt at the breaching of limits; even the gods had to respect the boundaries drawn by the Fates. Nemesis brings down all immoderate good fortune, checks the presumption that attends it, and is the punisher of extraordinary crimes.

In Greek tragedy the refrain 'Too late I understand' is often heard. In Rome the triumph of a general is moderated by the words 'Remember you are mortal', whispered in the ear of the triumphant one. But classical hubris wasn't just a weakness of the ancient world, but a dangerous, recurring affliction that seems to be alive and well in our own days.

Some victims of classical hubris:

Arachne was a shepherd's daughter, a gifted weaver but boastful, even to the extent of challenging the skills of Athene, the goddess of crafts as well as wisdom. Shocked and enraged by Arachne's presumption – and the flawless quality of her work – Athene strikes her three times on the head with the shuttle. Arachne hangs herself in terror and shame, but still lives on, transformed by Athene into a spider, still weaving. The first written account of this myth was given by the poet Ovid, in exile from the reign of Augustus.

Icarus was the son of Daedalus, a highly skilled craftsman of great renown, who had built a labyrinth for King Minos of Crete. To retain the secret of its design, the King had imprisoned father and son in a tall tower. Daedalus eventually hit on a way to escape, by constructing wings from dropped bird feathers. The wings would be held together by wax – distinctly worrying I'd have thought. What sort of wax was it? No doubt a rather stronger substance than we are familiar with. But it could still be melted, so Daedalus warned his son not to fly too high, as the sun's rays could disintegrate the wings into a cloud of floating avian plumage.

The hubris of Icarus is seen in two ways: in not respecting the advice of his father, and in becoming over-excited by his ability to fly. Soon, young Icarus was keeping dangerous dizzy company with Helios, the sun god, whose chariot surged across the sky, whose crown radiated sunlight. The boy was at an altitude far above his usual station in life. The wax melts, his wings fall away; Icarus plunges to the waves and drowns.

A not-dissimilar fate awaited **Phaeton**, the son of Helios, who demanded to drive the chariot for a day, but was completely unable – as his father had warned – to control the mighty steeds that pulled it. Phaeton thus subjected the earth to sudden and capricious climate disasters, as the erratic course of the sun-chariot alternately scorched or froze the unhappy lands below. Obviously this state of affairs could not be allowed to continue. Zeus struck the chariot down with a thunderbolt.

Phaeton did not survive. But, bearing in mind his reputation as the most reckless driver the world has ever known, it seems a little surprising that his name was given in the eighteenth century to a successful open carriage, and by the early automobile industry to an elegant open touring car.

Salmoneus was King of Elis and founder of the city of Salmone. He was also arrogant and presumptuous, desiring that his people should worship him as Zeus and make sacrifices to him. Good luck with that! To intensify this bizarre idea he constructed a bridge of brass that would make a sound like thunder as he drove across in his chariot. The unpleasant effect of this was heightened by the resounding boom of cauldrons trailing behind. While this appalling racket was going on, fake lightning was conjured up by the hurling of torches. Such presumption could not be tolerated and Salmoneus and the city were destroyed, most appropriately, by Zeus himself, with another of those useful thunderbolts.

And more briefly:

Cassiopeia This vain queen, the wife of King Cepheus of Ethiopia, boasts that she, and her daughter Andromeda, are more beautiful than the sea-nymphs, the fifty Nereids. Poseidon gets to hear of this, and punishes her hubris in a grotesque way. This is reflected in the five-star shape of the constellation that still bears her name.

Oedipus In his pride and over-confidence, swollen by his success in answering the riddle of the Sphinx and becoming thereby the saviour of Thebes, Oedipus believes that he can avoid his own fatal destiny. This had already been prophesied on his visit to Delphi, where he asked the oracle who his real parents were. But the only answer he ever received was, that he shall kill his father and marry his mother… which he did.

Tantalus abuses the hospitality of his father Zeus by his theft of ambrosia and nectar, by the theft of a golden dog, and by indulging in the taboo atrocity of eating his own son, Pelops. Tantalus is thrown down to Tartarus where he is condemned to dwell in a pool, from which he can never reach the fruits that dangle above him, nor drink of the water that sinks away at his every approach.

Odysseus displays hubris in several episodes of the Odyssey, his long return journey from Troy to Ithaca, his island home. And he had stolen from the temple of Troy the Palladion of Athene, a sacred statue. But for this act of hubris he was forgiven by the goddess of wisdom, who was his protector.

THE GARDEN OF EDEN Hubris in aspiring to rise to a higher or god-like level is associated with Adam and Eve failing to obey the command of God: that they eat not from the Tree of Knowledge.

HUBRIS AS IT APPEARS IN THE PROVERBS OF SOLOMON 16:18 Pride goes before destruction, a haughty spirit before a fall.

THE WOODEN HORSE OF TROY, c. 1180 BC This story of trickery certainly involves a great and puzzling assumption by the city of Troy. Why did they allow the giant wooden horse, with its hidden elite of Greek warriors, to pass through the city walls? Why was there no investigation as to what might be found inside?

Well, such a very old story is likely to have evolved into a mixture of legend, myth and history. The original tale may have been factually overridden over hundreds of years of oral tradition. There are theories that the 'horse' may have been a battering ram, a ship or an earthquake. But as a metaphor it survives yet, and is often referred to in military history and elsewhere.

But taking the story just as we find it in Virgil and Homer, I humbly submit a possible explanation.

It would seem that King Priam and the citizenry both accepted the story of one Sinon, a cousin of Odysseus, who had been left behind by the now-departed Greeks. Sinon explained that the Greeks had had enough of the ten-year siege, and after the death of Achilles were ready to return home. And the horse? Oh, well, that was just a peace offering to the goddess Athene, in reparation for a statue stolen by Odysseus from her temple. Why was the horse so large? Well, to prevent it being taken *into* Troy; if it entered Troy then Athene would promote the city across Asia and Greece, explained Sinon.

At this point the Trojan priest Laocoon rushes down to the assembly of people and warns them in the strongest terms that this is all a trick of Odysseus: you fools, the Greeks will return, there are men hiding inside the horse, it is a machine to spy upon us, it will fall upon the walls, Sinon's talk sounds just like Odysseus! Laocoon couldn't have been clearer. Thus his famous utterance: 'Timeo Danaos et dona ferentes': 'I fear the Greeks even when they are bearing gifts.' But two sea serpents sent by Poseidon rise from the sea and fall upon the priest and his two sons, who they entwine in their coils and throttle to death.

King Priam's daughter Cassandra, the soothsayer that can never be believed – because of the curse laid upon her by Apollo – also predicts, in the same vein as Laocoon, that the Greeks will return. And the Trojans do not believe her. The gruesome fate of Laocoon and his sons suggests that it might be unwise to act on the priest's warning. Do then the King and populace find themselves drawn towards a coherent pleasing picture, a comforting assumption, a Troy achieving peace at last, with Athene's support – if the offering of the horse is taken into their city? Was this warming prospect too hard to resist? Perhaps to check the contents of the horse of peace may have been to risk the disfavour of the goddess.

The horse is drawn inside the walls.

Outside the city Sinon lights a beacon at midnight to signal to distant Agamemnon that Troy will soon be open. Within the dark city the warriors leap from the horse and the gates start to creak…

XERXES THE GREAT, 480 BC The invasion of Greece by the million-strong multi-ethnic army of the Persian Empire is an historic example of great hubris. In Herodotus' account, written some fifty years later, he mentions numerous omens of Xerxes' hubristic state, including the presence of the untrustworthy Mardonius. Particularly bizarre was the whipping of the waters of the Hellespont, punishment for their destruction of the bridges Xerxes had constructed. Was there some symbolic value in this? Could it have been a legend arising from the frequent use of whips to force the pace of troops and engineers marching towards Greece?

At first Xerxes' army succeeded in Greece; Athens was destroyed on his orders. What he wanted now was 'a decisive victory' – well, don't they all! But such victories are not so easy to arrange. And by some trick of misinformation the Greek general Themistocles may have excited Xerxes to move too soon towards the victory he needed.

Very little seems to be known about the details of the Battle of Salamis, but what is clear is that the Persians took a risk in bringing their vastly greater fleet into the narrow twisting Straits of Salamis – just where the Greeks had been waiting for them. The high point of Xerxes' hubris was his ordering a throne to be built on Mount Aigaleo, from where he could watch the progress of his presumed 'victory', and reward commanders who showed especial valour. But overcrowding in the constricted waters cramped the attack of the Persians and much of their force was neutralised. The Greeks were able to pick them off one by one, as it were.

Salamis was the sudden reversal of Xerxes' fortune, the *peripeteia*. A splendid canvas of this throne of hubris was painted by Wilhelm von

Kaulbach in the nineteenth century: *The Wrath of Xerxes*, a rare depiction of a great assumption exploding in full view.

After this defeat Xerxes retreated to the north and back across the Hellespont, before the Greeks could close it.

SUN-TZU, FIFTH CENTURY BC *The Art of War* by the Chinese general Sun-tzu is one of the most highly respected books ever written. His insights are still admired and used today. He proposed that it is possible to win a battle before you have to fight it, and that real victory lies in not having to fight at all.

The last chapter of *The Art of War* deals with intelligence matters. He declares that military success is dependent on knowledge of yourself, your aims and your resources, and knowledge of the enemy, his aims and resources. Without that knowledge, you are left guessing and making dubious assumptions.

Useful knowledge of such crucial matters can only be obtained from other men. Thus intelligence through spying is essential. There are five types of spy, who must all be working at the same time to confuse the enemy with an incomprehensible body of information.

Sun-tzu's conclusion is that 'All warfare is based on deception.' Spying is so important that the cleverest minds of the army must be employed and paid well.

Nevertheless, we shall encounter in later centuries dismal campaigning into which the clear rays of Sun-tzu's advice have been unable to penetrate, hubristic commanders being deaf to advice, and liable to lose any clear understanding of themselves, let alone of the enemy.

In warfare, then, there is a great need to know the assumptions of your enemy, and to be alert to assumptions in turn foisted upon you. Deception in warfare is a vast theme in itself, and has been extensively written about. It isn't the main theme of this book, but I have dealt with it up to a point because it often exploits assumptions that have already been made.

PLATO'S *DIALOGUES*, FROM 399 BC These Athenian dialogues seem to be the first accounts of discussion and interview known in Western literature. They owe a great deal to the philosopher Socrates (470–399 BC), whose ideas are mainly known through the medium of Plato's writing.

We can see that Socrates does not see discussion as an argument that must be won; or a matter of pressure and raised voices; or a way of rapidly reaching some conclusion. Instead he listens carefully to what others have to say, asks questions and creates an atmosphere in which the other person can begin to see for himself some of the weaknesses of his own position. He thus gains a better understanding of difficult problems, even if no conclusion is reached.

Socrates explains his method thus: 'I am questioning you not out of personal animosity, but simply to help the discussion proceed coherently. This will prevent us from getting into the habit of guessing at one another's views and anticipating what might be said, instead of allowing you to develop your own argument as you wish…'

Thus we see that two of the most eminent thinkers of Ancient Greece have both identified the making of assumptions, in the shape of 'guessing' and 'anticipating', as something to be avoided.

A FLAT EARTH? In early societies there were perhaps a majority of people who assumed the earth was flat or didn't extend much beyond their own horizons. But it seems that by the sixth century BC societies such as Greece and Egypt had accepted that the earth was, like the sun and moon, globular.

By the third century BC the polymath Eratosthenes of Cyrene, assuming that the earth was indeed round, had elegantly calculated its circumference with accuracy. At the summer solstice, knowing that the sun's rays on that day shone perpendicularly down a well at Syene (Aswan), he measured the angle of the sun's rays against a vertical pole in his home city of Alexandria, nearly 500 miles north of the well. The angle was about seven degrees from the vertical. These seven degrees represented both 500 miles on the earth's surface and a fiftieth of the 360 degrees of the earth's circumference. Therefore, 50 times the 500 miles between Syene and Alexandria would give the earth's circumference.

Eratosthenes' exact calculation does not seem to be known, but 50 x 500 brings it very close to the present measurement of nearly 24,901 miles.

AMBIGUITY OF THE ORACLES An oracle is both the place of prophecy, and the priest or priestess who speaks the words of the god directly to the client. In the Roman world they were called 'sybils'. Oracles must have served some useful purpose, for they lasted until around AD 300, having originated in Ancient Greece. They at least provided their clients with a calm atmosphere and drawn-out process, during which assumptions were perhaps more likely to be noticed and challenged. Their clientele was varied, from foreigners and kings to families and individuals, asking questions on subjects such as war, politics, family matters, duty, law, personal difficulties and so on. It was of course understood that their answers could be ambiguous, but perhaps that helped to open up discussion.

The oracles were generally trusted, it seems. Any failure of prophecy was put down to faulty interpretation. Socrates believed they played an important role in the state and its development. Cicero was critical of the oracles and in the eighteenth century, Bernard de Fontenelle disparaged them in his *Histoire des Oracles*, suggesting that the calm atmosphere owed something to hashish and intoxicating underground gas.

In a bizarre experiment King Croesus of Lydia tested seven oracles at the same time on the same day for their ability to predict what he was doing. The winning oracle, Delphi, had known that he was cooking a lamb and tortoise stew, needing a slow cook no doubt. Delphi was the oracle of the god Apollo, its priestess known as the Pythia, or 'pythoness'.

In 546 BC Croesus consulted the oracles of Delphi and Amphiarus as to whether he should invade the territory of the Persians. The oracles replied that if he crossed the River Halys he would destroy a great empire. Croesus seems to have assumed this to mean that he should indeed attack King Cyrus. Perhaps he had already made up his mind and used the oracle as the ultimate validation of what he was hell-bent on doing. But in the event it was own empire that was crushed.

HANNIBAL'S CROSSING OF THE ALPS, 218 BC This extraordinary achievement is a classic example of how a bold general can gain tremendous advantage from taking the initiative and from surprise. The boldness of Hannibal was combined with great attention to detail, careful forethought and the use of all available information.

After leaving Spain, Hannibal's forces had, in the early autumn, begun to march north up the valley of the Rhône. He knew that the Roman general Publius Scipio, having landed his army near Masillia (Marseilles), was a few days march behind him. But it was no part of Hannibal's strategy to fight against the Romans until he was on Italian soil. He moved fast, and further north turned east up the valley of the Drôme and over into the basin of the Durance river, from where he could begin to make out the autumnal snows of the Alps.

Scipio now knew that Hannibal would have to cross the Alps at some point – but *after* the winter, surely! He thus decided that it would be better to return to the Italian side. In the spring he could wait for Hannibal to come through the mountains and descend to the foothills and plains of Italy. There the Roman army could confront the Carthaginians, exhausted or at least weakened after the hardship of the mountain winter.

In the event, Hannibal's boldness lay not only in crossing the Alps – but in crossing them so quickly. Scipio was deceived by Hannibal's speed ('Quickness is the essence of war' – Sun-tzu). The ascent and descent of the very high and remote Col de la Traversette, nearly 10,000 feet above sea level, took just over two weeks. Hannibal was well-prepared to overcome all difficulties of terrain, climate and hostile tribes. He had been determined that the army should cross before winter set in; delay until spring would allow the Romans time to raise larger forces.

Hannibal was off the Traversette around the end of October. The plains of the Po are clearly visible from this pass, just as in Livy's account. Within a month he had massacred the hostile tribe of the Taurini, to broadcast his determination. The news spread quickly eastward. When Scipio heard of the massacre he was 'incredulous' that Hannibal was already over the Alps and now in Piedmont. The Senate and people of Rome were also astonished. Scipio's unprepared army was in winter quarters somewhere east along the Po.

Scipio nevertheless hurried westwards along the river to find Hannibal. The first battle between Rome and Carthage, now aided by supportive Celtic tribes, was fought in late November at Ticinus, near Pavia. Scipio was quickly defeated, and would have lost his life on the battlefield had it not been for rescue by his son, Scipio Africanus. A second defeat, at Trebia, soon followed. Thus began the protracted hostilities of the Second Punic War.

According to a recent field manual of the US Army, targets of deception (Publius Scipio in this case) tend to dismiss unlikely events as impossible events. Scipio was right to think that it was 'unlikely' that Hannibal would cross the Alps before winter, but he was wrong to assume it was 'impossible'.

In a slightly different wording it was an axiom much recommended by Sherlock Holmes. In the intervening 2,000 years there must have been many similar confusions of the 'unlikely' with the 'impossible'.

The accurate identification of Hannibal's pass by Sir Gavin de Beer (*Alps and Elephants*, 1955) has been confirmed by Bill Mahaney's 2016 archaeological discoveries on the Traversette.

THE BIRTH OF CHRISTIANITY I was rather dreading having to deal with the early momentum of this vast subject. But Christianity's origin and success have long intrigued me. I am drawn towards churches and cathedrals, their words, their music, their history. In the last twenty-five years I have sung in many London church choirs. I have engaged with the substantial volumes of Edward Gibbon's *History of the Decline and Fall of the Roman Empire*. Chapter fifteen on the origins of Christianity was controversial in its day, but shone a great deal of helpful light into my obscure notions.

Reflective moments in the choirstalls often set me wondering about the assumptions that loomed up amongst the Gothic arches and stained glass. I began to wonder…

about the fact that it's lasted for over 2,000 years. Has that given it an ever-increasing plausibility with each century that passes, despite the decline in faith in much of the West? I have heard people on this basis declaring that 'there must be something in it'.

about prophecy. Is it a way of creating authority and legitimacy? If an event was foretold by a prophet centuries ago does it seems as if some inevitable long-term process is at work? That the prophecy has been made a link in the chain of higher knowledge? But perhaps a very great number of prophecies were made that have *not* come true. These have fallen by the wayside and the surviving prophecy can be seen in retrospect as something remarkable, perhaps leading people to make an assumption when matched up with much later events. That was just my own generalising reflection, no doubt very naïve and unsubstantiated. But we shall find the subject properly explained further on when we reach the nineteenth century.

about the wider history of that time. One might assume that Roman history would reflect the larger events in the Gospels. I have been in church on Easter Day when the vicar assured us that the trial and crucifixion of Christ and its aftermath was the greatest event in the history of the world. But the Roman historian Cornelius Tacitus remarks that 'under Tiberius all was quiet'. The only mention he makes of Christianity is what he had heard from Christians near the end of the first century.

It was alleged by Tertullian that Pontius Pilate had made a report on the crucifixion, but Gibbon finds no evidence of it.

The naturalist Pliny the Elder was the leading observer of phenomena such as eclipses and eruptions. He received information from across the Empire. There is no report of darkness falling across the earth around the period of the crucifixion, not even in the chapter on 'Unusual Eclipses' in his *Natural History*.

Why were early Christians known as 'atheists' by the Roman authorities? Well, at the beginning they had no dedicated church buildings – so where was their god? When basilicas were built, the authorities could find no god inside. What aroused further suspicion? Their secretive meetings stimulated people to make assumptions about their practices, leading to the spread of dreadful rumours, though their secrecy was apparently based on the respectable Eleusinian Mysteries, pagan rituals of Greek origin that were admired by Cicero.

It seems they also offended society by their predictions of calamities, their aloofness from mankind, their obstinacy, their refusal to serve in the military as part of the 'Pax Romana' and refusal to play any part in civil life. Pliny the Younger, a senior lawyer in the Roman government, was appointed governor of Bithynia, in Asia Minor. He had to rule on various outbreaks of what he described as 'this wretched sect'. He discusses this difficulty in business-like correspondence with the Emperor Trajan, who took a light-touch approach to the Christian communities. That Pliny knew so little about the Christians suggests that he had not come across the problem before, despite being a citizen of Rome and widely travelled in Italy.

This brings us to the persistent assumption that Christians were widely persecuted under the Roman Empire. I have heard an Anglican clergyman assuring the congregation that the Romans were *always* crucifying Christians. But Gibbon, in writing chapter sixteen of the *Decline and Fall,* had taken it upon himself to examine the subject. He calculated the number of deaths from persecution over the three centuries before Christianity became official under Constantine. Gibbon ended up with a figure of some 2,000, mainly attributable to a few emperors only. These included the paranoid Domitian, who persecuted Roman citizens just as easily; and much later, Diocletian (at his accession, though not throughout his reign), as well as his successors, Maximian and Galerius, who were not typical of Roman administrators. In between there were long periods during which Christians were tolerated and allowed to increase their presence. As for Nero's notorious public persecutions, Gibbon argued that those 'Christians' were in fact Jewish troublemakers or terrorists with the confusing name of 'Galileans'.

Gibbon suggests that the Christian ecclesiastical writers of the fourth and fifth centuries, who wrote of the alleged persecutions, had made a very natural mistake. By now imbued with unrelenting zeal against the heretics and idolaters of their own times, they assumed a likewise fanatical spirit had raged in the Roman authorities of the earlier days. But Gibbon's considered conclusion is that most magistrates across the Empire were certainly, as with Pliny in Bithynia, 'men of polished manners and liberal education, who respected the rules of justice and were conversant with the precepts of philosophy'.

But it would be interesting to know how many deaths resulted in the early centuries from the fanatical persecution of Christians *by other Christians.* The shocking brutality in the fourth century of the anti-Trinitarian heresy proposed by Arius is fully described by Gibbon, though he does not attempt an estimate of the number of martyrs.

PLINY THE YOUNGER Did the Romans and Greeks of those centuries actually talk of 'assumptions'? It would seem so. In a letter from Pliny to Pompeius Falco, between AD 97 and 102, we find that he was conversant with the idea of the assumption and that it might turn out be false.

Falco had asked Pliny's opinion on whether he should continue to practise in the law courts while holding the office of a tribune (an officer chosen by the people to protect their liberties). It depends, replied Pliny, what view you take of the tribunate. Is it an 'empty form' or 'mere title' or is it an inviolable authority?

> When I was a tribune myself, I acted on the assumption (which may have been a wrong one) that my office really meant something. I therefore gave up all my court work, for I thought it unsuitable for a tribune to stand while others were seated…

The translator of the Penguin edition of *The Letters of Pliny the Younger*, Betty Radice, tells us that Pliny's letters are the best source of information about Roman life at the turn of the first century, and also the fullest self-portrait which has survived of any Roman, with the possible exceptions of Horace and Cicero.

WEAKNESS IN THE LATER ROMAN EMPIRE: THE EMPEROR VALERIAN, AD 253–268 Here we find a strange error in the choice of successor to the imperial throne. Valerian, already revered for his great qualities in the service of the state, was elevated to the purple in 253, but as he was seventy years of age he announced that he would share the throne with a younger person.

Valerian was reckoned perfectly capable of making a judicious decision, but instead, 'consulting only the dictates of affection or vanity' in the words of Gibbon, he chose his own son Gallienus – already confirmed as an effeminate and vicious youth. His father somehow managed to assume that this would work well. When Valerian died in 261 Gallienus continued as sole Emperor for another eight years. These fifteen years amounted to 'an uninterrupted series of confusion and calamity' at the hands of the most dangerous enemies of Rome: the Franks, the Alemanni, the Goths and the Persians. It was found that Gallienus was talented at everything – except being present at, and attentive to, those great emergencies which continually pressed upon the Empire.

As well as the danger of weak emperors, there grew a fatal assumption that barbarian states could be paid liberally for keeping their distance. But the keen eyes of the newly swarming barbarian nations concluded from this generosity that Rome was not only wealthy, but weak. The secret was out…

THE INVENTION OF CHESS I remember reading, aged eight, the intriguing little tale that follows. My career as a chess player started then and has remained deeply obscure. My only moment of glory occurred on a skiing holiday in the French Alps. One of our party was something of an expert player and had published his own book on chess history. Each evening he kept badgering me for a game, a game which I knew I would lose pretty quickly. In a moment of weakness I relented. Imagine my astonishment when my opponent (white) opened by advancing two pawns in such a way that I was able to checkmate him in two moves: Fool's Mate, the fastest possible.

When he had recovered from the shock, the defeated expert insisted that I owed him another game —but I explained I'd had enough chess for now, and it was time to step out in search of some *après-ski*. This did not go down well.

But to return to the tale: some 1,500 years ago chess seems to have been invented in India. The then ruler, wishing to reward the inventor of such a brilliant game, asks him to name his prize. The inventor (perhaps one Sessa, a minister) requests that he would like a quantity of wheat, one grain to be placed on the first square, two on the next, and so on, doubling on each square until all squares are covered. Without calculating how much wheat will be needed, the ruler assumes there will not be any difficulty in meeting this request. Are you sure that's all you want?

Whether the inventor ever received his reward is not recorded, but it seems rather unlikely. The ruler would have needed to deliver 18 quintillion, 446 quadrillion, 744 trillion, 73 billion, 709 million, and 551,615 grains.

It would seem that the ruler's maths education had not put much emphasis on exponential growth. The ruler had probably assumed a more reasonable arithmetical increase, a few thousand grains perhaps.

As for the inventor, his fate or future does not seem to be known. Perhaps the tale is a legend, using the fact of the sixty-four squares to retrospectively enlarge and enliven its origins.

OCKHAM'S RAZOR A clever but lazy university friend of mine probably peaked in life as a schoolboy debater. He told me how in the final round of a debating competition at Bangor University he spent the short interval visiting the library, frantically looking up Ockham's Razor. Something told him it could be critically important, and sure enough, he used it in the last debate – and emerged triumphant.

But if we have heard of it, do we know what it entails? The Razor is an axiom which was prominently used by William of Ockham, an English Franciscan friar and philosopher, born in the late thirteenth century. He stated that when two or more explanations have been proposed for the same question or problem, one should select the simpler explanation. Over the centuries several versions have appeared, including one which states that you should select the explanation that depends on the fewest assumptions. In other words, let the razor shave away those explanations that rest on surplus assumptions.

Ockham's Latin original 'pluralitas non est ponenda sine necessitate' was translated as 'Pluralities should not be posited without necessity.'

This principle has evolved within numerous disciplines to the present day.

THE MIDDLE AGES Quite soon this experiment in the history of assumptions arrives at a major difficulty, to put it mildly! The ten centuries between the fall of Rome and the Renaissance seem to offer very little evidence of individual assumptions being made. In a sense the era was dominated by one vast assumption: the beliefs and authority of the Universal Church of Rome. And there was little escape from the suffocating medieval landscape of superstition, alchemy, astrology, witchcraft, necromancy… Sir Arthur Bryant writes that 'Behind all this superstition lay a conception shared by rich and poor alike, educated and ignorant. It was that the universe, from its greatest to its minutest part, was governed by divine law… Everything medieval man did was blessed or cursed, approved or disapproved, explained and solemnised by the Church.' Perhaps this is a partial explanation. Of course, assumptions were surely still being made, but perhaps not recorded as such, or not recognised as such within the mental framework of the times. And in the Middle Ages the word 'assumption' was not used in the 'taken for granted', 'jumping to conclusions' way that we are concerned with in this book.

Henry II may have made the reasonable assumption, after seven years of constructively working together, that Thomas Becket was a true friend and ally, before raising him to the throne of Canterbury. This led to unintended consequences that could scarcely have been imagined by anyone. The element in Becket that perhaps Henry had overlooked seems to have been a relentless overwhelming urge to excel, to which everything else could be sacrificed. Was it in fact a case of hubris? It is interesting that the Becket controversy is still a matter of historical debate.

I thought that the history of the Crusaders, men and women driven along by many motives, over a 500-year period, might be fruitful territory. But I found only the melancholy episode of The Children's Crusade, which in the light of later scholarship was probably not what it seemed to be; and the fate in 1270 of the Tunis expedition in which Louis IX, the saintly King of France, died of fever, having assumed it was safe to follow the lead of his notorious brother, Charles of Anjou.

But at least we have the cautionary tales from Chaucer, and others.

Stories such as the *Miller's Tale* involve the farcical explosion of some very down-to-earth assumptions indeed.

In respect of the aforementioned medieval superstitions, there is Charles Mackay's famous work *Extraordinary Popular Delusions and the Madness of Crowds*, published in 1841. This famous study stretching across some 2,000 years, presents a seemingly endless stream of fraudsters, fanatics, quacks and charlatans deliberately deluding the populace, rendered somewhat defenceless by their relative ignorance. Not that Mackay would have lacked similar material in our present age.

But I don't think his book duplicates the present work, for he deals with the manipulation of a passive crowd, rather than the active assumption-making of individuals. In crowds, writes Mackay, credulity is contagious… and always greatest in times of calamity.

Eventually the various Reformations in Europe, and the Renaissance in Italy, allowed the individual mind to flourish as never before. Examples of assumption, and the philosophers and scientists who warn against them, become more numerous and varied from that time onward.

AN ARCHITECT OF THE RENAISSANCE AND HIS ENEMIES, 1462 Aeneas Sylvius Piccolomini, Pope Pius II, being from a renowned but impoverished family of Siena, had settled on the small Tuscan town of Corsignano as the site for a future palace. In particular he wished to pioneer in the town the architecture of the Renaissance. He renamed the town 'Pienza' after himself. The palace and the new cathedral, apart from its bell tower, were completed quickly, in three years.

Pius II, pronounced as the English word 'pious', had always taken a great interest in the country districts around Rome and Siena, often holding papal councils and church festivals in carefully chosen rural scenes amid the relics of the Roman Empire. These he describes in his autobiography *The Memoirs of a Renaissance Pope*. In this rare and honest work, Pius is of course mainly concerned with weighty matters: the dubious loyalty of French cardinals, the great danger posed to Europe by the Turks and the shocking outbursts of criminal anarchy on the streets of Rome itself. But there is always space in the mind of Pius for humanist initiatives too.

The Pope had appointed as architect for his palace and cathedral one Bernardo Rossellino. He visited Pienza in the summer of 1462, to inspect the work for the first time. But there had been many envious voices raised against Rossellino: to the Sienese, the fact that he was a Florentine was enough on which to assume his roguery. These voices claimed that he had cheated, that he had erred in the construction, that his estimate had been only 18,000 ducats, though the real price was 50,000. Rossellino was not present at Pienza, but his name was being abused by everyone. After a thorough inspection Pius sent for the architect. Rossellino arrived in a state of intense anxiety, knowing what his enemies had been up to. They were now rubbing their hands in confident assumption of his imminent downfall. But Pius II was not a man to tamely please the crowd. When Rossellino appeared, Pius spoke thus:

> You did well, Bernardo, in lying to us about the expense involved in the work. If you had told the truth, you could never have induced us to spend so much money and neither this splendid palace nor this church, the finest in all Italy, would now be standing. Your deceit has built these glorious structures which are praised by all except the few who are consumed with envy. We thank you and think you deserve especial honour among all the architects of our time.

The Pope then offered financial rewards for both him and his son. We are told that the architect burst into tears of relief.

Today the town centre of Pienza is a UNESCO World Heritage Site and considered the 'touchstone of Renaissance urbanism'.

RICHARD III AND HENRY VII: HISTORY WRITTEN BY THE VICTOR There is still no conclusive evidence with which to exonerate King Richard (1483–85) of the accusation of murdering his nephews. But it seems clear that his reputation suffered drastically at the hands of the dictatorial Henry, after Richard's death at Bosworth. In the following five centuries the general assumption about Richard has scarcely shifted, though many books and studies have been published. They suggest that such a murder would have been well out of character for Richard, who had enjoyed a good reputation as an administrator and as a decent man in other walks of life. (For the most recent developments in this great mystery, see the year 2012.)

SHAKESPEAREAN TRAGEDY My school had a great reputation for its Shakespearean productions. One year we had a visit from Harold Hobson, a renowned theatre critic. In the space of a few years I had been bewitched by the Scottish Play, had studied *King Lear* and *Anthony and Cleopatra* and had seen *Othello, Hamlet, Twelfth Night* and *Romeo and Juliet* performed on our stage. And in these tragedies and comedies we find much dramatisation of hubris and its accompanying assumptions – of which the following play is a fine example:

THE SCOTTISH PLAY, *MACBETH*, 1606 It is striking that Shakespeare should have chosen to write and stage a play, *The Tragedy of Macbeth*, about a tyrannical King of Scotland so soon after James VI of Scotland's accession to the English throne. But it seems as if the playwright was well aware of James's views. In particular, James disapproved of all rebellion – and was bored by long-winded theatrical performances. The Bard had also read James's books, including the ones about demons and witchcraft. As James was a direct descendant of Banquo, he adjusted that role in the play with care.

Rebellion, and suspicion of Jesuits and Roman Catholics haunted the decade. The uncovering of the Gunpowder Plot the year before had shocked the populace. In these times there were many who found it necessary to 'equivocate', that is, to use language that could be understood in two ways. Thus ambiguity and trickery is found throughout this play.

One of the shortest of Shakespeare's plays, the pace of events is rapid, perhaps to reflect Macbeth's 'vaulting ambition' – and lest the King be bored. Returning from great victories with his colleague Banquo, Macbeth makes easy assumptions from the equivocation of the three Weird Sisters they meet on a lonely heath. When the sisters' first prophecy comes true, that he shall be the Thane of Cawdor, he is tempted to make more use of their knowledge.

By murdering King Duncan he swiftly fulfils their second prophecy, that he shall be King. His over-confidence swells at a third prophecy in which the Sisters show him the apparition of an armed head which cries 'Macbeth! Macbeth! Macbeth! Beware the Thane of Fife, Beware Macduff!' A second apparition declares that 'none of woman born shall harm Macbeth' and that 'Macbeth shall never vanquished be, until Great Birnam Wood to high Dunsinane Hill shall come against him.'

But these three prophecies also contain equivocation: in the final scenes of battle Macbeth learns that Macduff, his most feared enemy, was not in the strict sense 'of woman born' because he had been 'from his mother's womb untimely ripped'. And he learns that it is perfectly possible for an army to cut down branches in Birnam Wood to disguise their advance, in this case against Macbeth's castle of Dunsinane, fifteen miles away.

Holinshed puts Macbeth's death as 1057.

The triple format of these prophecies may have played a part. Chesterton's Father Brown observes that 'men will believe the oddest things if they come in threes…'

MIGUEL DE CERVANTES: *DON QUIXOTE*, 1605, 1615 A mad lust for adventures, derived from the obsessive reading of chivalric romances, sends Señor Quixada out into the world beyond his Castilian village. Promoting himself to 'Don' Quixote and attended by a labourer, Sancho Panza, as his 'squire', our hero assumes that a whole world of chivalric excitement awaits him. But he soon finds that 'adventures' of that kind are just about impossible to find. The only course of action, then, is to invent them. Thus, when he charges towards windmills, he shouts to Panza that he shall slay these 'giants'. He knows they are windmills, but proclaims that only this minute his enemies, malevolent giants, have been turned into windmills by the sorcerer Freston, who wants to thwart his plans. His madness must consist of simultaneously knowing they are windmills, but to attack them as if they were giants. And the Don is voluble and articulate in arguing his case, during the protracted debriefings that tend to follow his violent humiliation at the hands of outraged and law-abiding citizens.

On another occasion a great cloud of dust appears across the plain; soon, from the opposite direction, another great cloud looms up. Two great armies preparing for battle, explains the Don. Panza retorts that they are sheep, great flocks of ewes and rams. This does not prevent our adventurer from describing in staggering prolixity the appearance and titles of eminent heroes of chivalry as they come to terms in the swirling dust. He enlists himself on the side of the valorous Emperor Pentapolin of the Naked Arm and charges straight into the midst of the mingling flocks. He is quickly forestalled by stones hurled by irate shepherds. When it is all over, he explains to Panza that yet again his enemies – the sorcerers, the enchanters – have frustrated him by conjuring the armies into mere flocks of ewes and rams, of which seven were killed.

This bizarre tactic of inventing adventures was, I suppose, the only way, in a world bereft of romance, to achieve chivalric adventures and honour, a sort of deliberate and necessary self-delusion, almost a working assumption, a 'let's pretend'. What was the alternative? A quiet life in humdrum rural Castile…

A Castilian lady of my acquaintance, steeped in the literature of her land, declared that *Don Quixote* is 'very Spanish'.

SIR FRANCIS BACON, 1561–1626 In his fiftieth Essay – *On Studies* – Bacon advises: 'Read not to contradict or refute; *nor to accept and take for granted*; nor to find talk and discourse; but to weigh and consider.' That phrase above (in my italics) is a warning against assumption: best avoided by 'weighing and considering'.

Bacon is revered as the founder of scientific method, building on the work of Copernicus and Galileo. He deplored the existing Aristotelian method of inferring truth from broad ideas, from syllogisms, 'fanciful guessings' and the 'mere citing of authorities'. We can reasonably assume that such a method was heavily loaded with implausible assumptions. Bacon called them 'idols' or 'false images', to which the human mind is susceptible. He warned especially against these errors:

> thinking that the world is more orderly and regulated than the evidence shows

> failing to think for oneself; and thereby failing to challenge conventional dogma...

What did Bacon offer instead? Although his new scientific method (published as *Novum Organum,* 1620) is a complex process in practice, it can perhaps be summarised as beginning with observations, leading to the establishment of accurate facts. Patterns can then be found and conclusions can perhaps be drawn. This leads to the further establishment of accurate facts. Gradually, carefully, an edifice of firmer knowledge may be built.

This new way of inferring from facts was termed 'induction' by Bacon. It required hard work. It starts with the setting up of properly organised observation and experiment.

And all this careful meticulous work of observation was placed by Bacon in the context of his own religious faith. Sir Francis, one of the greatest liberators of the mind, considered his new method to be a way of retrieving the knowledge of nature that had been lost to man after the Fall.

SIR THOMAS BROWNE: *PSEUDODOXIA EPIDEMICA* ('ERRORS OF THE CROWD') 1646 Browne's muscular exhilarating English is put to the service of exposing all types of error – and not just those of the 'crowd' either. He was a committed follower of Bacon. Like him, he does not use the word 'assumption' – use of the A-word in English seems to arise in later centuries – but they still have their own corner within his scheme.

Right at the start he writes of the 'common infirmity of humane nature' and its 'deceptible condition'. We need, he says, no other example of this than the errors we ourselves commit so frequently.

It is in his fifth chapter – *Of Credulity and Supinity* – that he seems to really have the assumption in his sights. Credulity, then, 'allows an easy assent… or a believing at first ear what is delivered by others'. Although this is commonly found in 'vulgar heads', Browne has also found 'Credulity' in higher places, for example in the beliefs of the ancient Athenians in respect of the origin of their nation.

As for 'Supinity', he comes even closer. Supinity is 'neglect of enquiry, even in matters whereof we doubt: rather believing, than going to see; or doubting with ease and gratis, than believing with difficulty or purchase'. He puts this weakness down to 'temperamental inactivity' or by 'contentment and acquiescence in every species of truth'.

Browne, a doctor by profession, offers his vivid language not only for the guidance of everyday lives, but also in the search for scientific truth.

RENÉ DESCARTES, 1644 In his *Principles of Philosophy* Descartes proved his own existence through the axiom 'Cogito ergo sum': 'I think therefore I am.' He realises that thinking is the chief activity of mankind. He divides thought, when confronted with a new proposition, into two steps:

understanding

followed by

acceptance of its truth.

BARUCH SPINOZA, 1677 Spinoza was a Dutch philosopher of Portuguese Jewish descent, the son of a merchant family in Amsterdam. He was considered one of the finest examples of a 'virtuous pagan'. He died at the age of forty-four, perhaps from silicosis: minute particles of glass may have been inhaled in the daily pursuit of his profession as a grinder of lenses used in telescopes.

Spinoza is known as a deep examiner of human thought: 'In his thinking man has only an illusion of freedom. He dreams with his eyes open.'

In the second book of *Ethics* (published soon after his death in 1677) he makes an advance on Descartes' idea, above, of how we think when faced with a new proposition. Spinoza suggests that understanding cannot exist alone, without the person also unconsciously attempting to imagine the proposition as true, that is – in believing in it.

Thus he declares that Descartes' two steps are in fact one and the same thing, and chooses the term 'belief' to describe it. Spinoza calls this thinking 'effortless, automatic and passive'. After that moment it was possible for an individual to doubt and 'unbelieve'. But that was much harder work. (Subsequently, it has been shown that doubting is a more difficult matter than believing, and tends to be acquired only gradually in the course of human life.)

Well, that's interesting, this emphasis on 'belief'. He means, of course, 'belief' pure and simple, not necessarily religious. This 'effortless, automatic and passive' operation of the mind – 'belief' – sounds very much like a mechanism in which assumptions can be made.

In this period of Bacon and Browne, Descartes and Spinoza we surely find a sharpening focus on the working of the mind. A silver thread of enquiry now leads on through subsequent centuries.

JOHN MILTON: *PARADISE LOST*, 1667 It would seem that this great epic or tragedy is the first full and clear depiction of Lucifer (or 'Satan' as Milton names him). In earlier literature he is an obscure or symbolic figure.

Lucifer, an angel of exceeding stature and quality, is guilty of pride and rebellion. God hurls him from heaven for his intolerable hubris. Has the depth of his Fall ever been better measured than by the words of Milton, or better illustrated than by Gustave Doré?

PIERRE BAYLE, 1647-1706 This father of scepticism was admired by Voltaire, Gibbon, Hume, Leibnitz and Frederick the Great, amongst many others. He reflected to an extreme degree the trends of the later seventeenth century: restlessness, belief in individual experience instead of divine revelation, defiance of authority, an ardour for liberty and the examination of the rights of the individual. He was particularly known for incisive attacks on superstition, dogma and the kind of assumption known as 'conventional wisdom'. In the words of Voltaire: 'He was the greatest dialectician that has ever written: he taught doubt.'

Bayle was born in southwestern France, to a Protestant family. His own choice of a Roman Catholic education by the Jesuits proved very worthwhile intellectually, but he reverted to his family's position soon after. While in a teaching post at the Protestant College at Sedan, at the foot of the Ardennes, he witnessed the Great Comet of 1680. The general assumption then was that comets were harbingers of disaster, such as had been seen before the fall of Carthage and the invasion of England by Duke William of Normandy. They tended to cause panic in the populace, and created a need for immediate repentance. It must have been a tremendous sight, the Great Comet, one of the brightest comets ever seen, plunging to the horizon with a long almost vertical tail, at its brightest on the 29th of dark December. Its brilliance was partly the result of its parabolic 'sungrazing' course, exposing it to colossal solar radiation.

An eyewitness – 'an intellectual man' – reported his impression at the time:

> I tremble when I recall the terrible appearance the comet had on Saturday evening in the clear sky, when it was observed by everybody with inexpressible astonishment. It seemed as though the heavens were burning or if the very air was on fire. From this little star stretched out such a wonderfully long tail that even an intellectual man was overcome with trembling; one's hair stood on end as this uncommon, terrible and indescribable tail came into view... O wonderful almighty God! The heavens show thy might and the earth thy handiwork.

Bayle had been overwhelmed by requests to explain the meaning of the comet. This was an opportunity to further his campaign against superstition. He wrote a substantial pamphlet – *Various Thoughts on the Occasion of a Comet* – in which he emphasised that this was not a supernatural event, nor a message from which prophecies could be extracted, but a phenomenon of the solar system. It had been observed by Newton, Flamsteed and Halley and the parabolic course through the perihelion (the closest point to the sun) was now more clearly agreed between them.

Bayle supplied a great list of arguments against these superstitions. For example: *Comets have a malign influence on human life.* Bayle: but no scientist or philosopher has been able to explain how that could happen. *But that is the general opinion of the people.* Bayle: but the general opinion has no weight at all compared with that of people who have really investigated the subject; and so on, in a lengthy Socratic dialogue. The dialogue develops. To the notion that *God uses comets – and eclipses – to send a message of his displeasure at Christian mankind*, Bayle replied that a deity would be unlikely to use a comet as a message: it would be seen and interpreted similarly by other world religions who far outnumbered the population of Christians.

But as we read on through this pamphlet with its deceptively casual title, we find that Bayle gradually encroaches onto rather riskier territory than that of the heavenly bodies. Eventually he courageously argues against another stubborn assumption of the times: that a community or society of atheists must necessarily lead to a decline of morality. This, declared Bayle, was 'only a common prejudice…'

Not long after the comet pamphlet, he moved to Rotterdam, where his public scepticism was at least better tolerated than in the France of Louis XIV. In 1697 he published his *Historical and Critical Dictionary*. This continued his attack against unthinking prejudices, belief in the supernatural and the easy acceptance of superstition and dogma. Bayle was thereby a pioneer foe of assumptions. He considered written history to be always unreliable and the clergy closed to any questioning.

He was against constraint in religious matters, especially in 1685 when his family were re-exposed to persecution by the revocation of the Edict of Nantes.

He mocked religious sects, each with their favourite miracles and scorn for the miracles of others. He was surely one of the first to criticise the Bible as unhistorical. He attacked the doctrine of original sin. He alarmed even Voltaire…

Thanks to the plotting of an enemy, Bayle was removed from his professorship at Rotterdam and accused of 'corrupting the youth', that easily raised rumour so often used against the high-minded, such as Socrates.

In our day Pierre Bayle seems a forgotten figure. His rather exhausting tendency to digress may explain this. But he was undoubtedly the pioneer in his field.

LOUIS XIV: THE DECISION OF 16 NOVEMBER 1700 At an evening ceremony at
Versailles, witnessed by the diarist the Duc de Saint-Simon, Louis fulfilled
the will of the recently deceased and severely inbred Charles II of Spain.
Charles had, on the advice of the Archbishop of Toledo, left the crown
of Spain to Philip of Anjou, the grandson of Louis. Louis pointed to the
boy Philip and announced to the Spanish Ambassador that he could now
do homage to the King of Spain. The ambassador flung himself on his
knees in the traditional way and delivered a complimentary address in his
own language.

The Spanish crown also accorded the French boy-King dominion of the
entire Spanish Empire, consisting of most of South America, California,
Florida, the Philippines, the Canaries, the Spanish Netherlands, Milan,
Naples and Sicily. Voltaire, in his book *The Age of Louis XIV*, points out that
the unfortunate Charles II had very little idea of the extent of the Spanish
possessions and did not actually know what he was leaving to Philip.

> Thus, after two hundred years of wars and negotiations over certain
> frontiers of the Spanish states, the House of France, by one stroke of
> the pen, obtained the whole empire, without either treaty or intrigue,
> without even having entertained any hopes of the succession.

This acceptance of the will was a fine example of 'masterly inaction' by
Louis, but opened him to the accusation of extraordinary hubris, by
which the Bourbon family would obtain the rule of most of Western
Europe. Such an action, with its violation of treaties, would surely not
be countenanced by the Grand Alliance of England, Austria and the
Netherlands. It led quickly to the War of the Spanish Succession. But
what had allowed Louis, despite his abilities and achievements, to rise
to this level of provocation? Well, partly because he had good reasons to
think he might well succeed.

For explanation, we look back a few decades. From 1661, with the death of Cardinal Mazarin, Louis had been able to exert total authority, through Colbert, who directed the economy, and Louvois, in charge of the armed forces.

Louis had ordered the vastly expensive construction of a new palace, in the damp countryside of his father's hunting lodge near Versailles. Here he forced the leading nobles of France to attend his court, well away from the conspiratorial atmosphere of Paris. By the invention of the most elaborate ceremonial, he managed to hypnotise courtiers into assuming that they were fulfilling some useful function. He imposed a myth of his greatness on the court, pervaded by an unreal atmosphere. In the words of Harold Nicolson in his book *The Age of Reason*:

> Never since the days of the Roman Emperors had the rule of a single man been accepted with such acquiescence; never had the principle of monarchy and the Divine Right of Kings commanded such wide assent; and never again was any sovereign to create around his person a legend of equal awe, majesty and splendour.

And the Sun King's rigid and much resented dictatorship in matters of religion showed how far and wide his hubris could stretch: he had launched an anti-Protestant campaign against the Dutch; he hoped to re-introduce the Roman Catholic Church into England with the connivance of James II; he had encouraged the influence of the Jesuits over the puritan Jansenists. Most notoriously, in 1685, he had revoked the tolerating Edict of Nantes. Voltaire described this decision as 'one of the greatest disasters that ever afflicted France'. Some half a million Huguenots left the country.

And so we return to the consequences of that fateful evening of 16 November 1700. The war (of the Spanish Succession) had begun in 1701, but Louis' dominance did not receive its first and perhaps most decisive setback until 1704. At the Bavarian village of Blindheim on the banks of the Danube, the armies of the Imperial Alliance under

Marlborough and Prince Eugene won their 'glorious victory' over the French and their local allies. Louis could hardly have expected the emergence of two of the greatest military geniuses of all time – or the incredible speed of Marlborough's advance from Cologne to the Danube. 'Blenheim' had saved Vienna from the threat of the French forces. Louis had lost his best army and the whole of Bavaria and the Rhineland. Such a defeat seemed to the French to be incredible. Back at Versailles it was Madame de Maintenon who broke the news to the King that he was no longer invincible, for no one else at court had the courage to tell him.

After the battle of Ramillies the French were kept on the defensive for the rest of the war.

To ask if – and when – Louis reached the turning point of *peripeteia* and the retribution of *nemesis* might be to unjustly simplify the rest of his seventy-two-year reign. But Louis' death in 1715 marked also the death of the assumption: that the best form of governance was that of a single monarch – however 'great' he was. He may never have actually spoken the apocryphal words 'L'état, c'est moi,' but the tradition has persisted nevertheless.

THE LOSS OF GIBRALTAR, 1704   The rocky and precipitous peninsula of Gibraltar, at the southernmost tip of Spain, was thought to be impregnable. It had no harbour, the bay was open to the wrath of the Atlantic and it was assumed that a handful of townsfolk and a garrison of a hundred would be enough to defy any attack, by firing down from the fortress. But, as Voltaire observed, 'the very strength of the place was the cause of its capture'.

At the outset of the War of the Spanish Succession, a British and Dutch force led by Admiral Rooke attempted to take Gibraltar by a relentless bombardment, but to no avail. But there was a duty that the garrison had neglected, in the complacency suggested by Voltaire: to keep an eye on the southern mole that stretched into the sea south of the town. By chance some British sailors, just larking around in rowing boats beneath this structure, had not been noticed by the defenders. So they clambered up unopposed and in that one small step discovered the Achilles heel of the peninsula. Troops soon followed and a conventional assault on the town led to a Spanish surrender on 4 August.

By the Treaty of Utrecht, which concluded the war in 1713, Gibraltar was ceded to Britain in perpetuity. Military and diplomatic attempts by Spain to recover it have got nowhere; the issue still seems to rankle in the Spanish mind. Thus one small slip of attention, a complacent assumption of safety, had completely changed the life of the peninsula for over 300 years.

THE PATH TO MOSCOW I: CHARLES XII OF SWEDEN, 1708–09 Perhaps in this day and age Charles XII lacks the fame of two later enthusiasts for Russian campaigning. Let me first give a brief picture of this extraordinary monarch. Then we shall find out how it all went so wrong.

Born of a Swedish father and a German mother, he inherited the throne of Sweden in 1697 at the age of fifteen. Sweden was then the strongest nation of northern Europe, ruling both north and south of the Baltic. The boy-King's vulnerability was pointed out by the Swedish renegade Patkul to several neighbouring powers who had lost territory to the Swedes. But at eighteen Charles suddenly realised who he was, displaying extraordinary aptitude in military matters, inspired by the examples of Alexander and Julius Caesar. A succession of astonishing battles against the allied neighbouring nations left him the victor in the first Great Northern War. At the Battle of Narva, identified and revered as the 'Thermopylae' of the Swedish army, he defeated the huge but chaotic forces of Peter the Great.

As an absolute monarch Charles led the army in person. His ideal way of life was to be with the army. He was of the Lutheran faith, austere in his habits, even spartan. He hardly ever touched alcohol. He never married, admitting that he had a fear of strong emotion and the length of the commitment. He needed discipline and self-control because he had great ambitions for the Swedish Empire. His genius as a military commander was abundantly clear. He was known for his almost suicidal indifference to danger on the battlefield, and tolerance of injury and pain.

Mathematics was Charles's intellectual speciality. He comes across as a humane ruler at home – *when* he was at home, that is. He was a devout follower of Martin Luther. I wonder if that Church's mysterious doctrines of Predestination and Grace had supported a sense of his own destiny? His troops apparently lived with 'a pious fatalism'. 'A man,' declared Charles, 'should not worry about being killed in battle; you would not die unless God had decreed it was your time to die.'

The awe and admiration of this modern Alexander resounded through Europe. He was uncompromising. Voltaire records that in his first address to the Swedish parliament he had stated: 'I have resolved never to start an unjust war, but never to end a legitimate one except by defeating my enemies.'

For an absolute monarch so quickly elevated to such a great height, it would not be surprising if the heady perspective of hubris had somewhat affected the young leader. Loren Carrica has recently studied the background of Charles and the progress of his campaign against Peter the Great. And sure enough, she finds many causes and symptoms of the hubris known to the Greeks. In particular, a general assumption or 'false narrative' that Charles was invincible had been spread through the populace over the years of the Great Northern War. And Charles shared that view. Invincibility was a systematic element of his leadership, in tandem with another assumption: that all Russian forces were to be held in contempt. The constant repetition of this belief within his army boosted the morale of his soldiers – but detached them from reality. What if the Russian forces became stronger over the years, trained by imported British and European generals? And Russian casualties could always be replaced from the population of that vast land, but an invader had to rely on minimal losses. Indeed, Peter the Great had observed after the Battle of Narva: 'I know that the Swedes will long beat us, but in time they will teach us to beat them.'

Charles now calmed the turbulence of the ongoing Great Northern War and installed Stanislaus I as King in Poland, his own choice of monarch. Charles, aged twenty-five, was at last able to turn his ambition towards Russia.

During this campaign Charles was to receive many chance setbacks: personal injury, attacks by Cossacks, and unreliable reinforcements and allies. But our real subject is the fatal attraction of Moscow and the assured dangers of the route itself. It is like the difference between 'insurance', against events that *might* happen, and 'assurance', against events that *shall* happen: retirement, death and the Russian winter.

The Swedish King began his Russian campaign from Poland with an army of over 40,000. Voltaire described it as 'now shining resplendent in gold and silver, and enriched with the spoils of Poland and Saxony'. By January 1708 Charles had crossed the Vistula, despite the dangerous state of ice on the river. Half the force was cavalry, Charles believing in quick advances. It is unlikely he expected to spend a *second* winter on Russian earth.

By late January they had reached Grodno through ice and snow, Swedish troops being accustomed to campaign in the dead of winter since the reign of Gustavus Adolphus. A short battle with some of the Tsar's forces led to the perhaps ominous retreat of the Russians.

Charles pushed on eastwards through marshes, empty plains, immense forests and grain-growing steppe where all produce was kept hidden by the country folk. It took *four months* to get as far as the Berezina river, about 300 miles east of Grodno: for the winter lasted longer than expected and the Russians had been laying waste the lands along their line of retreat. There was nothing new about 'scorched earth'. It's an ancient tactic that Charles must have known about.

Despite these problems, an encounter with the Russians at Holowczyn led to what Charles called his 'favourite victory'. Tsar Peter then proposed a truce through a Polish nobleman sent to the Swedish headquarters. Charles replied: 'I shall treat with the Tsar at Moscow.' That was a haughty assumption, that he would get to Moscow at all.

By September the Swedish army was in the wasted country leading to Smolensk, about 200 miles from Moscow. But now the lack of provisions became serious. General Levenhaupt's reinforcements and supply train were lagging far behind.

Charles at last admits that Moscow is impossible to reach.

Ignoring all advice to wait, or return to Levenhaupt's position, Charles astounds the whole army by turning off the Moscow road, and heading south into the Ukraine, thus getting even further away from the supply train.

An assumption that the hardened Swedes could cope with a second winter now has to contend not just with an average Russian winter, but the coldest for 500 years: the Great Frost of 1709. In one night away from camp over 2,000 of his soldiers died.

By the end of this terrible winter, his army was depleted by nearly half, and suffered from sickness, exhaustion and despair. The Russian army had meanwhile gained experience, skill and unlimited reinforcements, and had now, as Peter the Great had predicted, already learnt how to beat the Swedes. Yet in June 1709 the irrepressible Charles laid siege to the town of Poltava, hoping to capture an ammunition magazine and find much-needed provisions. But he was shot in the foot while on reconnaissance and was now unable to direct his forces.

By the time he had recovered it was too late to avoid defeat. The assumption of his invincibility was exploded. *Peripeteia* cast its shadow across the scene, and in a state of fever from his wound, even Charles lost the will to plan further action.

Most of the army ended up as prisoners of the Tsar. The King, though, escaped with a small troop. Somehow they found their way through the harshest terrain imaginable, crossed the Berezina again and eventually came to rest in an obscure outpost of the Ottoman Empire, near the Black Sea. It took long, wearying years for Charles to extricate himself from this backwater.

> The vanquished hero leaves his Broken Bands
> And shews his Miseries in distant lands;
> Condemned a needy Supplicant to wait
> While Ladies interpose and Slaves debate.

His Russia campaign had been doomed by factors not exactly unpredictable. The chief of these seem to have been:

– exhausting, hellish terrain
– the policy of scorched earth
– the Russian winter
– his underestimation of Russian improvement under Peter the Great
– the vast reserves of Russian forces.

Captain James Jefferyes, a British diplomat accompanying the campaign, considered that even more fatal than these factors was that 'The King would not hearken to any advice that was given him by his Counsellors, who I can assure you were for carrying on by another method.'

Charles was guilty of 'reckless assumptions', that is, very high risk and lacking enquiry beforehand. But I can't help thinking that more enquiry would have been unwelcome. The results might have forced him to abandon the whole project. Being such a fatalistic military machine of a man, what on earth was he going to do instead? He had no interest in society. At dinner with Charles it seems there was a rigid ban on conversation. Civilian life had no value for him. He was the shark who must keep swimming onward, lest he die from inaction.

Voltaire, in his vivid and rather romantic biography, judged him a hero whose 'only fault and misfortune was taking things to excess'. For example, what had once been his admirable resolution degraded into obstinacy. Voltaire concludes that Charles was certainly an extraordinary man, but not a great one.

Charles XII died at the age of thirty-six in mysterious circumstances during a local campaign against Norway. He earned the ambiguous distinction of featuring in Samuel Johnson's famous poem just quoted above, *The Vanity of Human Wishes*, of which the last verse tells of his death:

> His Fall was destined to a barren Strand,
> A petty Fortress, and a dubious Hand;
> He left the Name at which the World grew pale,
> To point a Moral or adorn a Tale.

THE QUEBEC EXPEDITION, 1711 A naval expedition to fight against the French at Quebec was agreed by the government of Robert Harley. It would defend New England, and in the process establish a policy of British dominance of the sea. The naval element of the plan was led by Admiral Sir Hovenden Walker, well-experienced in leading convoys across the Atlantic. Bolingbroke was the politician in charge. By cloaking it in secrecy he created many problems for those who would carry it out. The provisions were kept to three months' worth, suggesting a European adventure, to hide its transatlantic purpose from spies. Even the Admiralty was kept in the dark, thus depriving Admiral Walker of the navy's knowledge of the northeastern American seaboard. However, the navy had never charted the St Lawrence and it remained a 'dangerous enigma'.

After several weeks of delay they sailed first to Boston, Massachusetts, where the fleet – the largest ever seen in North America – expected to be able to replenish supplies. An assumption seems to have been made that this would be a matter of course, but in fact the city of Boston and the New England countryside were unable to meet their demands. The governor of the state even ordered days of fasting to ease the problem. Eventually supplies were obtained, to be carefully husbanded so as to last the whole voyage. Walker also had difficulties in finding pilots with any experience of the area, and any accurate charts of the St Lawrence gulf, estuary and river. This concerned him and in due course he switched his flag to one of the smaller ships, the *Edgar*.

The fleet, supplemented by colonial troops, and consisting of some 14,000 soldiers and sailors in all, sailed from Boston at the end of July, much later than had been anticipated. This added further time-pressure, as the river would begin to freeze by November. Walker was increasingly concerned about the many dangers in the St Lawrence. Even compass needles were at risk from iron-bearing hills along the shore.

Admiral Walker led his fleet from the front. Things began to go wrong once they had left the Gulf of St Lawrence. They passed south of the long arc of Anticosti Island into the estuary, the largest in the world, where fresh and salt water mingled. Here low-lying fog could form at any time. Navigation was reduced to complete guesswork, based on the last sighting of land (This was the era before the Harrison chronometer and the sextant). Beyond Anticosti they turned southwest, aiming at distant Quebec. Here the estuary was about seventy miles wide, though after Sept Iles it would narrow considerably on the northern side, where the isleted coast turned sharply south.

By 23 August, after two days in fog, Walker had assumed from his last sighting of land that he was in the mid-stream of the estuary. He retired for the night, seemingly comfortable in the expectation of steady progress on an uncharted route. He had set a slight sail and a tacking course to the southwest, which would indeed have led the fleet down the centre of the estuary. Unfortunately, he was not in mid-stream at all, but twenty miles further north. Worse, a powerful unseen current was shifting the fleet northward.

By now a gale had sprung up from the east and was blowing hard. The fog had disappeared. He was told by his flag-captain that land had been sighted ahead. But their communication seems to have been vague. Assuming that his course had gone too close to the southern shore he adjusted the fleet's direction – to the north. Thus the islets, rocks and reefs of the northern coast crept ever closer.

During the night a soldier, Captain Goddard, was horrified to see breakers ahead and aroused Walker from sleep, but the admiral dismissed his observation as the hysteria of a non-sailor. Goddard insisted he come on deck and see for himself 'or we should surely be lost'. When Walker appeared he immediately ordered evasive action. Ships in severe distress could be seen ahead, and during the rest of the night the dreadful sounds of shipwreck and drowning could be heard. Seven transports and two other ships were lost. After saving as many soldiers as possible, some 500, Walker guided the rest of the fleet to safety.

Not until three days later could the full extent of the disaster be realised. Some 700 soldiers are estimated to have drowned, and a number of sailors too, a total of almost 900. Walker's log showed that the fleet was now forty-five miles further west than expected. The gale and current had soon exploded the assumption he had been forced to make of his position. But who can say what pressure Walker was under, by this stage of such a voyage? And yet... Was it odd that a soldier, rather than one of his officers, first discerned the danger of the breakers in the darkness?

It was one of the worst British naval disasters. Walker had already had to deal with an accumulation of dangerous assumptions made by Bolingbroke and others: that the fleet would sail in good time; that there would be enough supplies at Boston; that the Admiralty need not be involved; that accurate charts could be obtained; that pilots with knowledge could be engaged; a chain of disappointments steadily weakening the progress of the operation.

And in fact Walker was not blamed for the disaster, because the government were keen to divert attention from the whole sorry tale of the Quebec Expedition, now quickly abandoned. But the Admiralty made life difficult for him later and his career did not end happily.

THE ELUSIVE NORTHWEST PASSAGE, 1714 The quest for a sea passage from the high latitudes of the North Atlantic across to the Pacific had exhausted the energy and patience of Tudor and Stuart explorers. They finally gave up in the reign of Charles I. Straits, bays and islands now bore the illustrious names of Davis, Baffin, Hudson, Frobisher, Foxe and James. Minimal interest was shown over the next eighty years. On reaching the reasonable and scientific eighteenth century, it was presumed that the quest was dead. But in fact it was about to be resurrected.

Starting with the 1714 voyage of Captain Knight, a bizarre edifice of delusion was being constructed by the optimistic promoters of voyages to the same region. They were assisted by what became known as 'speculative' mapmakers. Hundreds of ordinary sailors and fairly sane volunteers were tempted to embark on largely futile, miserable and dangerous journeys to find the 'The Strait of Anian'. This mythical strait was thought to be the final exit of a northwest passage into the Pacific. Perhaps it was somewhere north of California, then thought to be an island, or much further north in the unknown spaces of Canada and Alaska. It kept appearing on maps, though it had never been found. The identity of whoever first dreamt up this desirable waterway remains unknown.

In the revived search for a northwest passage, the focus was on Hudson Bay. The Hudson Bay Company had been quietly exploiting a trading monopoly given to them some forty years earlier. The directors of the company in London looked askance at these new ventures. James Knight, however, had been the company's governor of the Bay since 1692. By

1714 he was too old really for the exertion demanded by the treacherous Bay, but he was still ambitious for further riches.

The attraction of a more direct passage to the Pacific lay in a great increase in trade, and in the prospect of finding gold and other minerals along its imagined route. Against this was the stubborn fact that the ice of the Bay only opened up for exploration for a couple of months each summer. But by then the energetic relationship between ice floes and tidal streams became dangerous. During the rest of the year the brutality of the weather was way beyond the imagination of the British sailors. And it was not until much later in the century that scurvy was vanquished by sauerkraut, and before longitude was properly calculated using John Harrison's magnificent chronometer.

In the event, James Knight's expedition vanished without a trace somewhere in the Bay.

Next, an engineer and a member of the Irish parliament interested in the trading potential of the passage, Arthur Dobbs, published a seventy-page prospectus in 1731. It contained over-confident vague remarks such as: 'There seem to be strong Reasons to believe there is a passage Northwestwards of Hudson Bay, and that Passage no way Difficult by being pestered with Ice.' And 'In the north west corner of Hudson Bay the presumptions are strong for a Passage.' Dobbs used the impersonal language of 'reasons' and 'presumptions', since he had no evidence from human sources, except an uncertain report of big tidal movements in Hudson Bay. These might suggest a link with the Pacific, on the wild assumption that the Bay was nearer to the Pacific than the Atlantic. And someone's single sighting of black whales had allowed him to assume that these must have somehow come from the Pacific. Dobbs himself had never experienced the unimaginable difficulties of Hudson Bay and the mazes of choked-up ice along its west coast. He suggested that it would be comparatively easy to survey. But of course there was no need for him to take part himself.

Both of his projects ended unhappily in enquiries and controversy. He then retired, leaving other promoters to spread their own brands of delusion.

Thus the glowing prospect of finding the passage and reaping its rewards was constantly aired. The crews were sufficiently seduced by likely success. Elsewhere, the speculative mapmakers were flourishing on the proceeds of elaborate and grandiose maps that seemed to impart a growing knowledge of northwest America, yet were based on an almost complete lack of evidence. What little they did have was gleaned from the returning voyagers themselves, in the form of unreliable observations of tides and ice, and from the murky travellers' tales of previous centuries. And it seemed that a place can enjoy a plausible existence merely from being featured on a map, especially if the map has been published by such an eminence as the Royal Geographer to the King of France.

Meanwhile, an expedition under Vitus Bering, his second, had set out from the coast of Russia to search for two large landmasses, Yezo and de Gama, in the North Pacific, and, east of them, the elusive 'Strait of Anian'. Unfortunately this whole project, supported by the Russian government, was under the guidance of Joseph Delisle, a highly speculative French cartographer employed at St Petersburg. The landmasses turned out to be imaginary, but managed to split the expedition in two. They both reached the Alaskan coast, but could not land, nor did they find any strait. The expeditions lost their purpose and both suffered dangerous return journeys through the Aleutian Islands chain, leading to the death of Bering and others in a shipwreck.

One of Bering's surviving officers, Sven Waxell, a Swede, put the blame on cartographers such as Delisle, 'who obtained all their knowledge from visions… it would only be reasonable were such unknown lands first to be explored before they are trumpeted abroad as being the coast of Yezo or de Gama… my blood still boils whenever I think of the scandalous deception of which we were the victims.' Delisle, though, moved to Paris and, with Buache, published ever more fantastical and dangerous maps.

Thus the interplay of 'information' between such parties, though personal communication was sadly lacking, ignited a sort of Infernal Assumption Engine, running for the rest of the century, until the more expert mariners – James Cook, La Pérouse and George Vancouver – put a stop to the nonsense. The fury of the deluded had expended itself in the air of remote frozen regions. Cook himself had harsh words in his journal for the 'speculatives'. Too much of his Third Voyage had been devoted to an exploration of the Pacific coast right up to the Bering Strait, where he found huge sheets of ice blocking any waterway to the east. This discovery, so far north, pretty well finished off the Northwest Passage as a reasonable proposition.

The Passage was finally identified some three centuries later by Roald Amundsen, but not as a continuous unfrozen waterway suitable for shipping. It is the rise in sea temperatures since that has finally begun to open the passage.

LOUIS XV'S 'DEERPARK' His better-informed subjects might, at first, have assumed that when Louis retired to the 'Parc aux Cerfs,' he was riding out near Versailles beneath the dappled shade of ancient trees, admiring or hunting the deer. But the King was after other game. The Parc aux Cerfs was the name of an ordinary house in a smart street in the town of Versailles. It housed Louis' private brothel. Here, writes Harold Nicolson in *The Age of Reason*, 'he did much damage to his repute, his constitution and his powers of application.'

CHARLES VII, HOLY ROMAN EMPEROR, 1742 As Elector of Bavaria, Charles Albert of the Wittelsbach dynasty aspired to become Holy Roman Emperor. This was rather ambitious considering that the role of Emperor had been fulfilled by the Habsburg family for an unbroken 300 years. But he managed to get himself acclaimed as King of Bohemia after a short campaign of invasion; and he managed to get elected Emperor on 24 January 1742. He succeeded Charles VI, the father of Maria Theresa. Although she ruled as Archduchess of Austria and Queen of Hungary, as a woman she was unable to become Emperor. But it was more of a symbolic role by this time.

But on the very day of election, Charles suffered the loss of his own capital, Munich, to an Austrian force sent by Maria Theresa. She had wept at the loss of Bohemia and considered his election as Holy Roman Emperor a catastrophe. But by insisting on a campaign in the dead of winter she had surprised Charles, who had assumed there was no danger in that season – and perhaps no danger from a woman?

Charles fled from Munich and settled at Frankfurt, another Imperial city. But from there he had no control over either Bavaria or the Empire. He was mocked as 'an Emperor and nothing', a play on the words of Julius Caesar that he would have 'an Empire *or* nothing'.

Charles died from gout in 1745, aged only forty-eight. The Imperial throne was now held by Francis, the husband of Maria Theresa, who could at last be entitled 'Empress'.

COLLAPSE OF A VAST ASSUMPTION, 1755 Until this time thinkers such as Leibniz, Voltaire, Shaftesbury, and an accumulated fair-weather impetus within society, had sustained a vast general assumption: that this was, on careful consideration, the best of all possible worlds. They looked back on the seventeenth century aghast at such destabilising events as the Thirty Years' War and the English Civil War. The 'enthusiasm' of that century was now replaced by the idea of 'Deism', a calm optimistic belief that there was a Supreme Manager or Geometrician benevolently inclined to mankind; he was not the Christian God, but a being who was present but had not revealed himself. Mankind was the measure of all things and the centre of the universe. Thus evil could be tolerated when seen within this context. The Augustan Age in England was believed to have reached a perfection of society, the end of history, the language 'fixed' within the majestic and grave sentences of John Dryden, Dr Johnson and Alexander Pope. The still-powerful Church seemed to co-exist with these ideas and Deism offered a refuge for those who no longer believed Christian theology.

But one single event of 1755 was to shatter these comfortable dreams, beginning at twenty to ten on a Sunday morning, 1 November, All Saints' Day, in the city of Lisbon. At least 10,000 citizens were killed in six minutes beneath the bells and towers of the packed churches, by an earthquake of extreme intensity. How could a beneficent Being or Supreme Manager allow such a catastrophe to injure and kill those who were about to offer worship? To crush the lives out of children and babes? And the one part of Lisbon not suffering much damage turned out to be the red-light district…

Fires from toppled candles added to the destruction. Tidal waves from the epicentre of the quake, off Cape St Vincent, flooded the lower city and also caused damage as far away as the Azores and western Ireland.

People interpreted the disaster in various ingenious ways. Voltaire lost at a stroke his Deist beliefs. No longer could he think that 'all was for the best in the best of all possible worlds'. His famous poem and his satire *Candide* followed. He adopted an agnostic view, not clearly defined.

Dismay and doubt spread across Europe.

But a distinctive feature of the relief and rebuilding in Lisbon was the enlightened and vigorous practical leadership of the prime minister, the Marquis of Pombal. He overruled the Church, imposing his own novel ideas. For example, he sent a questionnaire to every affected settlement in order to understand better what had really happened.

VOLTAIRE, DEFENDER OF FREE SPEECH, 1758 'I disapprove of what you say, but I shall defend to the death your right to say it.' These famous words are taken to be Voltaire's own, but are in fact a supposition of his likely point of view, expressed in the 1906 biography of Voltaire by Evelyn Hall.

It arose when she was describing his reaction to the condemnation and burning, by the College of the Sorbonne, of a controversial and heretical work by Helvetius. Voltaire did not admire Helvetius, but deplored even more the attempts to silence him by French institutions.

PARLIAMENT AND THE NORTH AMERICAN COLONIES, 1763–1783 In these two decades a Gordian knot of linked assumptions had entangled the collective mind of parliament. They were almost paralysed by their ignorance and confusion. How did that arise?

The early history of westward exploration and the search for the Spice Islands had led men to imagine the coast of America as mainly a trading venture; the parallel naval conflicts with Spain and France along these coasts had reinforced the idea of plantations as prizes of war.

Alongside these limiting views, a notion had sprung up somehow that Britain was becoming over-populated with the idle and wretched and that the colonies were a convenient dumping ground. Over the course of time, this undermined respect for the quality of the colonising populace.

Parliament held to the plausible yet deranged creed of mercantilism, by which a colony could sell raw materials only and the mother country sold them its manufactured goods. When the colonists objected to this formula, they were accused of being 'unreasonable' and of resisting the unquestioned assumption that mercantilism was the 'gospel' of commerce. Adam Smith had not yet demolished this theory in *The Wealth of Nations*, published in the appropriate year of 1776.

And then there was the sheer distance. 3,000 miles of ocean, rudimentary coastal charts and a paucity of more extensive mapping left the British ignorant of the hinterlands beyond the Appalachians and their great potential. But the population of the Colonies had risen from 339,000 in 1720 to over two million by 1763.

It was this compounding ignorance that prevented parliament from making proper decisions about the future of the colonies. Some of their opinions might have been understandable if the colonists had been as feckless as they imagined. But they simply did not know who they were dealing with.

Another unhelpful assumption was that the colonies were all different and lacking in morale. It seems they didn't know that the colonies had imported British political traditions, with elected assemblies. They had no idea that their rising populations had already developed a patriotic sensibility about their American hills and plains, forests and rivers. These feelings were stronger than their fading memories of the mother country.

Who and what cut the Gordian knot? The genius and courage of Benjamin Franklin, the verdict of the American War of Independence and the loss of thirteen British colonies.

JEAN-JACQUES ROUSSEAU, 1712–1778 Whatever else he was, this strange genius was by no means a foe of assumptions.

In the later decades of the eighteenth century, Rousseau was probably the most influential voice after Voltaire. But where Voltaire had aimed to be sceptical and rational, Rousseau tended towards the sentimental and exaggerated. Was the Age of Reason going soft in the head?

His idea of the Law of Nature was based on a myth: that man had been born virtuous, a 'noble savage' in fact, but had been undermined by false education, corrupt institutions and bad laws. This myth was hard to refute as there was little evidence from the past: it was a kind of assumption. But myths may be needed by a society; they can gain power and develop an appetite for 'facts' to support them; if the facts cannot be found they may be invented for the purpose. In the case of the noble savage, 'Utopia' was imposed upon the past.

Then there was his famous antithesis: 'Man is born free, but is everywhere in chains.' Well, I'm afraid I don't go along with this idea. When out skiing I often stayed in a Swiss hotel named after the great man. The hotel cat was 'Rousseau' too. The décor of my agreeable room included lists of quotations from Jean-Jacques. So I had ample opportunity to ponder the 'born free' notion.

Au contraire, I reckon we are born instantly into networks of 'chains' – chains can be useful as well as oppressive – made up of family, dwelling-place, schools, society, the law, the nation, humanity. Rousseau is on surer ground if by 'chains' he is referring to the Bourbons continuing to pile up trouble for themselves by their over-repressive regimes.

Rousseau also gave us 'All men are born equal.' This has been described by Harold Nicolson as 'a dangerous fallacy that could lead only to incompetence and the despotism of the mob'.

Thus Rousseau had a talent for creating superficially plausible phrases, only too likely to swell within uncritical minds into undermining assumptions.

He strode further onto shaky ground with his pernicious idea of the *Contrat Social*, 1762, which states that the individual must surrender his personal rights to the community, who were the holders of the 'General Will'. The People as Sovereign could never be wrong. This sounds precariously close to totalitarian dictatorship. It was a source of much muddled thinking and injustice. For example, during the Terror the Jacobins exploited this concept to blur the fact that they did not command a majority of the French people. In the Declaration of 1793 they proclaimed the Rights of Man and at the same time proclaimed Rousseau's Right of the People to violate those rights.

Such phrases of Rousseau, once set free, are greeted cheerfully by rebels and revolutionaries who have no interest in their original meaning and intention. The clichés of Rousseau are perhaps some of the most dangerous in history.

Madame de Staël was the first to challenge Rousseau: 'He inflamed everything, but discovered nothing.'

Compared with minds such as Bayle and Voltaire, both vigorous enemies of assumption, Rousseau was seen by many as a menace. Harold

Nicolson accuses him of somehow managing to destroy the age of reason and to substitute in its place a 'universe of fantasies that introduced much confusion, much unhappiness, much cruelty and many illusions into the civilised world'.

J.W. VON GOETHE: *THE SORROWS OF YOUNG WERTHER,* 1774 Written by its young author in five weeks as a confession of, and release from, a stormy emotional period, Goethe was also aware of the wider value of this work as a cautionary tale, against the evils of introspection. He assumed it would function as a warning, offering 'a comprehensible expression of an inner sickly and youthful delusion'.

Well, imagine his surprise when young men in Germany – from Breslau to Frankfurt, from Leipzig to Cologne – popped up in the streets all wearing Werther's blue coat and buff waistcoat and contemplating imminent suicide.

'This little book,' wrote the author in later years, 'which helped me so much personally, may have done great harm to others.' Indeed, suicides were reported after its publication and the book was banned in Leipzig, Weimar, Copenhagen and Italy. This behaviour became recognised in psychiatry as the 'Werther Effect' or 'copycat suicide,' and the problem seems to persist in varying forms to this day.

EDWARD GIBBON, 1776 *The History of the Decline and Fall of the Roman Empire,* published over twelve years in six volumes, is an astonishing achievement. The width and depth of his perspective is exhilarating, the energy within his eloquent prose seemingly inexhaustible and its vast resources well-referenced for re-excavation.

Gibbon was what in the eighteenth century was called a 'philosophic historian', one who rises above the overwhelming minutiae of historical facts: 'one damn thing after another'. Instead he attempts to build an impartial, clear and unique image in which the causes of things can be discerned. Gibbon had understood the secret mechanism – 'secret' in the sense of not being easily visible to the populace – whereby human society flourished or declined, 'Decline' of course being the ultimate subject of his book.

Adam Ferguson, a Scottish Enlightenment friend of Gibbon, had explained this mechanism in his *Essay on the History of Civil Society*:

> Mankind, in following the present sense of their minds, in striving to remove inconveniences, or to gain apparent and adjoining advantages, arrive at ends which even their imagination could not anticipate, and pass on, like other animals, in the track of their nature, without perceiving its end… Every step and every movement of the multitude, even in what are termed enlightened ages, are made with equal blindness to the future, and nations stumble upon establishments, which are indeed the result of human action, but not the execution of any human design.

The 'blindness to the future' is taken by Gibbon to mean that history is a series of unintended consequences. These are derived from many accidental causes, not just from the divine or the heroic. These causes surely include forgotten or outdated large assumptions of previous administrations and cultures. But these may have survived in altered or distorted forms. People and nations were thus gradually and 'insensibly' (an adverb frequently used by Gibbon) caught up in changes and evolutions that they were unaware of and could not wholly understand.

Using this unintended consequences theory, Gibbon was famously able to progress beyond the previous assumption of historians that the barbarians were the destroyers of the Roman Empire. His far more subtle appreciation showed how the two 'sides' needed the strengths of each other and in so doing encouraged the development of European civilisation.

To take a more domestic example, who would have imagined that the suffragettes, so stubbornly convinced of their cause yet so unappreciated in the Edwardian years, would find their greatest, if unconscious, proponent in Kaiser Wilhelm II? For by the end of the First World War, the position of women had changed vastly, the result of their ability to fulfil new and vital roles demanded by an unprecedented struggle.

Thus the philosophic historian needs to be alert to such ironic or paradoxical relations between cause and effect.

LOUIS XVI: THE FLIGHT TO VARENNES, 21 JUNE 1791 Having given up on air travel and car rental for getting to the winter Alps (I just can't be doing with those in-car 'infotainment' systems), I drive my own capacious motor through the profound depths of Champagne and Lorraine. I love those backroads, poplar-lined, empty for miles ahead. One spring evening I approached a small town in the Argonne called Varennes. There are several towns of this name in France, but could this be *the* Varennes of Louis XVI and his family's 'Flight to Varennes'? This was soon confirmed by several clues in the main street.

But the event is misleadingly named: Varennes was not the intended destination of Louis and his Austrian queen, Marie Antoinette and their children; it was just a place along their route from Paris to Montmédy, near the northeastern border of France. Up there, troops loyal to the Bourbon monarch were stationed: the Marquis de Bouillé's 'Army of the East'. This force consisted of some 10,000 soldiers of the Old Guard and auxiliaries from Switzerland and elsewhere. There Louis would be protected, and could campaign to wrest power back from the revolutionaries in Paris.

One assumption that Louis had made before this escape from the Tuileries Palace was that there was considerable support for him in the country at large. But this was not so. And the journey itself was badly managed: too conspicuous, too late, too slow. They did not follow the route recommended by Bouillé, or take his advice to split the party between different conveyances. Eventually they were recognised and arrested when they reached Varennes.

Not long after my chance route through the town, I came across this quotation from the mouth of the unfortunate monarch: 'The French people are incapable of regicide.'

JOSEPH HAYDN: *MISSA IN ANGUSTIIS (MASS IN TROUBLED TIMES)*, 1798 This mass was composed – with good reason – in the dark key of D minor. Napoleon's armies had won several battles against Austria and were now attempting to wreck British trade routes from Egypt. Vienna itself, now Haydn's home, had been threatened the year before. Austria was in a state of constant anxiety.

In September 1798 the mass was first performed, at Eisenstadt. The orchestral forces had been reduced by Haydn's patron, so the woodwind and brass sections were represented only by trumpets. The opening Kyrie is an intense interpretation of 'Lord have mercy upon us', with its relentless motion and virtuosic solo for the soprano. Other movements also fight vigorously through darkness and despair in their own way, except the final Dona nobis pacem.

Haydn had written the mass during the summer, but – and possibly on the very same day as the first performance – news had arrived in Vienna that, seven weeks ago, the British under Nelson had won a major battle against the French, the Battle of the Nile.

Somehow the title of 'Nelson Mass' began to attach itself to the D minor mass and the 'Troubled Times' fell away. Indeed Haydn and Nelson met two years later when the admiral visited Eisenstadt. And they got on very well. But the change of title surely amounted to a distortion and a simplification. I wonder how many listeners over the years have assumed that this anxious fearful music was intended as the music of victory and tried aurally to wrestle, as it were, dark D minor into joyful C major.

In support of this notion, H.C. Robbins Landon, in *Haydn, his Life and Music* laments that performances of the mass in subsequent periods were 'over-inflated'. He blamed this on the 'heroic nickname'.

JANE AUSTEN: *NORTHANGER ABBEY,* 1799 So far this history has had to rely on assumptions mostly made by public figures. But now, in the era of the novel, we can ransack literature for examples of the vulnerability of private individuals. Otherwise we would need access to the diaries and letters of ordinary private citizens, rarely available and not necessarily revealing the diarists' mistakes.

In *Northanger Abbey*, the plot is advanced by two bold assumptions, which I paraphrase here.

Catherine Morland, the seventeen-year-old daughter of a Wiltshire clergyman, visits Bath with her landowning neighbours and close friends, a Mr and Mrs Allen. Catherine settles into Bath's social life with a certain amount of enthusiasm. The first friendship she makes is with a Mrs Thorpe and her three daughters. Soon they meet her son John, down from Oxford. But he is the hearty type of undergraduate that is interested in horseflesh, hunting, frantic outings in gigs – and not much else. His contradictory and ill-disciplined banter becomes tiresome, and causes confusion and embarrassment for others. But because he has brought with him her own brother, James – a friendship made at Oxford, but only just known to Catherine – she feels obliged to treat John Thorpe civilly. This only serves to encourage him in his sudden notion of marrying her – about as likely as the re-appearance of the dodo.

Catherine's more successful friendship in Bath is with a brother and sister just a few years older than herself: the Reverend Henry Tilney and his sister Eleanor. She soon finds herself very drawn to Henry, amusing and witty, yet possessing real depth and manners.

Their father, General Tilney – handsome, decisive, impatient – is the owner of Northanger Abbey in Gloucestershire. It has been in the family since the Dissolution of the Monasteries. He joins them at Bath for a while and notices the warmth between Catherine and his son. At the theatre some time later Catherine notices him talking with John Thorpe. She is surprised at this, and even more surprised to find that she herself seems to be the subject of their animated conversation. But once out of the theatre, she manages to pin down Thorpe about the General:

'But how came you to know him?'

'Know him! There are few people much about town that I do not know. I have met him forever at the Bedford [a London coffee house]…'

A while later, his military colleagues having failed to join him at Bath, the General decides to return home to the Abbey. Thorpe has already let on to Catherine that the General has a high opinion of her, and now she finds, to her great happiness and excitement, that the General has invited her to the Abbey for an indefinite stay, and to be the especial companion of his daughter Eleanor. And Henry will also be there some of the time.

After several happy weeks – always more relaxed when the General is absent, she finds – and with the prospect of many happy weeks to follow, disaster suddenly strikes. The General arrives back one night from London in an agitated state. He immediately arranges through his daughter that Catherine shall leave the Abbey by carriage at seven the next morning, without the offer of any servant – or any explanation. Eleanor is all sympathy, but powerless; she can throw no light on the matter. Henry – who Catherine can never forget – is away, supervising affairs at his parish. So she returns to Wiltshire in a wretched state. After three days of silence and sadness, all is suddenly turned upside down again. Henry unexpectedly arrives, his immediate purpose to inquire if Catherine had returned home safely; his deeper purpose soon vouchsafed to Catherine. From then on the story begins to show signs of 'hastening towards perfect felicity'.

The mystery of the General's harsh decision is explained by Henry. It turns out that Catherine was guilty only of being less rich than the General had supposed. That conversation with Thorpe at the theatre had led the General into a welcome delusion, that Catherine had great prospects on account of her own family and connections. Thorpe, heady with the reflected glory of such an eminent acquaintance as the General, had got carried away and concocted a very misleading picture of Catherine's position. It was his habit, it seemed, always to inflate the status and success of any friend or connection: 'As his intimacy with any acquaintance grew, so regularly grew their fortune.' In the grandeur of this moment, Mr Morland's preferments were doubled and his fortune trebled. The General had assumed that Thorpe's connection with Catherine's brother guaranteed his word. It was not until his recent visit to town and a chance meeting that he learnt the truth, for Thorpe, irritated by Catherine's rejection of his marriage offer, had angrily reversed the Morlands' wealth and Catherine's prospects. The General, 'enraged with everybody in the world but himself,' had set out next day for the Abbey.

Within and alongside the above plot, runs the **other assumption**, which is made by Catherine herself. In the isolation of a Wiltshire parsonage she has acquired a rather perverse ambition to become a 'heroine', in the fashionable neo-Gothic manner of Ann Radcliffe's *The Mysteries of Udolpho*. At Bath she has been attempting to excite others with this obsession: ruined castles and pointed archways hint at a world of delightful horrors, of midnight assassins and drunken gallants.

When finally on the way to Northanger Abbey (some thirty miles north of Bath, in a remote fold of the Cotswolds) the General suggests that she should ride in Henry's open curricle, to better appreciate the passing scene on such a fine day. Catherine's mounting enthusiasm for the Abbey of her imagination, 'just like what one reads about,' is answered by Henry with a hilariously exaggerated introduction to the horrors of a building such as 'what one reads about'. Has she the nerve? he asks, to cope with gloomy passages… conducted by Dorothy the ancient housekeeper… a remote bedroom not used since the death of a cousin twenty years before… the feeble rays of a single lamp… looming tapestries… the secret tunnel to the chapel of St Anthony… 'Can you stand such a ceremony as this?'

In fact the Abbey proves quite cheerful, busy and modernised. Yet Catherine had been more intoxicated by imagining herself a 'heroine' than she realised, to the extent of really needing to be swept up in some dangerous saga or scandal. The death of General Tilney's wife nine years ago, and the General's apparent indifference to the fact, ignites an overheated imagination. Soon she is constructing her own mystery about what really happened to Henry and Eleanor's mother. In the grip of lurid suspicion, she embarks on a risky investigation of Mrs Tilney's old room. But Henry, appearing unexpectedly on the landing, finds her in an agitated state. With superb tact he realises something of her delusion and gently brings her back to a saner view, laying out the circumstances of his mother's death. Without inquiring into exact details, he leaves her with 'Dear Miss Morland, consider the dreadful nature of the suspicions you have entertained. What have you been judging from? Dearest Miss Morland, what ideas have you been admitting?'

Catherine is deeply mortified by this exposure, and – even worse – feels she may have lost Henry's respect and affection. But as we know, this was not the case, and that evening she finds Henry ever kinder.

These two assumptions are made, as it were, against each other: the General deluding himself about Catherine and her family, and Catherine being led by her imagination. She had confused the General's modern residence in the English shires with the wind-blasted perils of an Apennine pass and the guilt-haunted castellations of Italy. In each case the assumption (though Jane Austen does not use that word) is developed from several sources over a period of time and inflated by wishful thinking. In both cases the assumers kept their thoughts rather to themselves, in unhealthy isolation. By contrast, Henry Tilney is a model of rationality, with an open perspective.

(Henry's character may have been partly inspired by the young Sydney

Smith, a clergyman who the Austens knew of, and may even have met, at Bath. Sydney Smith later founded *The Edinburgh Review* and was renowned and loved for his wit: 'My living in Yorkshire was so out of the way that I was twelve miles from a lemon.' He was later a canon of St Paul's Cathedral.)

J.W. VON GOETHE: *FAUST, PART ONE*, 1808 This play focuses on the somewhat obscure figure of the German alchemist Johann Georg Faust, who may have studied at Heidelberg University at the start of the sixteenth century. A legend had grown around him that he had made a pact with the devil, risking his soul after death. Many versions had appeared before Goethe's, notably by Christopher Marlowe. But Goethe's version, with *Part Two*, is considered one of the greatest works of German literature.

Faust, an intelligent yet dissatisfied scholar, is guilty of hubris in making a bargain with the devil – and in thinking that he might yet outwit him. Thus he is breaching the limits of the divine order allowed by the Fates. But Faust, unable to properly engage with humankind, tied up with futile solitary investigations, has also made a terrible assumption: that he can spend the rest of his earthly life in worldly pleasures, in repulsively regular contact with the devil's agent, Mephistopheles; and without causing any harm to other people. But this is clearly not possible, which is immediately proven during the early scene at Auerbach's beer cellar in Leipzig. Far worse, the dreadful fate of Gretchen and her family lies at the heart of Goethe's *Part One*.

THE PATH TO MOSCOW II: NAPOLEON BONAPARTE, 1812 To dominate Europe with a Napoleonic 'peace', Bonaparte had become gripped by the finalising idea of a 'decisive victory' over the Russia of Tsar Alexander.

The notorious disaster of 1812 certainly involved many dangerous assumptions, propelled in part by the hubris of Napoleon and his extraordinary track record of driving his soldiers through the 'impossible' to eventual success. His big expensive campaigns could not be predicted in every detail, but he had developed such confidence in his ability to improvise, that he was not afraid of blind adventures.

I relate the march to Moscow simply in terms of Napoleon's apparent thoughts and actions. The Retreat from Moscow is more famous and dramatic; the Advance is perhaps more intriguing.

Napoleon had a poor opinion of the Russian Army, recently vanquished at Austerlitz. By early 1812 he had recruited several allies including Prussia and Austria. With these he created a new Grand Army of some 600,000 strong. He had hoped to fight the Russians if and when they made an expected move into Poland. But by March, with no sign of that happening, he decided to attack them in Russia itself. He imagined joining battle not far over the border. He was gambling on a quick victory, which would not require a march all the way to Moscow.

He already knew Alexander, liked him and respected his intelligence, but he considered him indecisive and somewhat feminine. He went so far as to jest that if Alexander had been a woman he should have married her. But in fact Alexander *had* been decisive – choosing a different kind of war, avoiding pitched battles in favour of long retreats leading to entrenched camps, as used by Wellington in Spain. By the end of March, Napoleon had learnt that if his army took a stand on the Vistula, the Russian army would deploy on the Niemen, to the east, not far from the Tsar's headquarters at Vilna. And an entrenched camp was being prepared behind, at Drissa.

Yet Napoleon still anticipated the 'big battle', which he believed would lead to the longed-for 'decisive victory' in twenty days. He did not seem to have taken the alternative threat of a long tactical retreat seriously, even though his respected aide-de-camp, Count Narbonne-Lara, had heard it from Alexander himself, during a diplomatic visit to Vilna. The Count had warned Napoleon not to invade Russia – but his advice was unheeded. How could Napoleon so easily assume that the enemy would stand and fight, and thereby give him his decisive victory? Had he misunderstood the Alexander he thought he knew?

Preparations for the invasion proceeded. But assuming a quick victory, winter clothing was not included in the supplies, nor the spiked horseshoes essential for a horse's grip on snow and ice. Napoleon had read Voltaire's account of Charles XII's failed campaign. And he had already experienced the difficulties of the Polish winter during his campaign of 1806–07. But he still went ahead…

The march to the east started with the crossing of the River Niemen on 23 June. From here on, though, things start to deteriorate and Napoleon's persistence becomes puzzling. After five days the Grand Army reached Vilna, and found the Russian army evacuating the city and retreating to the camp at Drissa. Napoleon had hoped he would be able to use huge supply magazines left behind, but all he found was a pile of ashes, and the bridge across the river destroyed. But should this have been a surprise to him?

Already the weather had turned, wet and chilly even in mid-summer. Roads had become quagmires. Rations were utterly inadequate, the land providing little nourishment. The advance guard lived pretty well, but the rest of the army behind was dying of hunger and exhaustion; 10,000 horses had already perished. But Napoleon's mind seemed ever more haunted by the all-important 'decisive victory' over Russia. That victory would force Alexander to see reason and allow Napoleon to achieve European dominance.

Summer now reverted to hot and dry weather. Brutal Cossack raids were a constant grievance. To the east, the retreating Russian Army was getting closer to the high road leading to Moscow. Would the Tsar reach Vitebsk and bring on the desired battle there?

Napoleon has been described as a perennial optimist. Thus his dispatches to Maret on 25 and 26 July: 'The entire Russian Army is at Vitebsk. We are on the eve of great events… I am heading right now for Vitebsk… things could not go better… the country is beautiful, the harvest superb and we find food everywhere…' This was all fantasy: the Grand Army was in a dire strait.

Thus the fateful pattern of retreat by the Russians and deeper advance by the Grand Army continued through Vitebsk and then through Smolensk, now left to burn. The Russian general Barclay de Tolly was clearly enacting the policy of 'scorched earth'. Most of the actual 'scorching' was delegated to the Cossacks. Yet Napoleon tells General Cailancourt: 'We shall be in Moscow in a month; we shall have peace within six months.' This confident statement assumed that the Tsar would defend Moscow and give Napoleon his chance. That happened earlier than he expected, at the small town of Borodino.

But even that notoriously destructive battle was not decisive. The Russians continued to retreat, even from Moscow itself, evacuated and burning by the time the Grand Army entered on 15 September. Alexander had withdrawn from the city, and never replied to any communication from Napoleon. All Napoleon's efforts had ended at indecision, his purpose vanishing as water runs into the sands of the desert.

By the time the French had escaped from Russian territory some 400,000 of the Grand Army had died and another 100,000 were taken captive, though these figures are still a matter of dispute. Napoleon placed the blame on the weather. It was agreed that his time would now best be spent in Paris.

In contrast to Napoleon's high stakes assumptions and inexplicable risk-taking, we return to a rural England where assumptions on a personal level are just as important for those involved.

JANE AUSTEN: *EMMA*, 1815 Emma is a clever, rich and handsome twenty-one-year-old. As the doted-upon daughter of the nervous and long-widowed Mr Woodhouse, she has charge of the household (And that is 'what all women want', according to Chaucer's Wife of Bath in *The Canterbury*

Tales). For someone on such a seemingly confident pedestal in the society of Highbury, her Surrey village, she is oddly anxious about questions of class; in other respects she is liable to over-confidence. She takes a close interest in people, and is dutiful, kind and active, though tending to know what is best for others. In the case of Harriet, an innocent protégé of hers, she is convinced that a match with the Reverend Philip Elton, the good-looking young vicar, is very much on the cards. Emma herself rates him as the 'most good-humoured and gentle of men'.

It soon emerges that Mr Elton is indeed aware of Harriet, expressing to Emma with great warmth how cleverly she, Emma, has brought her forward by her wise encouragement. He becomes involved in some of Emma's schemes, such as a portrait of Harriet, to be painted by Emma. Mr Elton praises this picture extravagantly, while Mr Knightley, Emma's mentor and long-standing friend, merely notes that she has made Harriet too tall. Mr Elton eagerly puts himself forward to arrange for the portrait's framing, which requires a visit to London. She puts down his rather excessive sighing compliments to his gratitude for her scheme.

Meanwhile Harriet is astonished to find that she has received a proposal of marriage from Robert Martin, a local yeoman-farmer. Well, she had spent the summer very happily on the Martins' farm, and had built a warm friendship with the whole family. Harriet shows his letter to Emma, who is surprised to find herself admiring the quality of his expression. She, nevertheless – so aware of gradations of class – firmly steers Harriet away from any thought of accepting. When Mr Knightley gets to hear about Emma's role in the refusal, he is very cross with her. Being a landowner, he has already established a good friendship with Robert Martin, and admires his professional ambitions. A bruising conversation between them leaves Emma somewhat vexed about her judgement, but she manages to rationalise her behaviour – and to downplay the arguments of Mr Knightley. She is able to carry on as before with the Harriet-Mr Elton scheme.

Then a lot of froth is generated by a charade written specially by Mr

Elton for Harriet's commonplace book. Emma's confidence that he is the man for Harriet swells accordingly.

Another day she and Harriet bump into Mr Elton after they've been engaged in charitable visiting, perhaps a promising subject on which the assumed lovebirds could converse. But she can't help but notice that Mr Elton's progress in the matter is 'Cautious, very cautious'.

Christmas approaches and with it arrives the family of John Knightley, the younger brother of Mr Knightley and the husband of Emma's sister: a clever reflective man, a lawyer practising in London. In the course of some casual conversation about the vicar and his agreeableness and goodwill – to the ladies especially – John Knightley suggests to Emma that Mr Elton 'seems to show a great deal of goodwill towards you'. Emma is astonished at his implication, and refutes the notion strongly. As she walks on, she reflects that John Knightley has only a partial knowledge of the circumstances. She takes refuge in recalling 'the mistakes which people of high pretensions to judgement are for ever falling into…'

Emma's assumption about Mr Elton is not exploded until Christmas Eve. After an evening at the home of her beloved former governess, a confusion about the carriages means that Emma and the vicar find themselves sharing a carriage and 'that the door was to be lawfully shut on them and that they were to have a head to head drive'. Though adopting as calm a conversational tone as possible, Emma finds herself the sudden object of Mr Elton's violent love-making. Embarrassment is soon replaced by angry clarifications, and by the time he is dropped off at the vicarage, Emma has gained a very much clearer idea of Mr Elton and his ambitions.

Reflecting on the fiasco back in her bedroom, it is poor Harriet that is painfully uppermost in her mind. Emma asks herself how *could* she have been so much deceived? She casts her mind back over the preceding weeks, but all now seems confused. She had taken up the idea, she supposed, and made everything bend to it.

A few chapters later, a Miss Bates, in general conversation, happens to come up with a very similar usage: '... one never does form a just idea of anybody beforehand. *One takes up a notion, and runs away with it.*' (My italics)

Thus both Emma and Miss Bates use the verb 'take up'. This is a synonym of 'assume', which is formed from the Latin preposition *ad* – 'towards, up' and the verb *sumere* – 'to take'. Emma also describes her mistake as 'a series of strange blunders', perhaps reflecting the role of unconscious thought in the matter.

In the course of Jane Austen's novels quite a few other notions are 'taken up' and 'run away with'. It seems pretty clear that Jane Austen considered assumption (though she does not use the word, which barely features in Dr Johnson's dictionary fifty years earlier) to be a real risk in the social life she knew so well. The examples I have given come from her earliest novel and her penultimate one. She knew that the results of such errors could be painful and embarrassing. They amount to a failure of human understanding, and the plots of her novels gradually rectify these mistakes, to the benefit of those characters sufficiently strong in mind and humility to make the necessary adjustments. Emma herself, confessing her error to Harriet a few days later, resolves to be 'humble and discreet, and repressing imagination all the rest of her life'.

My pedestrian paraphrasings were only written to demonstrate those assumptions. But I always encourage friends to sample the fascinating way in which Jane Austen writes. In her determined pursuit of writing effectively and entertainingly about human society she became the first author to hit on a new technique – free indirect speech – in which the thoughts of the narrator, or an anonymous voice, are mingled with the thoughts of the fictional character. This technique or style was able to convey subtle shades of thought, to encompass dualities, making for a much more realistic picture of humanity. It became the typical style of the nineteenth-century novel. Robert Clark, in his introduction to the Everyman edition of *Emma*, suggests that 'the free indirect style is one of the fundamental ways in which modern consciousness represents its experience.'

THOMAS CARLYLE AND THE HISTORIAN'S ILLUSION, 1830 In his essay *On History* Carlyle writes of difficulties facing the historian. One of these is what he calls a 'fatal discrepancy' between how we observe and record things, and how these things actually occur. A historian, he notes, tends to assume that the base unit of history is a series, but the actual occurrences are often simultaneous. The things done were not a series, but a group. This group is a part of what he calls a 'Chaos of Being, wherein shape after shape bodies itself forth from innumerable elements'. The historian's narrative of cause and effect is linear, but the action he is describing is 'solid' and deeply interconnected beyond his ability to reach.

Carlyle is not against the writing of history – on the contrary, he encourages it – but does stress that vigilance and humility must be vital qualities for the historian, who is merely one link in a longer chain of gradual understanding.

DR DAVID STRAUSS: BIBLICAL PROPHECY AND EXEGESIS In 1835 one of the most significant of all works of theology was published: *The Life of Jesus Critically Examined* by the German theologian David Strauss. This was available in English from 1846, in a translation by the young Mary Ann Evans, better known in literature as 'George Eliot'.

I consulted this famous book partly to remedy my ignorance about biblical prophecies, which I mulled over earlier. Since then I've also found the opinion on prophecies of Voltaire, who with breathtaking directness declares: 'They have been in every age a means of deluding the simple and inflaming the fanatical.'

Strauss was what was known as 'an alienated theologian'. He hoped to reach deeper truths about Christianity by identifying what was mythical rather than historical in the Gospel texts, but this approach, though very influential, lost him the favour of the German theological establishment.

For example, he examines the ancient prophecy of Isaiah (written in Hebrew) which is later quoted in the first gospel (Matthew), at the

Annunciation to the Virgin Mary. Research by Strauss's contemporaries had found that Isaiah had been merely making a secular short-term prediction, using the image of the stages of childbirth to illustrate to King Ahaz of Judah 'a lively assurance of the speedy destruction of his much dreaded enemies [Syria and Ephraim]'.

But by the time this prediction makes its appearance in the first and third (Luke) gospels (written in Greek), it has changed from being historical to mythical, to foretell the birth of a Messiah. His supernatural nature is indicated by the critical word 'virgin'. The centuries pass, and this is how it reads in the King James Bible, translated from Greek:

> All this was done, that it might be fulfilled which was spoken of the Lord by the prophet: a virgin shall be with child, and shall bring forth a son, and they shall call his name Emmanuel.

But this Messiah was, for the first time perhaps, given supernatural form. For the Jewish people though, the Messiah had been a longed-for human, secular leader, in the tradition of Moses and David. Gibbon suggests that a supernatural Messiah would have been a grave disappointment to the majority of Jews. Even the early Christian sects, Jewish in composition, saw Christ as pure man.

It would seem that prophecies and the myths following in their wake were a vital part of presenting the new religion. The prophecies of an imminent Second Coming, the End of the World and the Kingdom of Heaven, loomed largest and most welcome among the first Christians of Judea. A prophecy believed is a kind of assumption, of perhaps deep import. Yet prophecy has its slippery, unstable side. It can be further complicated by prophets or evangelists being credited with making a 'prophecy' *after* the event prophesied, known in the theological world as 'vaticinium post eventu'. As somebody once wrote, the most accurate way to make a prophecy is to predict the past.

In the case of the Second Coming, Gibbon, rather more tactful than Voltaire, suggests that 'The revolution [the passing] of seventeen centuries has instructed us not to press too closely the mysterious language of prophecy and revelation.'

Strauss then inquires into the accuracy of the Gospel genealogies, and points out that if the conception was supernatural then Jesus cannot also be descended from David through his father Joseph. Reading Strauss I quickly felt overwhelmed by the complexity of these exegetical investigations, but struggled on, fascinated. *The Life of Jesus* is not an easy read, and there are many quotations in Latin, Greek and Hebrew. Mary Evans herself found the level of detail tried her patience, though she liked Strauss's clarity and fertility of mind. 'But I do not know one person who is likely to read it through, do you?' she wrote to a friend.

Well, I've read most of it. I remain fascinated. Initially it was a surprise to find Strauss treating the persons involved – for example, at the Annunciation: Anna, Elisabeth, Joseph, Mary – as historical people, until proved otherwise; as contemporaries of Roman citizens and the subjects of an emperor. I'd never quite seen it like that before.

Strauss approaches all the many Gospel stories like a counsel for both the prosecution and defence, examining in relentless detail each episode of the Messiah's life as it appears in the three Synoptic Gospels, in the later St John's Gospel and sometimes in the Apocryphal Gospels.

He asks firstly how much of an episode can be validated as historical (whether supernatural or natural) and then investigates how much is in the service of the Messianic myth, such as that modification of Isaiah's prediction. He finally concludes that the majority of the Gospel stories are not historical but mythical. But Strauss did retain his belief in the existence of Jesus as a historical person, and the reality of some of the later episodes in his life. He was in fact drawn towards Jesus. Separating the historical from the mythical was not done from a negative sentiment but, as already emphasised, to gain a deeper understanding of the religion.

As for the four Gospels as a whole, Strauss believed he had exposed an ancient assumption still persisting even to his own time. It may be described as the belief that the Gospels were written by eye-witnesses whose names were Matthew, Mark, Luke and John. Thus he first searches for external evidence to confirm this assumption. He examines a well-known testimony of Papias, Bishop of Hieropolis, martyred under Marcus Aurelius, and formerly the church officer of John the Evangelist. This seems to point toward there being some kind of an account of Jesus's life, though no particular author is mentioned. Papias also states that the evangelist Matthew wrote in Hebrew. But it is mere assumption, says Strauss, for the Christian fathers to conclude from that sliver of information that the Greek text of the first Gospel was translated from Matthew's original Hebrew. The cold rejection by the Jews of the miracles of Christ meant that there was little or no demand for a gospel in Hebrew anyway.

No further evidence was found by Strauss. All he can say with certainty is that 'an apostle or some other person who was acquainted with an apostle, wrote a gospel history; but not whether it was the same as that which came to be circulated in the church under his name.' Secondly, there were other writings similar to the four Gospels, but these named no author and are highly uncertain. They were written from AD 130 onward. Three of the four evangelists had all died well before the year AD 100, when John is said to have died. Thus Strauss postulates that the four Gospels were circulated only in oral form until eventually, towards the end of the second century, they were deposited into anonymous manuscripts in different cities of the eastern Mediterranean.

LEGEND AND MYTH These two forms often include assumptions. Strauss, above, offers a clarification, stating that 'legend' originates with some historical facts and builds a fiction upon them to perpetuate a particular and valuable idea; 'myth', on the other hand, begins with the idea.

Karl Otfried Müller was a pioneering enquirer into Greek mythology and primitive history. In 1825 he published his *Introduction to a Scientific Mythology*. He explains that the complex nature of myths springs from them having been formed for the most part not at once, but by successive degrees, under varying influences and circumstances. They were orally transmitted and not restricted to any written document. In the course of long centuries they were thus open to every new addition deemed valuable in the myth's creation. Thus a myth is founded by the more elevated and general conception of a whole people. Since this thinking is spread over long periods of time by people who never met, the successive layers of thought are likely to include all kinds of earlier thoughts and judgements, including assumptions, which may shift or distort the evolving myth.

LORD JOHN RUSSELL, AN ASSUMPTION IN HIMSELF, 1838 Sydney Smith, Canon of St Paul's Cathedral, in an open letter that was highly critical of the Ecclesiastical Commission, launched an accusation against Lord John Russell, the Whig Home Secretary. Lord John had believed that the recommendations of the Commission were fair, and that Church property was not being confiscated, but only remodelled and re-divided. Canon Smith did not agree:

> I accuse him not of plunder, but I accuse him of taking the Church of England, rolling it about as a cook does with a piece of dough with a rolling pin, cutting a hundred different shapes with all the plastic fertility of a confectioner, and without the most distant suspicion that he can ever be wrong, or ever be mistaken; with a certainty that he can anticipate the consequences of every possible change in human affairs. There is not a better man in England than Lord John Russell: but his worst failure is that he is utterly ignorant of all moral fear; there is nothing he would not undertake. I believe he would rebuild the stone of St Peter's or take command of the

Channel Fleet; and no-one would discover by his manner that the patient had died – the Church tumbled down – and the Channel Fleet had been knocked to atoms.

Russell was it seems not surprised by this, but he was annoyed, because the vivid incongruity of Smith's outspoken comments (for which he was well known) was gleefully quoted by Tory members and acquired wide currency.

THE FIRST ANGLO-AFGHAN WAR, 1839–1842 This war was an almost total catastrophe, finishing with the massacre of the retreating British forces. A famous painting by Lady Butler, *Remnants of an Army*, portrays the sole survivor, the exhausted Dr Brydon, miraculously still astride a pony as he approaches the walls of Jalalabad.

The war had begun when British policymakers decided that Afghanistan, insignificant in itself, opened up India to the threat of invasion from Russia. Thus began the 'Great Game' between the two empires. Matters were needlessly complicated when the British ignored the present ruler and brought in a former king who had been exiled in India for thirty years. Kabul fell easily, but gradually the population resented the entrenching and meddling of an infidel invader. Despite growing rebellion, the British somehow assumed that the conquest of the country was now complete. Much of the army was withdrawn to China. But then a jihad was declared against the British and the depleted army retreated through the Khyber Pass to disaster.

This war gave rise to the imperial maxim 'Don't invade Afghanistan'. Nevertheless, this advice has been ignored ever since, in the demands of the Great Game and its more recent manifestations. The only exception seems to have been the brilliant intervention of Major General Roberts at Kabul and Kandahar in the Second Afghan War.

It would seem that a persistent assumption has contributed to the failure of these adventures: that in such a diverse, unstructured land of shifting allegiances, with safe havens over mountain borders, with hardly any co-ordination between the Afghan forces, it was nevertheless still possible for a foreign power to understand the unstable loyalties of Afghan tribes and their warlords.

MARXISM, 1848 I used to be puzzled by the ability of Marxism or communism to spread within turbulent nations in various parts of the world. I thought there must be some sort of catch or trick involved. Thus on getting round to reading Karl Marx's *Communist Manifesto* (1848) – it's not long – I noticed something in the later chapters that brought me up short. My eyes scrutinised again a paragraph that seemed to contain a very dangerous assumption: 'that although violence will have to be used to bring about the revolution *there will be no further need for violence and society will develop on revolutionary principles*.' (My italics)

Well, if Marx really believed that he must have been very naïve – or profoundly cynical. What he had really done with those words was to give every tin-pot revolutionary and vile dictator his ideological blessing for the initial use of force and violence against their own nation. But which regime has then ever voluntarily given up its apparatus of violence to allow society to develop on revolutionary principles?

I was later interested to read in a biography of Marx that he was not averse to attending political meetings at which there was a good chance of some physical violence breaking out, for which, it seems, he had a taste. And what might a visit to the barber have revealed about the man?

MAZEPPA, 1852 This refers only indirectly to Lord Byron's verse legend of Ivan Mazeppa, who was strapped to a wild horse and carried vast distances over the Ukrainian steppe. This *Mazeppa* was an engine of the London and North Western Railway, but she too made a wild journey. This is the first of five railway accidents I've found in which assumption played a fatal role. We know a lot about what happened because of the painstaking inquiries made by determined accident inspectors, often army officers with engineering qualifications.

A certain Joseph Thompson was a night cleaner at the Shrewsbury shed. One night near the end of May his duties included making a simple repair to a blowing regulator gland on *Mazeppa*. She was a new and sprightly engine, one of the first of a long line built at Crewe, distinguished by huge single driving wheels. By four in the morning Thompson was getting *Mazeppa*'s firebox coaled up and lit for the day's work. Gradually the fire took hold; a head of steam was building. His shift was due to end at 6am, but he decided to leave some ten minutes early, perhaps assuming that Daniel Tinsley, his relief, would be on time. But Tinsley did not arrive until ten past, so *Mazeppa* was left alone for some twenty minutes... Had Thompson checked that he had put on the brakes, disengaged the forward gear and turned off the regulator? Did he consciously reflect on the situation at all?

When Tinsley entered the shed at ten past six, looking for *Mazeppa*, he could not find her; he reckoned that she must have been taken out earlier that morning.

This comfortable conclusion was soon exploded when a breathless platelayer rushed in to assert that he had just seen an engine running along the Stafford line with an empty footplate. The die was now cast: *Mazeppa* had left the shed unseen and was set on her wild journey over eastern Shropshire. A hue and cry was raised, she was chased down the track, but all that could be seen was flying steam rising some way ahead. They could not catch her. After some fourteen miles she finally ended her escapade at Donnington station, demolishing all three carriages of a waiting train, steam still blasting from her safety valves, her energy seemingly inexhaustible. There were only three passengers in the waiting train: two were injured, the third was killed.

What would it be like to awake from slumber and find yourself accused of the manslaughter of a person fourteen miles way, while you had been asleep? That was the fate of Joseph Thompson a few hours later, confronted with the results of his inattention earlier that morning.

An official inquiry followed, but of the fate of Thompson I have found no trace. L.T.C. Rolt in *Red for Danger* concludes his chapter on this kind of accident with a 'cautionary moral':

> Safety on the railway is the responsibility of all and there is no item of railway equipment, from a wagon sheet or a porter's barrow to a stationary locomotive, that carelessness cannot convert into a potent instrument of disaster.

LADY DEDLOCK'S FATAL ASSUMPTION, 1852 In Dickens' novel *Bleak House*, a brief moment, a loss of reflection perhaps, leads to the exposure of Lady Dedlock's shameful secret, and to her downfall. Not long after the start of the book, in which the author has laid before us the horrors of the Court of Chancery, Lady Dedlock and her older husband, Sir Leicester, are in parley with the family's lawyer, a Mr Tulkinghorn. The lawyer is reputed to have become rich through his discreetly held knowledge of the secrets of prominent families. There is an air of quiet ruthlessness about him.

Perhaps Lady Dedlock has momentarily forgotten that? Mr Tulkinghorn takes out some affidavits for Sir Leicester's consideration, places them on a small table and begins to read aloud. Lady Dedlock, uninterested in affidavits, now finds her place by the fire too hot.

> My Lady, changing her position, sees the papers on the table – looks at them nearer – looks at them nearer still – asks impulsively: 'Who copied that?' Mr Tulkinghorn stops short, surprised by my Lady's animation and her unusual tone. 'Is it what you people call law hand?' she asks.
>
> 'Not quite. Why do you ask?'
>
> 'Anything to vary this detestable monotony. O, go on, do!'

And that's all: a tiny morsel of information, but enough to seal my Lady's doom. For Tulkinghorn, while she and Sir Leicester are now away in Paris, has not forgotten her unusual interest in the handwriting. He has, without any further prompting, made enquiries: he has found the address of the law-copier who copied the affidavit; he has visited his shabby room; and he has found the person in question lying dead, from what turns out to be an overdose of opium.

A public inquiry follows. It is only a matter of time until Tulkinghorn will find out the full story of her Ladyship's connection with the law-copier.

In that one moment of impulse, she gave herself away. Perhaps if the fire had not been so hot she could have held her tongue. She does not seem to have imagined that the lawyer would follow the connection so assiduously; that he would openly mention his discovery, in the course of a letter to Sir Leicester. Lady Dedlock seems to have assumed that the lawyer would protect her interests as much as he would Sir Leicester's.

PIONEER ALPINE MOUNTAINEERING, 1854 In the mid-nineteenth century English pioneers of mountain climbing began to appear in Switzerland and Savoy. But continental mountaineers, mostly educated men from the cities, had been active for the previous hundred years, seeking first ascents especially.

Judge Alfred Wills arrived at Grindelwald in 1854. He engaged the guide Peter Bohren to accompany him on a first ascent of the Wetterhorn (formerly known as the Hasle Jungfrau), which towers above the village to a height of 3,692m. Bohren had in fact climbed this peak at least twice, but he kept quiet about that because *first* ascents could command a higher fee. Wills thus assumed he was making a first ascent. The village also went along with this seemingly harmless delusion, so as to indulge these foreigners in finding success on their mountains.

In the ensuing controversy, Arnold Lunn and other historians concurred that Wills had not made the first ascent of the Wetterhorn.

This news first appeared in print in Lunn's book *The Alps*, 1914. But Wills had died in 1912.

ALEXANDER BAIN: *THE EMOTIONS OF THE WILL,* 1859 Bain was a pioneer in psychology, and his observations, below, show an awareness of assumption as a basic element in human thinking:

He describes early man as having 'intense primitive credulity' and then evolving into a state of 'acquired scepticism'.

He refers to 'the generalising impetus of the untutored mind…'

He suggests that 'the great master fallacy of the human mind is in believing too much'.

He reflects Spinoza when he declares that 'we are scarcely able to feel or act without the operation of belief, or without making assumptions in anticipation of the reality.' (This is the *first* occasion in English that I've seen the word 'assumption' used in this sense, though the usage is reckoned to date from the 1620s.)

What Spinoza described as 'effortless, automatic and passive', Bain terms 'intuitive'.

Bain describes memory as a 'flash of recovery from the past' and 'a store of previous beliefs'.

CHARLES DARWIN: *ON THE ORIGIN OF SPECIES,* 1859 At the suggestion of Alfred Russell Wallace, Darwin agreed to use the phrase *survival of the fittest* (originated by Herbert Spencer) as an alternative to *natural selection*. This duly appeared in the fifth and sixth editions of Darwin's famous book. But eventually, it was realised by biologists that *survival of the fittest* is too ambiguous to be used in this way. The word 'fittest' can mean, as Darwin intended, 'best adapted for the immediate local environment', or can mean 'strongest, healthiest', a less subtle idea. But that second meaning of *survival of the fittest* was taken up by many to justify or legitimise social theories of unrestrained competition and aggressive nationalism.

Thus the luminous exquisite concept of *natural selection* and its delicate operation through geological eras was in danger of gross simplification, leading towards an easy assumption that evolution was a matter of the raised clubs and bared teeth of tribal warfare.

JOHN STUART MILL: *ON LIBERTY*, 1859 This philosopher, political economist and member of parliament was one of the greatest foes of the making of assumptions. His essay *On Liberty* is one of his most famous works.

He states the necessity for plural debate, for taking absolutely nothing for granted, but holding all our dearest assumptions up for national scrutiny.

There must be 'protection against the tyranny of the prevailing opinion and feeling, against the tendency of society to impose… its own ideas and practices… on those who dissent from them; to fetter the development of any individuality not in harmony with its ways'.

After only a few pages we find Mill coming up with 'a very simple principle':

That the sole end for which mankind is warranted, individually or collectively, in interfering with the Liberty of Action of any of their number, is self-protection. That the only purpose for which power can be rightfully exercised over any member of a civilised community, against his will, is to prevent harm to others.

He adds that (to interfere with someone's liberty of action) for his own good, either physical or moral, is not a sufficient warrant.

Moving from liberty of action to liberty of speech, another memorable idea is expressed:

The peculiar evil of silencing the expression of opinion is, that it is robbing the human race; posterity as well as the existing generation;

and robbing those who dissent from the opinion, still more than those who hold it.

In this continuing discussion of the value of discussion, Mill soon reaches another principle:

All silencing of discussion is 'an Assumption of Infallibility'.

He points out that even the Roman Catholic Church, the most intolerant of churches, before the canonisation of a saint, nevertheless admits, and listens patiently to, a 'devil's advocate'. Similarly, if no one had been permitted to question the ideas of Isaac Newton, mankind could not feel as sure of those truths as they do now.

And if we think we can sometimes overlook the silencing of an opinion because we perceive it to be so disgracefully 'impious' or 'immoral', Mill urges us to think again – because this is the case *above all others* in which it is fatal. 'This is exactly the occasion on which the men of one generation commit those dreadful mistakes which excite the horror and astonishment of posterity.' This kind of mistake led to the execution of Socrates (executed for impiety and immorality), Christ (executed for blasphemy) and the persecutions of Christians by the Emperor Marcus Aurelius (for undermining the stability of society). These mistakes show that even the most enlightened possessors of power are capable of making huge errors as a result of alternative opinion being silenced. But in these cases, Mill asks:

What was the real mischief? I must be permitted to observe, that it is not the feeling sure of a doctrine which I call an Assumption of Infallibility. It is the undertaking *to decide that question for others*, (Mill's italics) without allowing them to hear what can be said on the contrary side.

Has Mill's liberty of speech ever been more relevant than now, when some British universities and public institutions seem spinelessly to allow the silencing of opinion by the bullying behaviour of 'activists' in their precincts? Or blocking the production of newspapers they don't approve of?

John Stuart Mill concludes his thorough and muscular reasoning by stating that 'without the collision of adverse opinions' the truth has little chance of being discovered, and what is found is more likely to be held by prejudice rather than with confidence and conviction. The human race is thereby 'robbed' of the truth.

Thus he notes that as a lawyer, Cicero, one of the greatest of all orators, always studied his adversary's argument with as great an intensity as his own, if not more so.

At a less exalted level, perhaps, but similarly, in all real markets the true price of an asset can only be discovered by the free opinions of buyers and sellers.

CHARLES DICKENS: *GREAT EXPECTATIONS*, 1860 The plot of this famous novel turns upon an assumption that germinates and grows inexorably in the mind of young Philip Pirrip, known as 'Pip'. We meet Pip at a tender age, six or seven perhaps, living on the Kentish marshes with his sister and her husband Joe, a blacksmith. At many moments in the first half of the novel he hears hints and clues that Miss Havisham – a lady seriously disturbed by a failed wedding day – has become his secret benefactor. She will allow him to be transformed into a gentleman and also to be united with the beautiful but heartless Estella, her adopted daughter. But Estella has been brought up by Miss Havisham to feel contempt for all men and 'to break their hearts'.

These are the moments which encourage Pip's self-delusion:

– When Miss Havisham tells him that she will support the expense of apprenticing Pip to his blacksmith brother-in-law.

– When a lawyer, Jaggers, visits Pip's village and imparts news of a secret benefactor who will make his fortune.

– When Jaggers asks him if he will accept a Mr Matthew Pocket as his tutor, Pip remembers that this person is a relation of Miss Havisham.

– When Pip wonders if this plan will somehow bring Estella and he together.

– When he takes leave of Miss Havisham in new clothes, on his way to live in London. She appears to know Jaggers, adding fuel to the flame of his hopes.

– When he learns the full story of Miss Havisham's disastrous wedding day from a close friend, Herbert Pocket. Herbert has no doubt that she is Pip's benefactor.

– When he receives a message from Miss Havisham that Estella has returned from further education abroad and would be glad to see him.

– When he reflects that if Miss Havisham has adopted Estella, 'she had as good as adopted me. She must be intending to bring us together.'

– When he goes down to meet Estella and feels even more painfully remote from her, on account of her progress in life. They walk in the garden and she admits to having no heart, as a warning to Pip, 'as we may be thrown together'. He does not ask her to explain that remark, but takes it as confirmation of his hope.

– When Miss Havisham teases him about his love for Estella. Again he takes this as further confirmation.

– When his friend Herbert also assumes that Estella is allotted to Pip. (He also tells Pip that he is 'a good fellow… action and dreaming, curiously mixed in him'.)

– When Herbert's father also mentions Estella's role in Pip's future, remarking 'it's settled and done or Jaggers wouldn't be in it'.

– When Pip meets Estella off a coach and finds she is 'never more delicately beautiful'. As they converse about arrangements – she is to reside for a while in fashionable Richmond – Estella remarks, 'We have no choice, you and I, but to obey our instructions. We are not free to follow our devices, you and I.' Pip hopes there is a hidden meaning here.

On reaching the age of twenty-one Pip waits in vain for news of 'expectations'. He is miserable in respect of Estella, but cannot retract from the painful emotional dilemma. Two more years pass and finally he discovers to his profound dismay that his benefactor was not Miss Havisham; it was in fact an escaped convict he had once helped when he was a child living on the Kentish marshes. 'Miss Havisham's intentions towards me, all a mere dream; Estella not designed for me.'

This is by no means the end of the story, but certainly a vital turning point. There is a great deal of pain in *Great Expectations* – and some happier relationships.

Pip's assumption has been built on sand. He has indulged in dreams and wishful thinking, been reluctant to investigate the evidence further, has 'built castles in Spain', has too easily gone along with the easy assumptions of friends, and did not want to mention the matter to his relatives at home. Only his clear-seeing friend Biddy, a marshland neighbour, is strong enough to give him the straight tip, but to no avail.

THE BATTLE OF BULL RUN, JUNE 1861 In the first major conflict of the American Civil War the two armies were facing each other over a broad stretch of Virginia, just southwest of Washington. A sluggish stream, Bull Run, wandered across the roughish terrain. McDowell, the Union commander, was ready to attack the Confederates, on the understanding that the experienced Union general, Robert Patterson, would prevent any further approach by other Confederate troops from the Shenandoah Valley. Patterson was given clear orders to detain these troops and he was expected to be successful, since he had some 20,000 men to the 12,000 Confederates.

But from Patterson nothing was heard for three days. A sharp admonition was sent by General Scott, who now worried that Patterson had let the Confederates take an escape route over the ridges, to join with their main force at Bull Run. And though Patterson denied that possibility, that was exactly what had happened.

It seems that General Patterson was not quite himself during this time. Since 9 June he had been requesting for reinforcements and sending messages of complaint. Worse, he'd failed to make a thorough reconnaissance of the enemy's movements. Lacking evidence, he became prey to exaggerated rumours and was finally doomed to fall into the grip of a dangerous assumption: that the enemy was far superior in numbers. In this conflicted state of mind he shifted eastwards, failing to make any engagement with the Confederates. As a result, McDowell and the Unionists were unexpectedly defeated at Bull Run. Patterson, by his mysterious inaction, was held partly responsible for this.

But the issue was never resolved it seems. Patterson, no longer employed by the army, published his own account of the episode, and even arranged to visit the White House to explain the curious matter to President Lincoln.

PROFESSOR TYNDALL, 1861 The Victorian scientist John Tyndall had made discoveries in many fields. As a pioneer mountaineer he was also able to make physical experiments at all heights in the Swiss Alps. On reaching Meiringen he visited the deep vertically-sided chasm through which the River Aar plunges, breaching a transverse ridge, the Kirchet, stretched like a dam across the valley of Hasli. But he was told by locals that the chasm – the *Finsteraarschlucht* – was understood to have been created by an earthquake. Shocked by this easy assumption or, as he phrases it, 'ready hypothesis' and 'off-hand theoretic guess', Tyndall notes that mankind longs for causes and explanations and that weaker minds will assuage their hunger all too quickly with a simple answer. But with more effort they might have found the truth through patient enquiry. Some 240 years after

Bacon's discovery of inductive thinking, Tyndall still needs to warn his readers of human weakness:

This proneness of the human mind to jump to conclusions, and thus shirk the labour of real investigation, is a most mischievous tendency.

Tyndall then patiently takes us through the eight or so steps, based on observation, evidence and knowledge of glacier movements, that can explain how the impressive ravine was formed.

ABRAHAM LINCOLN PROVOKED BY HIS GENERALS, 1862–1863 Two of the bloodiest battles of the American Civil War were fought in persistent close combat: at Antietam (Sharpsburg), Maryland in 1862 and at Gettysburg, Pennsylvania, the year after. These were both in Union states, penetrated by Confederate armies under Robert E. Lee.

On both occasions the ultimately victorious Union generals, McClellan and Meade, had earnt the opportunity to chase their beaten opponents back into Virginia and finish the rebellion decisively. But after Antietam, McClellan was so overwhelmed by what he had seen on the crowded field of battle, that he assumed the enemy could not also have sustained such terrible numbers of dead and wounded as his army had. But this was not the case. Yet the enemy was still the stronger force in McClellan's mind. Thus he procrastinated, until he witnessed with relief Lee's rearguard, on the second morning after the battle, retreating south across the Potomac. He then sent a joyous telegraph message to nearby Washington: 'Our victory was complete. The enemy is driven back into Virginia. Maryland and Pennsylvania are now safe.' But President Lincoln had decidedly mixed feelings about this piece of news.

The following July, after the Battle of Gettysburg, in which the status of General Meade's victory had not been immediately clear, Lincoln had been urging him to press hard upon the retreating Lee. The Confederate leader had now taken up a position on the north bank of the Potomac, uncrossable in its temporarily swollen state. Meade gradually approached until the two armies were less than a mile apart. But he did not attack.

Anxious messages from Washington urged Meade to attack Lee's army: Meade was to make up his own mind, he should *not* call a council of war: 'It is proverbial that councils of war never fight.' Lee must not be allowed to escape.

All to no avail, for the next morning it was seen that Lee had crossed the Potomac in the night, the waters fallen and a pontoon repaired.

Lincoln was infuriated, bitterly disappointed: 'We had them within our grasp, we had only to stretch forth our hands and they were ours, and nothing I could say or do could make the army move.'

With his lawyerly respect for words he had noticed a revealing phrase in Meade's general order after Gettysburg, in which he referred to 'driving the invader from our soil'. On reading this the President realised that this phrase – 'our soil' – revealed the same confused spirit that had moved McClellan to declare a victory because Maryland and Pennsylvania were safe. In other words, they had somehow fallen into an assumption that the purpose of the war was to defend 'our soil', meaning the North. 'Will our generals never get that idea out of their heads?'

But to Abraham Lincoln 'our soil' meant the entire nation of the United States, both North and South, and the purpose of the war – to extinguish the rebellion in the seceded states – had not changed. He regretted that he had not gone down to address the armies himself and to issue personally the orders for an attack into Virginia and farther south. In the following week he was heard to make such remarks as 'Our army held the war in the hollow of their hand and did not close it… We had gone through all the labour of tilling and planting an enormous crop and when it was ripe we did not harvest it.'

Lincoln had made his vital point, but then it was time to show his immense gratitude to Meade for what he *had* done at Gettysburg, and to let go his criticism of what he had *not* done.

That dangerous assumption of the generals had somehow remained hidden from view, only emerging into the light when it was almost too late.

THE MATTERHORN ILLUSION, 1864 Climbers who visited Zermatt in the mid-nineteenth century with an eye on the Matterhorn usually examined it from up on the Riffelberg, to the east. From here the east face of the mountain looks almost vertical. It did to Edward Whymper when he went up to see for himself – though he also noted large patches of snow lying on the centre of the face. This assumption of excessive steepness meant that Whymper, the most dynamic and successful British alpinist of that period, made all his first attempts on the Matterhorn from Breuil on the Italian side. But none of those attempts were successful, though they make for dramatic reading.

Those large snow patches Whymper had seen from the Riffelberg haunted him still. He decided to check the appearance of the Matterhorn from the north. From Zermatt he walked up a few miles to the high pastures of Stafelalp. Here the east face can be seen in profile, as Whymper writes in *Scrambles Amongst the Alps*:

> Its appearance from this direction would be amazing to someone who had seen it only from the east. It looks so different from the apparently sheer and perfectly unclimbable cliff one sees from the Riffelberg, that it is hard to believe that the two slopes are one and the same thing. Its angle scarcely exceeds 40 degrees.
>
> A great step was made when this was learnt.

Whymper thus chose a new route from Zermatt which would cross the east face from left to right and reach a high corner, giving access onto the north face for the final attack. He also saw that the dip of the rock strata favoured the climber. He tells us that he would have made an immediate attempt at this route with Adams-Reilly, if that fellow mountaineer had not been obliged to return home. So it was not until July 1865 that Whymper made his eighth attempt. The Matterhorn was duly conquered, though the victory was overshadowed forever by the deaths of four of the seven-man party. But that catastrophe was not due to the choice of route, but to a breaking rope.

Today, Stafelalp is passed by one of the quieter of the Zermatt ski-runs and the prospect of the Matterhorn from its lunchtime terrace I can heartily recommend.

DISCOVERY OF THE ALPINE WINTER, 1864 In the earlier nineteenth century an assumption ruled that the Alps in winter would repel any visitor mad enough to venture over them, on account of the vast quantities of snow, the savage storms and the fierceness of frosts which must surely prevail. Lacking evidence, the worst was assumed.

But a few men had faith that this might not be the case. In the spirit of Sir Thomas Browne, they went to see for themselves. They returned with lively accounts of the wonders they had seen. They had found that the mountains were as beautiful in winter as in summer.

Johannes Badrutt, founder of a hotel dynasty at St Moritz, may have made the first attempt at popularising this change of perception. He is said to have made an experimental bet in 1864, in which he invited his summer guests to return in winter. Then they could appreciate the sun, snow and amiable climate of the high-lying valley of the River Inn (known as the Upper Engadine). If any were dissatisfied, Badrutt would refund the cost of their visit. But it seems that all were content, and that some of his guests stayed on until Easter.

Winter sports now began to appear, and the Swiss Alps began to rival Egypt as a winter destination. Later, the detailed examinations of Professor Roget showed that the winter climate of the High Alps consisted of friendly paradoxes or surprises, such as warm frost, dry snow and temperature inversion. He also proved that it was easier to ski glacier routes in winter than to walk them in summer. Bad weather might intrude now and again, but its effects were soon cleared away by the mechanism of the winter atmosphere. In fact, he pronounced, winter up in the Alps wasn't really winter at all.

A later assumption about the Alpine winter, mainly affecting 'ski-runners' – as skiers were then known – was that Christmas coincided with good snow conditions. But Christmas was usually too early for that, and only a change in the Vatican Calendar could have provided the solution: shifting Christmas to 25 January.

THE STAPLEHURST ACCIDENT, 1865 Staplehurst is a village in Kent, on the railway line to London from the cross-Channel port of Folkestone, a fact of great significance in this accident.

A low railway bridge over the River Beult needed replacement of the wooden lengths which supported the rails. John Benge, a foreman, was contracted to carry out this work, in which he was well-experienced. He brought with him a gang of workmen and good progress was made, until by 9 June there remained only one more section to replace. Of course, this had meant much temporary taking-up of the rails. The work had to be fitted into gaps in the railway timetable. Benge was used to this arrangement, though his deputy at Staplehurst had lost his timetable, rather worryingly, leaving Benge as the sole source of knowledge. For safety reasons, two men were supposed to stand at a distance of 1,000 yards either side of the bridge, with flags and detonators to alert each train to the presence of the works. However, Benge stood them at only 500 yards, and told them not to use detonators unless it was foggy.

On the fatal day, he had arranged to replace the wooden lengths between 2:51pm and 4:15pm, ample time for the work to be done. But this timetable had an unusual feature, in that express boat-trains also ran on this line. The timing of these trains was dependent on tides in the

Straits of Dover. Their timings still featured in the timetable, but were irregular. Benge had looked up what was known as 'the Tidal' and found – or thought he had found – that it was scheduled to pass at 5:20pm, well after the replacement period. Well, railway timetables can sometimes be a little confusing and it's generally a good idea to double-check that you've got it right. It is especially worthwhile to do this if a train of several hundred tons is likely to invade your particular patch of Kent at a speed of some fifty miles per hour. In fact you must double-check the fact until there is no shadow of a doubt. It is only too clear that John Benge did not take this view, for the train was shown in the timetable as passing at 3:15pm, twenty-five minutes into their work plan.

The southeastern route across the open Kentish countryside is one of the longest straight lines in England. Did John Benge experience an eerie, chilling moment when he first heard the distant beat of an unexpected train? The wooden lengths had been renewed, but there was still twenty-one feet of rail to replace. Red flags were furiously waved, whistles blown, brakes applied – but they could not bring the thirteen-carriage train to a stop within 500 yards. To the surprise of the petrified onlookers the engine and first coach managed to cross the rail-less section, but the girders below broke under the strain and five carriages fell into the muddy waters of the Beult. Forty-nine were injured and ten killed. Charles Dickens, travelling in the first carriage, was not injured, and helped those who were; but he later suffered some kind of mental trauma, and never fully recovered. He died five years later, aged fifty-eight. As L.T.C. Rolt observed, Benge deprived the world of the solution to *The Mystery of Edwin Drood,* and who knows what further literature from that great pen.

At the subsequent inquiry Benge was severely criticised. If he had stuck to the rule of 1,000 yards distance for the red flags, the train could still have pulled up in time. He was sentenced to nine months imprisonment for manslaughter.

VICTORIAN BANKING, 1866 In mid-Victorian London a comforting assumption seems to have taken root in the minds of investors and the market: that the Bank of England would never let a big bank or lender fail. Indeed, when Overend and Gurney, a gigantic discount house (a firm that lends money at 1 per cent below the Bank of England's rate) got into trouble in the uncertainties of 1857, they were allowed to borrow from the Bank to see them through.

But in the following year the Bank adopted a new policy requiring the discount houses to rely on their own cash reserves. Thus when Overend and Gurney again got itself into trouble in 1866, the Bank refused to rescue them. It was a rare case of the state reducing its support to financial institutions. This caused a certain amount of chaos and financial loss. But many historians credit this decision with leading to fifty years of financial calm in a London stripped of 'moral hazard'. This is defined as a lack of incentive to guard against risk, because a company can be protected from the consequences of its actions by being bailed out.

MR CASAUBON, IN *MIDDLEMARCH*, 1871 The Reverend Edward Casaubon is a middle-aged scholar whose life is devoted to proving that all ancient myths and erratic fragments of myth are corruptions of a tradition already revealed. The similarities of all these myths would suggest a single origin, which Casaubon assumes is God. The working title of his *magnum opus* is *The Key to All Mythologies*. The underlying problem of this project is that Casaubon, as a clergyman, has already decided that his thesis must be correct and that the evidence for it can be found, given enough effort and time. This is a somewhat heroic assumption, which may lead to failure after years of work. And so it proves in George Eliot's novel. Casaubon finds himself working with several handicaps: not knowing the German language, in which the most advanced theological research was being written; the tensions of his marriage to Dorothea Brooke, who initially wanted to aid him in his work, but comes to doubt its importance; and poor health, which leads to his early death. The stiffness of his intellectual framework is reflected in his dry, unsympathetic character. He does not rise to the status of a tragic figure, but is merely self-centred and empty. His unusual surname comes from the renowned seventeenth-century scholar, Isaac Casaubon, of Geneva and Paris.

We already know of the feat of translation achieved by Mary Ann Evans ('George Eliot') for the English edition of David Strauss's *Life of Jesus Critically Examined*. Strauss was part of the German theological movement which had already left Casaubon behind. Both he and Casaubon were examining the relationship between myth and Christianity. Thus Eliot must have contrasted in her own mind the relative success of Strauss with the doomed approach of Casaubon. And whereas Strauss began with the acquisition of evidence and gradually discerned some underlying patterns, poor Casaubon had assumed the pattern, but cannot, even in the archives of Rome, lay his hands on sufficient evidence.

THE MENHENIOT ACCIDENT, 1873 At Menheniot station, in the southeast corner of Cornwall, two goods trains were being held on the passing loop. This route, running from St Germans westwards to Liskeard, was only a single-track line. There were no signals at this station, so instructions were given verbally.

The train about to head west was awaiting a verbal order from the porter-signalman to proceed. The other train, eastbound, had been told to wait. The porter-signalman was in the telegraph office. Receiving the 'all clear', he shouted from the office door to the guard of the westbound train, 'Right away, Dick!' Unfortunately the guard of the other train, out of sight, shared the name 'Dick'. On hearing the shout he immediately waved a 'proceed' message to his driver, and the long heavy train hauled by two engines was off towards St Germans. The porter-signalman had just learnt that another goods train was on its way from St Germans along the single track and desperately tried to get the attention of this guard, but to no avail. One locomotive destroyed, three engine crews badly injured and one driver killed was the result of the 40mph head-on collision.

That there would be only one guard called 'Dick' was an assumption that many of us might have made; but was it unprofessional to shout the instruction from a distance? The other guard seems to have been a poor communicator, yet too quick to react to a signal heard but not seen.

The inquiry insisted on the immediate replacement of verbal orders by proper signalling.

THE BATTLE OF THE LITTLE BIGHORN, 1876 This is often put forward as a classic case of rash assumption. The total massacre of General Custer's force is usually blamed on his decision to divide the 7th Cavalry into three, with each unit too far apart to support the others quickly. And his information does seem to have been at fault, as to the number of opposing Plains Indians and the quality of their rifles. Yet there seems to be much uncertainty about Custer's plans, and the final massacre left no witnesses other than Comanche, a notably courageous horse who was found badly wounded, but was brought back to health. The politics of the aftermath of battle further clouded the understanding of this event. A myth grew around the idea of Custer as a heroic warrior against a barbaric foe. Subsequently, the legendary Comanche always appeared on parades of the 7th Cavalry, but riderless. He became a symbol of the battle, its only survivor. And Custer's wife actively pursued a long campaign to exonerate the general.

Although the battle is also known as 'Custer's Last Stand', it was almost the last stand for the independence of the Plains Indians, whose last major conflict came at the Battle of Wounded Knee in 1890.

THE TAY BRIDGE DISASTER, 28 DECEMBER 1879 An ancestor of mine perished in this catastrophe. It seems astonishing that a train was allowed to cross the bridge during such a powerful storm. The signalman at the southern end, Barclay, after giving the driver the single-line staff, could only return to his box by crawling on the ground.

In photographs of the time I am struck by the insubstantial appearance of Sir Thomas Bouch's narrow, skeletal supporting towers.

Out of the sinister distant observations of the drama as it unfolded in darkness, and the inquiry that followed with a welter of technical details, I have attempted to focus on only the most critical factors in this apocalyptic event. But I also reckon that an earlier assumption had sown the seeds of disaster.

The collapse of the High Girders, the highest section, was found by the Court of Inquiry to be the result of wind. The surface area of the train passing inside the girders caught the wind like an elongated sail. The wind was from the west, blowing at right angles to the bridge, force ten or eleven on the Beaufort scale. The inquiry that followed calculated that this was about twice the wind pressure that the structure could resist.

Within each cast-iron tower were diagonal ties and lugs that held the six vertical columns together, but they could not take the strain of their compression and stretching in the wind. The whole structure leaned to the east in the storm. As the ties and lugs snapped and broke, internal rigidity was lost, and the towers toppled, pulling all thirteen High Girders down. A diver sent into the estuary found most of the train still inside the fifth girder.

The inquiry also found that Henry Noble, the maintenance 'engineer' – in fact a bricklayer – had already heard the sound of loose ties some months before. He had ordered them to be 'packed' to regain tension. But he had not mentioned the matter to Sir Thomas Bouch or the railway company.

Sir Thomas was severely criticised by the inquiry. The bridge had 'inherent defects' which would sooner or later have brought the bridge down. The inspectors judged that the bridge was badly designed, badly constructed and badly maintained. How could Sir Thomas, whose previous projects had worked successfully, have ended up presiding over such a flawed enterprise? We may find the answer at the start of the project, in 1871.

An inexplicable assumption From only some of the estuary borings, Thomas Bouch had somehow assumed that the whole bed of the estuary was formed of solid rock. He based his design on that notion. After fourteen tall brick towers had been constructed from the south side, he made a worrying discovery: that the bed in the middle of the estuary was formed of gravel and sand, and that the estuary was very much deeper out there. It would seem that he had a detached relationship with the survey contractors.

Well, to start a project to build the world's longest railway bridge – nearly two miles over a turbulent estuary, the first he had encountered – without having a thorough knowledge of the very foundations on which the project will stand is, shall we say, extraordinary. One source suggests that the fifty-seven-year-old Bouch was not well at this time. Or had he perhaps been infected with a touch of hubris from his successful career? Whatever the exact cause of this assumption, I think we can say that one thing led to another, in various and malign ways:

Such an oversight might well have undermined the respect of his colleagues and work force; this may have isolated him from vital contact about operational matters.

He was led to build the remaining majority of the towers from cast-iron columns, to reduce weight; he also had to build much deeper foundations below water. (The inquiry decided that this 'makeshift modification' was a very grave mistake; the whole bridge should have been redesigned instead.)

This change incurred greater expense and delayed the completion of the project. His client, the North British Railway, were pressing him to economise on these extra costs, and he does not seem to have wholly resisted this.

The new towers look vertical, though in fact lean very slightly inward towards the top. But in his impressive 1860 Belah viaduct near Kirkby

Stephen in the Pennines, one can easily see that the pier towers had a greater inward lean for stability, especially for the highest section. He had also used a type of lug superior to that used on the Tay Bridge. Protection against wind was on his mind upon the high moorlands, so why not in the middle of a notoriously exposed Scottish estuary?

Two years before completion a sudden gale blew up and a stretch of the High Girders was blown down during the process of construction, but this does not seem to have been taken as a warning.

DR ARTHUR CONAN DOYLE AND THE SCIENCE OF DEDUCTION, FROM 1881

This great son of Ireland, and hero of my boyhood library, was, in himself and through his creation of Sherlock Holmes, another great foe of the making of assumptions: assumptions that, when made by the police, could cause real harm through faulty convictions.

Conan Doyle had learnt from Dr Joseph Bell, of the University of Edinburgh Medical School, how to observe minute details for making a diagnosis and how to deduce a patient's work and habits by close observation. Bell had been invited to help in several police investigations. Conan Doyle (graduated in medicine, 1881) himself investigated in later years, most painstakingly, at least two notorious miscarriages of justice: the cases of Oscar Slater and George Edalji.

Until the era of Bell and Conan Doyle, police forces seem to have assumed the likelihood of guilt according to what was obvious, circumstantial, hearsay – or even plain convenient. But Doyle scorned such methods.

For example: in one of the earliest Holmes stories, *The Boscombe Valley Mystery,* the local police quickly establish a serious case on the circumstance of the son being in the same place as his murdered father, but Holmes dismisses that as mere conjecture. He himself will take nothing for granted until he has the opportunity of looking personally into it. 'There is nothing more deceptive than an obvious fact,' he laughs.

In *The Reigate Squires* he explains further:

The Inspector had overlooked the role of the younger Mr Cunningham because he had already assumed that these county magnates had had nothing to do with the matter. Now, I make a point of never having any prejudices and of following docilely wherever facts may lead me, and so in the very first stage of the investigation I found myself looking a little askance at the part played by Mr Alec Cunningham.

These county magnates are duly maddened by the thorough double-checking of Holmes; they are arrogant people, not used to this kind of careful and polite inquisition; finally they resort to violence against Holmes in person… and are promptly arrested.

Such open-eyed docility might lead anywhere, and so might require greater moral and physical courage – qualities not lacking in the character of Sherlock Holmes or his creator.

Then, in *The Naval Treaty,* Holmes is being quizzed by the impatient Miss Harrison about his progress.

'You suspect someone?'

'I suspect myself—'

'What?'

'Of coming to conclusions too rapidly.'

In the course of the sixty Sherlock Holmes stories – criminal cases and some non-criminal mysteries – Holmes reveals to Watson the elements of his Science of Deduction, which he describes as 'systematised common sense'. Here I divide these elements into Axioms, Skill and Knowledge, all harnessed in the endless battle against jumping to conclusions.

AXIOMS

1. The first rule of criminal investigation: 'One should always look for a possible alternative and provide against it.' *Black Peter.* This reflects, consciously or not, John Stuart Mill's notion that the truth is more likely to emerge from a clash of differing opinions than from one point of view alone.

2. 'It is a capital mistake to theorise before one has data. Insensibly, one begins to twist facts to suit theories, instead of theories to suit the facts.' *A Scandal in Bohemia* and elsewhere.

3. 'Crime is common. Logic is rare. Therefore it is upon the logic rather than the crime that you should dwell.' *The Copper Beeches*. The 'you' in that advice may also refer to Dr Watson as the recorder of Holmes' cases. Holmes then accuses him of degrading 'what should have been a course of lectures into a series of tales'.

4. 'It is an old axiom of mine that when all other contingencies fail, whatever remains, however improbable, must be the truth.' In other words, what is improbable or unlikely can still be possible: as in *The Bruce-Partington Plans,* when the only remaining explanation is that the body of Cadogan West must have been somehow placed on the roof of the underground train.

SKILL

1. Seeing is not enough. Holmes admonishes Watson in *A Scandal in Bohemia* that 'You see, but you do not observe.' Watson has climbed the stairs in Baker Street frequently, but does not know how many steps there are. He has not observed, he has only seen. And in *The Blanched Soldier* Holmes remarks 'I see no more than you, but I have trained myself to notice what I see.' Thus observation is the first critical skill.

'You know my method. It is founded on the observation of trifles.' *The Boscombe Valley Mystery*. 'There is nothing so important as trifles.' *The Man with the Twisted Lip*.

As examples of such trifles, I recall in particular: the curried mutton served to the stable lads in *Silver Blaze;* the overhearing of Mrs Barclay's curious use of the name 'David' in *The Crooked Man*; the tobacco-pouch found next to the dead man in *Black Peter*; in *The Six Napoleons* the significance of the street lamp in Campden House Road; and in *The Golden Pince-Nez* the fact that adjoining corridors at Yoxley Old Place were both lined with coconut matting. In *The Abbey Grange* there is the puzzling accumulation of sediment in one of three wine glasses, allegedly the impromptu refreshment of a trio of burglars. The landlady in *The Red Circle* brings Holmes two burnt matches and a cigarette-end because she has heard that Holmes 'can read great things out of small ones'. In *The Disappearance of Lady Frances Carfax* Holmes is 'haunted by the thought that somewhere a clue, a strange sentence, a curious observation, had come under my notice and had been too easily dismissed'. After a sleepless night, he does indeed dredge up the strange sentence: 'It took longer, being out of the ordinary.' This was the remark of the undertaker's wife: the 'it' was a coffin. A similar moment occurs in *The Lion's Mane* as Holmes ransacks his knowledge of natural history to recall the *cyanea capillata*, and also uses a lens to examine very carefully the wounds made by the lethal filaments of this jellyfish. In *The Creeping Man* the wolfhound, Roy, has taken to growling at his master, Professor Presbury. What can this mean? To Watson it is of no import, but Holmes takes this dog very seriously. In *The Valley of Fear* the finding of a single dumb-bell in the study at Birlstone Manor immediately arouses his suspicion. In *Silver Blaze* there is 'the curious incident of the dog in the night-time'.

'But the dog did nothing in the night-time.'

'That was the curious incident,' remarked Holmes. What did *not* happen can be a trifle of huge significance.

Holmes is very aware that his clients and colleagues are not accustomed to his degree of attention to small things. He finds that he often has to use soothing words such as 'Well, well, it was worth making sure, anyway…' In *The Three Students* there is a moment when Holmes stands on tiptoe outside

Hilton Soames's study and cranes his neck to see if it is possible to get a look at the don's desk. But Soames dissuades him, assuming he is checking how the miscreant might have entered the room; he does not think of *asking* Holmes what he is doing. Holmes rather enjoys the irony of these moments, and goes with the flow rather than explaining too much too soon:

> 'Dear me!' said Holmes, and he smiled in a singular way as he glanced at our companion. 'Well, if there is nothing to be learned here we had best go inside.'

In the final Sherlock Holmes story, *Shoscombe Old Place* (1927), the importance of the microscope in producing evidence from 'trifles' is now recognised by Merivale of Scotland Yard. To assist him, Holmes had identified the type of glue in the cap of an accused man, a glue-handling picture framer, and had identified zinc and copper filings in the cuff of a suspected coiner.

2. Inference must follow observation. *The Adventure of the 'Gloria Scott'* is Holmes' first case, dating from his undergraduate days (was it Oxford or Cambridge?) before he had come to London. Within the college his remarkable gifts of observation were becoming known. During the long vacation the respectable father of a college friend asks Holmes, over the port, to demonstrate his gifts upon himself. Holmes obliges, though the results are painful for the subject.

'What do you say to a ramble through London?' asks Holmes of Watson one October evening, after the air has been refreshed by rain. 'For three hours we strolled about together, watching the ever-changing kaleidoscope of life as it ebbs and flows through Fleet Street and the Strand. Holmes' characteristic talk, with its keen observance of detail and subtle power of inference, held me amused and enthralled.' *The Resident Patient.*

'Well, Watson what do you make of it?' Many of the stories begin with a client just departed or having left some belongings behind. Holmes generally offers Watson first shot at deducing from the all-important 'trifles' what can be learnt. This amounts to a ritual in which Watson is finally congratulated by Holmes, to find only that the 'congratulations' refer to the enormous value Holmes finds in the stimulus of Watson's entirely erroneous conclusions.

In *The Hound of the Baskervilles* the examination of Dr Mortimer's lost stick is a classic example. Watson confidently infers 'an elderly medical man, well esteemed... a great deal of his visiting on foot... worn down ferrule of stick... CCH engraved on the silver band... the local hunt... to whom he has perhaps given assistance...' Yet Watson has jumped too easily to conclusions. As Holmes so frequently reflects: if Watson had been a confederate who could predict his conclusions and course of action, he, Holmes, would be in danger of complacency, 'but one to whom each development comes as a perpetual surprise, and to whom the future is always a closed book, is indeed an ideal helpmate.'

(Well, yes, but what about the good doctor's patients, and the accuracy of his diagnoses?)

A *tour de force* of observation and inference occurs in *The Greek Interpreter* when Holmes and his brother Mycroft, seated in the bow window of the Diogenes Club in Pall Mall, compete in rapidly assessing and analysing the 'magnificent types' walking past – to the astonishment of Dr Watson: 'Come, this is a little too much!'

KNOWLEDGE

Holmes makes it clear that observation and inference should be supported by a third leg, as it were: a breadth of education and knowledge. This helps in all sorts of unexpected ways.

Special knowledge is needed too. Holmes has written many monographs on subjects such as footprints, handwriting, writing paper, cigar ash, trades and their effect on the hand, newspaper type, perfumes etc. Of the up-and-coming French detective, François Le Villard, Holmes notes his gifts of observation and inference, but regrets that he is deficient in knowledge. But at least Le Villard is now translating Holmes' monographs into French.

Holmes has a filing system of previous cases from all over Europe and North America which furnishes him with analogies for the crime of the moment, a huge advantage. Does Inspector Gregson (*A Study in Scarlet*) remember the circumstances around the death of Van Jansen in Utrecht in 1834?

'Read it up – you really should. There is nothing new under the sun. It has all been done before.'

Aided by imagination and perception

The value of imagination – 'the one quality which Inspector Gregory lacks' – is seen in *Silver Blaze,* where Holmes uses a working assumption that the missing racehorse has wandered across the moor to the other training stable. 'We imagined what might have happened, acted upon the supposition and find ourselves justified. Let us proceed.'

At the start of *The Six Napoleons* Inspector Lestrade, of Scotland Yard, turns up one evening at Baker Street, as he was wont to do: to keep in touch, to swap police news for advice from Holmes and so on. On this occasion Lestrade speaks of the weather, the news, and then falls quiet, 'puffing silently at a cigar'.

Holmes observes him closely.

'Anything remarkable on hand?'

'Oh, no, Mr Holmes, nothing very particular.'

'Then tell me all about it.'

PARADOXICAL WORDS OF OSCAR WILDE In his novel *The Picture of Dorian Gray*, 1890, the narrator declares that 'It is only shallow people who do not judge by appearances.' Elsewhere Wilde has boasted that 'My first impressions are invariably right.' Wilde made great play with reversal and paradox in his humour, but these two epigrams – haughty assumptions, at first sight – can now be seen as consistent with later discoveries of how the mind works.

The tragic ending of his life looks like a classic case of hubris leading to a legal *peripeteia* and eventual nemesis. He would surely have recognised the danger, for Wilde had been a brilliant classicist at Dublin and Oxford. Did he make the very dangerous assumption that he, with his great theatrical success and general fame, could break the taboos of Edwardian society with impunity? By his hubris – it seems he was too proud to be seen to flee from England – he lost almost everything.

THE PUBLIC MOODS OF THE LATER NINETEENTH CENTURY The long era of post-Napoleonic peace from 1815 to 1854 and the short Franco-Prussian war of 1871 had led to a general and optimistic assumption: that peace was now the natural state of history. Previous centuries had accepted war as an inevitable part of human affairs, though mostly fought by professional armies far beyond the ear of the city.

Now, there might still be occasional wars but they would be short, an extension of politics by other means, and would lead to negotiations which would usher in another period of peace.

Some other assumptions of the period:

The past is an indication of the future.

Greater wealth precludes conflict.

There is inevitable progress towards ever greater liberty and enlightenment ('The Whig View of History').

But, as the turn of the century approached, the holders of such agreeable illusions had to face up to hard cases such as Kaiser Wilhelm II and his military intentions.

DIARY OF A GERMAN PRINCE, 1898 A sharp portrayal of Kaiser Wilhelm, a man in a state of hubris, appears in *Rudolf the Last*, a highly critical book written anonymously by a member of the house of Saxe-Weimar. This prince had spent most of the previous decade studying the Kaiser, conferring with him, disagreeing with him and travelling all over Europe in an attempt to understand the developing anxieties of the time. He found that no single blow could ever shatter 'the boundless self-conceit of this man'.

> The Kaiser is not a modern monarch. He believes that he is God's anointed, and his belief in himself, his mission, his genius and his achievements is studiously fostered by his entourage, so that he is not accustomed to contradiction or strong expression of other views than his own. These he hears with astonishment and resentment. He would like to convert the whole world into a barracks. Everything must be cut and dried, standardised, labelled and tabulated.

A BOOK ABOUT ASSUMPTIONS, 1902 *On Assumptions* by Alexius Meinong was published in Germany. I quickly realised that this was a philosophical work that was going to be way over my head, but I did note that Herr Meinong drew a distinction between two major categories of thought: 'assumptions' and 'judgements'. Assumptions, he wrote, 'lack conviction'. With this division of thought was Meinong on the same thread of enquiry as Descartes, Spinoza and Alexander Bain? I felt an illustration would be helpful, but it was in grappling with his chosen example – involving a doughnut – that he left me way behind.

PIONEER ALPINE SKIING, 1902 Edward and William Richardson, sons of David Richardson – the 'sugar king of Scotland' – had this winter begun to explore the country around Davos, in eastern Switzerland. Pioneer skiing there was in a lull at this time, and the brothers, who had visited Norway, became the most vital force for persistent organisation of the sport.

They spotted a promising-looking mountain called the Brehmerbühl, which has since become a much-loved skiing ground, its bold domes of snow bulging above spacious larch forest. In this rosy dawn of the sport the Richardsons had set off 'thoroughly imbued with the idea that you could go anywhere at any time on ski'. They admitted only having the vaguest ideas about avalanches, knew very little about snow and nothing at all about föhn winds. Above the larches they began to traverse steeper ground. 'Suddenly there came a loud, dull report, something like the cracking of ice on a large lake, and before we realised what had happened we found ourselves on our backs with masses of snow surging about us.' They were carried down some hundred feet. Edward Richardson found himself buried up to his neck, unable to move. If it had not been for his brother, he believed he would have perished.

They dusted themselves down – and continued the climb! But inspection of the wall of snow from which the avalanche had peeled away suggested alarming instability and they decided to give up the Brehmerbühl for another day. 'We went back to Clavadel with a wholesome respect for steep slopes and new snow which neither of us has ever lost.'

In such an unfamiliar environment, pioneering and assumption inevitably must work together.

SKI RACING BEFORE THE FIRST WORLD WAR I came across this kind of assumption while researching the early history of skiing in Europe. The years before the war saw the first downhill ski races. At that time the competitors raced as amateurs. Thus in Austria it was assumed by the authorities that ski teachers were professionals and therefore should not be allowed to compete in the important races. But in Switzerland ski teachers *were* allowed to compete – because some thoughtful observer had pointed out that their profession was not in fact skiing – but *teaching*. Thus the great Austrian pioneer Johann Schneider was unable to compete in his own country, but was able to demonstrate his great abilities over the border in Switzerland. The assumption was due to a confusion of categories: skiing or teaching? Category assumption is very easily made, I have found.

MILITARY HUBRIS OF THE RUSSIAN EMPIRE, 1905 In the conflict over the territories of Manchuria and Korea, the Tsar continued hostilities against the Japanese for a second year. Japan had only recently emerged as an aggressive force in Asia. But within the Tsarist regime there was an assumption of racial superiority over the Japanese and ignorance of their war-like character, their abilities and the modernity of their British-built fleets. How could this small obscure nation offer any real resistance to the might of Holy Russia and its expanding empire in the east? And Nicholas II was at this time being encouraged by his German cousin, Wilhelm II, to gain further glory by addressing the imagined problem of 'The Yellow Peril', that is, China and Japan. This state of ignorance and hubris was soon to reap a terrible harvest of misfortune.

Port Arthur, Russia's only warm-water port on the Pacific and home of the First Russian Fleet, had been leased from China a few years before. But Port Arthur was now under siege by the Japanese. Thus in October the Baltic Fleet, later renamed the Second Pacific Squadron, was dispatched by the Tsar on an ambitious journey of up to 18,000 miles to relieve the besieged port.

No sooner had they passed out of the Baltic than an extraordinary incident occurred in the North Sea, on the Dogger Bank. Such was the official Russian paranoia about attacks by Japanese torpedo boats – even this far from Japan – and so jumpy were the crews, that a number of trawlers from Hull were assumed to be torpedo boats and were fired upon. Two fishermen were killed and much damage sustained. This almost led to hostilities between the UK and Russia.

Meanwhile, the decision to send a second fleet had aroused strong reactions in Russia. Its wisdom was severely questioned, and helped to fuel the revolution of 1905 and the continuing unrest thereafter.

During the seven-month journey the morale of the sailors had declined, what with rough seas and the difficulties and labour of re-coaling. The admiral, Rozhestvensky, seems to have achieved a miracle of logistics in very adverse circumstances. But the ships themselves were in poor condition and the long voyage fouled them with barnacles that slowed their speed.

On reaching Far Eastern waters it was discovered that Port Arthur had already fallen to the Japanese, during the fleet's rest at Madagascar. Now the only remaining place of refuge for the fleet was Vladivostok, further north, but free of ice, as it was now the month of May. It could be reached most quickly by passing through the Strait of Tsushima, which divides Japan from Korea, but vulnerable to attack by the Imperial Japanese Navy. Yet it was a mere careless assumption that was to doom the Russian fleet.

On the night of 27 May, the Russian fleet sailed through the strait without lights and outside the normal shipping lanes. Cloaking fog seemed to give the Russians extra safety. But the Japanese cruiser *Shinano Maru* was in the area and at 2:45am noticed in the distance one of the Russian hospital ships, the *Orel*, which by international law was required to keep its lights burning. By 4:30am the cruiser had drawn close and Captain Narukawa recognised her as an unarmed auxiliary vessel. But in the poor visibility someone on the hospital ship assumed that the cruiser was a fellow Russian warship and sent a signal that there were other Russian ships nearby. Narukawa then made out the shapes of ten more Russian warships lurking in the fog. At 4:55am he used the new technology of the wireless telegraph to send a message to Admiral Togo: 'The enemy is in square 203.'

In the subsequent annihilation of the Russian fleet, over 5,000 Russian sailors perished, and 116 Japanese.

Tsushima also held vast technical significance for the future of warship design – and the future of Russia. The Tsar's reputation was not helped by the story or rumour that when the news of the disaster was broken to him, he continued to participate in a tennis match.

But the Japanese success swelled to hubris over the next decades, and their stubborn and relentless ambition ended unimaginably forty years on. Tsushima led to Hiroshima.

PIONEER MOUNTAINEERING ON SKI, 1908, 1912 Arnold Lunn, an Englishman, was one of the greatest pioneers of skiing in Europe. In his youth he was a courageous and inexhaustible explorer of the Swiss Alps, venturing into districts which had never known the imprint of skis. The ski had only been introduced to the Alps two decades before, by engineers from Norway and Sweden studying in Switzerland.

On New Year's Day 1908 we find Arnold Lunn at the winter resort of Montana, high above Sierre in the canton of Valais. He had just completed his first term at Balliol, Oxford. In the freedom of the mountains his fierce hunger for ski exploration quickly led to a productive crisis, the Incident on the Rawyl. I have retold the whole story in my books on skiing, but here of course it is the presence of assumptions that we look for. Pioneers in such an environment are bound to make assumptions, consciously or not, and must rise to the subsequent challenges – or retire from the scene.

Lunn had decided to make a crossing of the Wildstrubel range to the north, as a way of reaching Villars over the course of a few days. He and a new acquaintance, Cecil Wybergh, left Montana at 4:15am and reached the Plaine Morte glacier eight hours later, a tough climb on account of the heavy snow, and skiing up without the grip of sealskins. Here they split up for a while. Lunn had his eye on the summit of the Wildstrubel (3,244m) across the glacier. Wybergh opted to go straight to the mountain hut close by, a very reasonable decision – for until he had met the persuasive Arnold Lunn he had only skied for an hour on the practice ground!

By the time Lunn rejoined an anxious Wybergh at the hut, he had been on ski for fifteen hours. His experience of overnighting in huts in winter was minimal, and this January the temperatures were exceptionally low, -20°C down in the valley, even lower at their altitude. His assumption that they could leave the hut in good time next morning came to nought, for when the stove went out, everything in the hut refroze. They awoke to frozen tea, frozen lamp oil and rock-hard frozen boots, amongst other icy delights. Re-igniting the stove proved difficult and they could not get into their boots until midday. This ruled out making an ascent of the Wildhorn, so Lunn decided they should go down to Lenk directly by the Rawyl Pass. He had read in the Alpine Club guide that there was a mule track over the pass: 'I had never crossed this path in summer, but did not anticipate any difficulty in finding the way.' This was his second pioneering assumption.

After an anxious search Lunn discerned the snowbound path below. It lay above a precipice.

> We shouldered our ski and hurried down the steep track. For a time all went well; then suddenly the path turned a sharp corner at a point where it was cut out of the precipice. In summer one would have passed this point without comment. As we found it, the wind had drifted the snow into an icy bank of extraordinary steepness, abutting onto the precipice.

They were forced to cut steps, without an ice-axe; the top layer of snow was liable to slip away; the skis had to be carried over the steps one by one. They very tentatively advanced. The snow looked horrifyingly unstable, the path disappeared into a steep couloir, darkness fell and their hopes of surviving the freezing night sank very low indeed. But – beyond the couloir they could discern the long slope of snow down to Iffigenalp; hotel and dinner at Lenk was now merely a matter of time. Lunn admits they were lucky to survive.

The two assumptions made by Lunn about the conditions in the hut, and using a summer path in winter, were venial sins, likely to have been made by other pioneers too, though Lunn certainly had the impulsiveness of youth. But the episode did not remain a private matter. There were consequences. A telegram confirming their safe arrival sent to Lunn's father, Sir Henry, was never passed on. A search party was then sent up from Montana and one of the party's guides was very badly frost-bitten; a second search party was sent out to call back the first search party, once it was discovered that Lunn and Wybergh were on their way to Villars. The choice of route was severely criticised in the *Lausanne Gazette* by a well-known mountaineer, who described the northern outlet of the Rawyl Pass as 'a most precipitous and ice-bound region'. Later in the year Lunn was also criticised in the journal of the Ski Club of Great Britain.

Arnold Lunn was most definitely under a cloud. But within three months he had founded the first British club for ski-mountaineers, and the following year he made the first crossing of the Bernese Oberland on ski with the author of the critical letter, Professor Roget. It seems that Lunn understood the principle of not wasting a good crisis.

Four years later, in dark December, we find Lunn in the Engadine, a region he did not know. He and his guide Maurice Crettex had planned a tour into the Bregaglia range on the Italian border. A Lieutenant Burton and his sister Frances were to join them. Crettex, a Swiss giant with the swagger and confidence of one of Dumas' musketeers, was one of the first ski-mountaineering guides, though unfamiliar with the Engadine. This outing did not go well…

They assembled at Maloja where they settled down to a 'sumptuous lunch'. The plan was to ski up the narrow Forno glacier and overnight at the Forno Hut (2,574m), about six miles from Maloja. As Maloja is already some 1,800m above sea level this would seem to be a fairly easy climb. But that sumptuous meal, it went on a bit, and it was not until three in the afternoon that they set out. Darkness falls earliest in December and they were in twilight while still on the glacier. At this point Crettex stopped to examine the map. A first uncanny suspicion disturbed the serenity of Lunn's mind: that Crettex could not find the hut. Lunn became even more worried when Crettex asked for his opinion: 'When Crettex consults an amateur there is something very rotten in the state of Denmark.' An anxious few hours followed, during which Crettex disappeared on a quest for the hut, while Lunn and his two companions somehow managed to stay cheerful sitting on a small rock. But Lunn was painfully aware of the steady approach of bad weather. Softly and treacherously the snow began to fall. The wind would sweep away their tracks. Storm and darkness was a lethal combination that he had not yet experienced. At midnight Crettex reappeared in despair. A long retreat was now their only choice.

By some miracle of observation Crettex was able to follow their half-obliterated tracks. They skied roped together. The morale of the party gained vital confidence from the unflagging courage and cheerfulness of Frances Burton. Without that, Lunn reckoned, there could well have been a very different ending to their adventure. Crettex agreed: 'Tonnerre, quelle demoiselle solide!" (By thunder, what a tough young lady!)

By 2am they had found a draughty cowshed. The danger, if not the discomfort, was over.

How did they get it so wrong? The late departure obviously didn't help, but the real problem was that Lunn and Crettex were unaware of two critical facts about the Forno Hut. They do not seem to have consulted local knowledge, and thus had to assume that finding it would be straightforward. In fact the hut lies in a hollow, despite its high elevation. Secondly, there had already been severe snowstorms that season, and the hut had been buried in drifts. They had probably skied right over it, as has been known to happen.

But Lunn was a quick learner, and his total record over nearly forty ski-mountaineering tours and twenty mountaineering climbs was notably successful. He also wrote the first book on Alpine snowcraft for skiers. The exploding assumptions of his youth had not been wasted.

A TRIBUTE TO SHERLOCK HOLMES? A wording of one of Holmes' axioms is used by Rupert Psmith in the four *Psmith* novels (1909–1923) by P.G. Wodehouse: 'Don't confuse what is improbable with what is impossible.' I seem to recall some painful episodes, as a victorious Psmith kindly introduces his victims to this useful advice.

ASSUMPTIONS IN THE PLOTS OF SHERLOCK HOLMES STORIES The earlier Holmes section showed how assumption in general could be avoided or overcome by his focus on "trifles" and his "science of deduction". In this section individual assumptions are made within the action of the story.

When Inspector Lestrade finds the word 'RACHE' written in blood on the wall of the front room of a house in Lauriston Gardens, Brixton, he becomes excited. He immediately pronounces that there is undoubtedly a woman at the bottom of this case – with the name of Rachel. Holmes then makes his own gymnastic and intimate examination of the room. Afterwards, Lestrade, not knowing German, has to put up with Holmes advising him not to waste his time on the imaginary woman, for 'rache' is the German word for 'revenge'.

In only the second story, *A Scandal in Bohemia* (1892), Holmes himself makes a rather naïve assumption about the opera singer Irene Adler. As the *dénouement* of the story approaches, Holmes plans to call at her home in St John's Wood at eight in the morning. 'She will not be up, so we shall have a clear field' (for he and his client, the King of Bohemia, to reclaim a compromising photograph). But on her doorstep Holmes is rattled by the news that she has already left England that morning by the 5:15 train from Charing Cross.

In both *The Norwood Builder* and *The Retired Colourman* an embittered solitary criminal has assumed that he can get away with some false evidence with which to nullify suspicion. But they go just that little bit too far, Holmes observes, and are found out. They lack 'that supreme gift of the artist, the knowledge of when to stop'.

Lastly, we find an assumption pleasingly wound into the plot of *The Hound of the Baskervilles*. The story was inspired by the landscape of Dartmoor and its ancient history. Conan Doyle had got to know the district in the company of Devonian friends such as Sabine Baring-Gould and Fletcher Robinson. As a result, Doyle evokes 'the moor' so vividly and subtly, that it becomes one of the *dramatis personae* of the tangled story.

The middle three chapters – the two reports and the rain-swept days of Dr Watson's diary – move the drama steadily forward. The reports are duly sent to Holmes, who is still far too busy in London to be able to get down to Devonshire. He has not even been in touch. For a while, it is a puzzled Watson who is responsible for guiding the reader around the disturbed moorland community.

One night he and Sir Henry Baskerville are out on the moor searching for the escaped convict Selden, the notorious Notting Hill murderer. As they turn for home, the silhouette of a man, tall and thin, is briefly glimpsed on a granite tor, just as the moon rises up behind. This figure seems to haunt Watson in the following days, though Sir Henry dismisses it as one of the prison warders from Princetown. The next chapter – *The Man on the Tor* – raises yet more questions, and Watson keenly regrets the absence of Holmes and his decisive mind. Then, on a fine October evening, armed with fresh information about this 'other man – the man on the tor', Watson walks up to the part of the moor where this personage may be dwelling. This splendid chapter reaches a classic surprise when Watson discovers that Holmes has been living in a prehistoric hut circle for the last ten days, pursuing his investigations unnoticed. Everyone, including the suspected murderer of old Sir Charles, has found it easy to assume that he is busily engaged in London.

THE QUESTION OF FEMALE SUFFRAGE, 1899–1914 It is almost certainly the case that until the First World War, most women in the UK did not want the vote. That might seem at first glance pretty hard to believe. The twenty-first-century School of the Bleedin' Obvious will ask why on earth wouldn't they want the same voting rights as men, what's not to like? Well, to counter that conventional wisdom, here follows a list of some objections that were actually voiced by women of the time:

- 1889, the first big petition, signed by women: 'We protest against [women's] admission to direct power in that State which rests upon force – the State in its administrative, military and financial aspects.'

- A dislike of party politics and the risk of being manipulated by male politicians.

- So bound up with their real and fundamental work in the family that they considered they did not have the expertise to vote properly on imperial matters. Party politics would be a damaging distraction from their proper and vital areas of expertise in the domestic sphere.

- Female suffrage could undermine marriage and family.

- What would India make of a Britain partly governed by women?

- Resentment against being bossed around by middle-class suffragettes, mischievously spreading the idea that domestic work was despicable.

Not such a simple matter, then. The suffragette campaign was suspended on the outbreak of war. But in February 1918 women aged thirty or over did obtain the vote, reflecting the value of the roles that women had filled during the war.

THE SHIFT IN NATIONAL MOODS, 1914 In a noted inaugural lecture at the London School of Economics in 1968, the historian James Joll suggested a tentative explanation of a much-asked question: how on earth was it that, by 1914, the idea of war had become generally more acceptable across Europe?

The lecture was titled *1914: The Unspoken Assumptions*. It later formed part of his book *The Origins of the Second World War*.

These shifting, unarticulated assumptions identified by Joll, these swings of the national mood, are not the most straightforward matters to describe, as Joll himself emphasised. I summarise briefly, hoping not to simplify. The 'unspoken assumptions' fall into three broad categories.

Firstly, in the previous three decades, a mood of simple patriotism and solidarity had been sown into every level of life across Europe. This had been achieved mostly through the medium of school history and by organisations of an outdoor or military character. For example, in Britain Lord Roberts had founded the National Service League, Baden-Powell the Scouts and Empire Day. There were various Church 'brigades' for the young. Conscription was universal in Europe, though not in the United Kingdom – until 1916. In Germany there was a strong emphasis on nature and hiking in the forested landscapes. A youth army – the *Jugendwehr* – was formed. In the Black Forest skiing rapidly developed through the formation of clubs, becoming a source of health in winter for all levels of society.

Secondly, in the higher levels of society and academia, there had been a change in the discussion of international relations. It seems that Charles Darwin's discovery of natural selection, and especially its simplified and misleading form as 'survival of the fittest', had encouraged a mood of revolt against the long-held values of peace and rational solution. The idea of 'liberation through violence' was countenanced. Patriotism began to acquire a nationalist edge, for example in the formation of Navy Leagues in the UK and Germany. For some the war was not only inevitable but desirable. The French novelist Emile Zola was writing that 'War is life itself. War is the school of discipline, sacrifice and courage.' Germany was under the influence of Friedrich Nietzsche and his gospel of liberation. It was said that the assassins of Franz Ferdinand had quoted Nietzsche amongst the café tables of Sarajevo.

The third unspoken assumption was an image of what the next war would look like. Focusing just on the British here, the prospect may have been seen in terms of the recent South African and Russo-Japanese wars, and only two years before, the Balkan Wars against the Ottoman Empire. Others may have imagined German naval threats across the North Sea. There had been many 'prophetic novels' about German ambitions, such as *The Riddle of the Sands*, *The Invasion of 1910* and *The Battle of Dorking*. But what the public probably did not imagine was the horror of a new kind of warfare, dominated by far more powerful weapons, in which defence and attack could become locked in prolonged brutal stalemates.

James Joll identified other reasons for war being acceptable for the individual: as an escape from the routine and tedium of ordinary life; as an opportunity for great adventure; even as a sporting challenge. When war broke out, some recruiting propaganda seems to have played on these unspoken assumptions.

THE SINKING OF THE *TITANIC*, APRIL 1912 The naval architect of this liner described it as 'almost unsinkable'. This was quickly simplified by the public into 'unsinkable', a widely held assumption.

Were there other assumptions involved in this apocalyptic tragedy? Probably, but one in particular stands out. Despite all the inquiry and investigation that has gone into this disaster for over a century, and the sinister discoveries of weaknesses – the steel was brittle, there was a fire burning next to the bulkheads during the voyage, the rivets broke under the strain, the transverse bulkheads weren't watertight at an angle – the strangest assumption remains this: that it was thought safe to be forging ahead at 22 knots (25mph) through a known iceberg zone, at night, in a ship 900 feet in length with limited ability to slow down or to change course.

In the inquiry this was claimed to be normal practice across the Atlantic, it was perfectly safe, Captain Smith was 'unlucky'. This was surely chancing the lives of thousands, and in Lord Mersey's original report he had suggested that what had become 'normal practice' in the trans-Atlantic crossings 'would in future be classed as gross irresponsibility'.

It was eventually confirmed that the critical damage (to the starboard bow) was from an outlying underwater spur of the iceberg. The damage consisted of just six narrow slits at intervals along the hull.

The United States set up a patrol a few years later in that quarter of the Atlantic, warning ships to give all icebergs a wide berth.

JOHN BUCHAN: *THE THIRTY-NINE STEPS*, 1914 The penultimate chapter of this famous eve-of-war adventure is built around the creation of a simple assumption. The chapter's background derives from Buchan's close involvement in high London circles and his successful legal career within government.

The scene is an evening in late July at Sir Walter Bullivant's house in Queen Anne's Gate, a street opposite St James's Park and his place of work, the Foreign Office. A meeting is being held for the visit of Royer, the French naval representative, who will receive a copy of the disposition of the British fleet on mobilisation. Four very senior officials are present, including the First Sea Lord, who arrives a little late. He inspects the plans without comment and leaves after about twenty minutes. The protagonist of the story, Richard Hannay, is also there, but has been requested by Sir Walter to wait in the hall. As the First Sea Lord walks out, Hannay catches his eye and receives an unmistakable sense of recognition between them, suggesting this man is not the First Sea Lord but someone else, someone that Hannay has met recently. But in the meeting room the other participants had taken his presence for granted, an assumption assisted by the fact that the First Sea Lord was notoriously taciturn. Thus a master of disguise in a German spy ring that Hannay has already partially uncovered, has had a good twenty minutes memorising the naval plans and has now left the premises.

Hannay first telephones the First Sea Lord's house and learns that he has not left home that evening, being unwell. He then strides into the meeting room, not received well by Sir Walter: 'This intervention is ill-timed, Hannay.' But he puts it to them that the First Sea Lord was not who he appeared to be. All are aghast, but the Frenchman, Royer, backs Hannay's perception: they had assumed his presence because they were all too interested in other things.

I don't know if the scene ever featured in film versions of the book. I looked up who the First Sea Lord was at that portentous date: Prince Louis of Battenberg, who was indeed somewhat taciturn, liable to answer questions with little more than 'Quite concur'. He had dwindled somehow to being a mere cipher to Winston Churchill's irresistible leadership of the Admiralty, and it was observed that most of Prince Louis' mornings were spent reading *The Times,* after a breakfast of gigantic proportions. He was replaced by Lord Fisher in the autumn of 1914. In fact Buchan has somewhat conflated both these men to create his own 'First Sea Lord'.

AN AGENT OF THE KAISER, 1914 An example of hubris, that may reflect Conan Doyle's own experiences before the war, occurs in the story *His Last Bow – the War Service of Sherlock Holmes*, in the person of von Bork, devoted agent of the Kaiser. Von Bork resides unsuspected in a country house in Suffolk. To cover his espionage in England he has adopted the character of a hard-drinking, hard-riding country squire, reinforced by his genuine love of sports such as yachting, polo, hunting, boxing. This is a milieu in which Conan Doyle himself often took part, or took an interest.

It is 2 August 1914. As von Bork prepares to follow his family's return to Germany, he remarks to Baron von Herling, who has been congratulating him on his years of espionage, that the English 'are not very hard to deceive. A more docile, simple folk could not be imagined.'

'I don't know about that,' replies von Herling, who is Secretary of the German Legation. 'It is that surface simplicity of theirs which makes a trap for the stranger.'

The conversation shifts to the coming hostilities against Belgium and France. The Baron suggests that England might well leave those nations to their fate, and that there is no binding treaty. Von Bork disagrees about the treaty with Belgium, which is definite, adding that England could never recover from such a humiliation, and would lose her honour.

'Tut, my dear sir,' responds the Baron. 'We live in a utilitarian age. Honour is a mediaeval conception.'

The two men, having now aired their very broad assumptions, stroll along the terrace in the dusk towards von Herling's one-hundred horsepower Benz, musing on the imminent catastrophe for England. 'Who is that?' asks the Secretary, for by a solitary lamp in the window a dear old lady in a country cap can be seen at a table, knitting. She pauses now and again to stroke a large black cat. She is Martha, the only servant left in the house. (But 'Martha' is not quite who she seems to be…)

The Secretary chuckles that she could be the personification of Britannia, with 'her complete self-absorption and general air of comfortable somnolence. Well, au revoir, von Bork!'

Von Bork is left to his packing, and to the final visit of 'Altamont', his Irish-American spy, who specialises in military and naval intelligence. Another assumption is about to be exploded.

A REASONABLE ASSUMPTION, AUGUST 1914 In a letter to *The Times* in August 2014, the historian Sir Michael Howard described the chief reason for Britain's entry into what became the First World War, according to the plentiful evidence at the time. He reckoned it 'a very reasonable assumption: that if Germany won the war and acquired a Napoleonic dominance over Europe she would set about building a fleet that would enable her to challenge Britain as a world power. She would destroy our empire, in what the Kaiser had described as another Punic War' (a war between superpowers, such as Carthage and Rome).

The German invasion of Belgium did indeed bring Britain into the war, on 4 August. Churchill became fascinated by the idea of 'The First Twenty Days'. He believed that the measured silent drawing-together of gigantic forces, the uncertainty of their movements and positions, the number of unknown and unknowable facts made the first collision 'a drama never surpassed'. The Germans mobilised according to the Schlieffen Plan; the French countered with Plan XVII. Everything was decided in the first twenty days.

THE SCHLIEFFEN-MOLTKE PLAN, 1914 Helmut von Moltke, Chief of the Great General Staff, had planned this invasion according to the Great Memorandum of his predecessor, the strategist Alfred von Schlieffen, who had died in 1913. The exceptionally detailed plan, on which Schlieffen had worked since 1891, showed an advance through the neutral territory of Belgium, fanning out to enter and envelop France quickly along a wide front, a tactic originating with Hannibal. This would lead to the defeat of France within forty days. Over the same period an eastern attack against Russia would also mobilise. To what end was all this warfare leading? It has been suggested by some that the outbreak of war in 1914 was just a matter of uncontrollable mobilisations. But the vast scope of Germany's imperial ambitions is clearly laid out in the *Septemberprogramm,* drawn up for the Chancellor, Bethman-Hollweg, in September 1914.

The historian Sir Max Hastings in *Catastrophe, Europe Goes to War* condemns the German plan as fatally flawed, yet which lured Germany into thinking that the war was worth starting. Schlieffen believed in the power of quick and highly organised troop movements. But he had created a 'collective delusion' that vast numbers of infantry, at a time when mechanical transport and signal communications were still fairly primitive, could march quickly from railheads through the complex network of French roads and back roads, following intricate directions calculated by the Chief himself.

Schlieffen had also been encouraging a habit of what we would now call 'brinkmanship', instilling a false confidence that wars could at the last minute be averted. The Kaiser himself had fervently encouraged Schlieffen to develop his plan, though he had been replaced as Chief by von Moltke in 1906.

Some oddities of the plan

Well, that 'collective delusion' certainly qualifies as an assumption of vast proportions. But in putting together the overview above, I became intrigued by the plan, especially by the amount of time Schlieffen had spent on it.

From 1891 he had constantly developed it throughout his time as Chief, that is, up to 1906. But it all sounded very theoretical. An odd aspect was that Schlieffen had first conceived it as a way of preserving his country's security rather than as a plan of conquest. Its aim had been to push southwards as far as needed to build a defensible line against France. The plan answered the threats pertaining after 1870, with the French still hostile, and nursing their loss of Alsace-Lorraine. Would this plan still be valid over forty years later for an attack leading to the capture of Paris? But it seems that Schlieffen was uninterested in foreign affairs.

I wondered whether he had ever put his theory of movement into practical use in any actual engagement. It seemed not, and his demonstrations had been confined to war games and staff rides through terrain. It appeared that for Schlieffen the plan was a pure chess-board exercise, unpolluted by the messy world of politics and human fallibility, worked out in fantastic detail through railway timetables for the first phase and road networks for the second.

By the time of his Great Memorandum (1905), Schlieffen had lost any respect for the treaty that guaranteed the neutrality of Belgium and Luxembourg. His plan required an advance of two-thirds of the army through their territory.

The historian Sir John Keegan has read the Great Memorandum and in his book *The First World War* shares with his readers that rather eerie experience. As he examines Schlieffen's dictates on the motions and intricacies of the campaign, wheeling down through Picardy towards a Paris to be captured in forty days precisely, he starts to find evidence of Schlieffen's doubts. Eventually a note of desperation enters the Memorandum, amounting to an admission of the logical impossibility of moving these vast forces through the tight capacities of the French roads.

There was also a curious estimate of likely British intervention to support the French. In an addendum Schlieffen wrote in 1906, he expected no more than a landing at Antwerp. But in the event, the British Expeditionary Force, directed by the dynamic Henry Wilson, landed in northern France in a focused strike on the 'decisive point' of the wheeling German forces.

The Great Memorandum was modified somewhat by von Moltke, pigeonholed for use, and re-animated by him in August 1914.

Distinct character of Schlieffen

The more I read about Schlieffen the more he seemed to conform to the fanatical, inflexible Prussian military man of caricature. He continued working on the plan for the rest of his life. He worked late hours, his only other interest in life being military history. Sir John Keegan tells us that he approached history in a wholly technical way: 'It was the disposition of armies on a map that interested him, not the spirit of their soldiers, nor the reasoning of governments that had brought them to the clash of arms... The routines of the map table seem to have possessed him completely.' How on earth did such a man exert so much authority for so long, even after death, so that his flawed plan could send the German armies into such a vast miscalculation?

A.J.P. Taylor throws light on this puzzle in his 1944 book *The Course of German History,* finding that in the political void of 1914 neither the Kaiser nor the Chancellor were actually in charge. No one ruled now in Berlin. The generals wanted a victorious war, but as an academic exercise only; they lacked political sense or ability, and were as aloof and innocent in worldly affairs as any monk. Taylor observed that Germany was now a runaway horse, or more accurately, an overpowered engine out of control.

Failure of the plan

In the event, the advance of the five German armies that were supposed to wheel round in the west and trap French forces north of Paris had become distorted. By September they were campaigning along the valley of the Marne instead. The First Army was now only thirty miles from Paris. An order was then received from the highest levels that Armies 1,2,3,4 and 5 should retreat to the valley of the Aisne, the next river to the north of the Marne. The forty days were up, and the Schlieffen Plan was now judged to have failed, after an on-the-spot assessment of the army positions by Lieutenant Colonel Hentsch. This military technician and intelligence officer on the General Staff was a Saxon within an institution dominated by Prussians.

The subsequent entrenching of the territory along the Aisne was the origin of the Western Front, a line of stalemate stretching between the Swiss border and the Belgian coast. A prominent rural route along a plateau above the Aisne was known as the 'Chemin des Dames'. This became part of the defensive line. The curious name comes from the daughters of Louis XV, who had used this route to visit the château of Vauclair, the home of an old friend. Their father had improved the road for his daughters' benefit.

'OVER BY CHRISTMAS', 1914 With the outbreak of war a dangerous assumption had emanated from Britain's senior military and government officials and other 'experts', and spread throughout the land, both verbally and by all sorts of printed media, to this effect: that the war would be 'Over by Christmas'.

Several reasons were given for this optimism. It would be a short war because governments and bankers would not allow so much money to be squandered. Recent European wars had been of short duration: in the Franco-Prussian War fighting had only lasted for eight weeks.

The Kaiser had himself told departing troops, 'You will be home before the leaves fall from the trees.' The comforting autumnal imagery no doubt referred to the Forty Days of the Schlieffen Plan.

Is it conceivable that, without the optimism of the 'Over by Christmas' and the 'Over by Autumn' assumptions, the First World War might have been postponed or never even have taken place?

WORKING ASSUMPTIONS IN WARTIME, 1916 From his experiences in India, South Africa and the Western Front, Winston Churchill assumed that 'in war nearly everything is a matter of hazard'. He also considered that 'war is a game that should be played with a smiling face'.

When Churchill was in command of the 6th Royal Scots Fusiliers on the Western Front in 1916 his adjutant was Andrew Dewar Gibb, a Scottish lawyer – who went on to a distinguished legal and political career. Gibb's two working assumptions were: that the army mostly operated on a series of 'cock-ups' and that this led to the second assumption: that most orders given from a senior to a junior officer were more likely to be wrong than right, especially if orders came from outside the battalion and involved staff officers.

But he also realised that Churchill was one of the most talented and conscientious of commanders, as told in his 1924 book *With Winston Churchill at the Front*.

HOW THE UNITED STATES ENTERED THE WAR, 1917 In January the German Foreign Secretary, Arthur Zimmerman, sent an encoded message to the German ambassador in Mexico. Zimmerman proposed that Mexico should attack the United States with German help, with the incentive that Texas and other US territory would in due course be ceded to Mexico. At that time the Germans believed that their exquisitely complex codes (pre-Enigma) were unbreakable.

That assumption proved fatal to Germany's ambitions. The message had been intercepted by British tapping of an Atlantic telegraph cable and passed on for decryption at the Admiralty's Room 40, founded by Churchill for signals intelligence. It was the forerunner of Bletchley Park. The German code was broken in two days by Nigel de Grey and 'Dilly' Knox. President Woodrow Wilson received the news of the plot and was persuaded of the danger. The 'Zimmerman Telegram' is thus famous for having been one of the triggers that brought the United States into the war, by assent of Congress on 6 April 1917.

Churchill believed that without the intercepted message and its effect on the American administration, the war 'would have ended in a peace by negotiation, or, in other words, a German victory'.

SIR ARNOLD BAX: *NOVEMBER WOODS*, 1917 This tone poem seems to be a long, detailed evocation of nature. Bax had lived through the troubles following the 1916 Easter Rising in Dublin. Bax being Irish, I made the naïve assumption that the woods in question were also somewhere in his home country, preferably far out to the west, unkempt and ferny, woods of the Celtic Twilight, solemn woods in the light and shadow of wild skies, somewhere out in Sligo or Clare. Some decades later I stumbled on the truth. Bax's inspiration had been the woodland in the outer suburbia of London, between Beaconsfield and Amersham, tall Chiltern beechwoods for the most part, through which Bax regularly walked from a railway station to visit a lady pianist to whom he was devoted, during a difficult period in his life.

THE ARMISTICE, 1918 AND THE TREATY OF PEACE, 1919 I didn't initially think of these events as involving assumption, but as I reflected further on their notoriety it seemed that they did, though not in a way that's easily measured.

This was a moment when common sense had a good chance of reaching a workable post-war relationship between Germany and the Allies, but it was not to be. Various large ill-informed assumptions about what Germany needed to do, or how she should be treated, took hold of the victorious Allied populace and leadership. These assumptions were characterised by a lack of evidence and knowledge, but plenty of emotion and the desire for action. They grew from the perceived atmosphere and from infectious public opinion, and most leaders seemed unable to clarify or defuse them. They were not held by everyone of course, but they were strong enough to sway events.

Now, in Paris, the victors debated and disputed, working swiftly at the complexities of the Treaty of Peace, signed off at Versailles six months later. But common sense began to lose its grip. The makers of the treaty faced an impossible task in reconciling nations and calming emotions so soon after the Armistice.

Retribution

For example, the public, and especially members of the armed forces, and most especially the oft-invaded French, were known to feel strongly that retribution should be imposed on Germany. This was expressed by an essential clause in the treaty, Article 231, which stated the guilt of Germany in starting the war.

This war had been the first fought by the people rather than by professional armies. The French had lost nearly one and a half million men. Yet the German birth-rate still exceeded that of France. Where was their security to be found in the future? In their millions the Allies demanded that reparations should be exacted to the utmost degree, 'till the pips squeaked'. Thus the treaty bowed to these demands, stipulating ludicrously vast sums to be paid by Germany, even though she did not possess the funds needed. The only way Germany could make payments was through enormous loans from the US and the UK. These payments were described by Churchill as 'insane transactions'.

Other forms of reparation using German services and products were likely to undermine the economies of the receiving nations. But knowledge of economics was not widely shared at this time, so the simple formula of retribution was easily swallowed, a dangerous assumption that led to economic damage in the Allied nations, huge German resentment and the destruction of the German currency.

Limitations

Only a drastically reduced regular German army of 100,000 was allowed; two territories, Danzig and the Polish Corridor, were ceded to Poland and any attempt by Germany to combine with Austria was prohibited. These sorts of limitations caused intense resentment in Germany. Most dangerously, they provided a cause around which Adolf Hitler would build his political base. He began to write *Mein Kampf* in 1923, while in prison, a book that would make it absolutely clear that his urgent purpose, once in power, would be to rip up the Treaty of Versailles.

The historian A.J.P. Taylor pointed out how the German mind generally had no real recognition of the Armistice, nor of the Treaty; surely some inexplicable mistake or bizarre misunderstanding had occurred. And it appears that Germany, far from making reparations, was expecting the Allies to reimburse her for damage done in the war, for example, to the German railway system.

It would seem that the treaty was conceived in a kind of vacuum, with little knowledge of the bitter and dangerous reaction it would cause among the German populace. Churchill was disappointed that there had been no German presence in the negotiations. Germans of all political shades denounced the treaty and refused to accept the admission of guilt clause. The eventual signing was performed under the threat of continuing starvation through blockade and an immediate Allied invasion of Germany.

The reaction soon came. For example, the limit on the size of the German army was circumvented by the growth of secret quasi-military bodies, such as the Freikorps and the Defence Leagues. When these were banned by the new German government, Hitler set up instead the Nazi Party's 'Gymnastic and Sports Division', an organisation whose activities would have been quite a surprise to those who took the title literally. In due course it became the SA, the stormtroopers, a vital element in Hitler's rise.

The German (Weimar)Republic

Another large assumption concerned the new constitution for Germany. The Allies, influenced by the prejudice of the United States against monarchies, blandly imposed through the treaty a republican constitution. It seems to have been assumed that this would be as suitable for Germany as it had been for the United States or France. But Germany had been a nation that had evolved through a long history of monarchy. The pan-German nationalists of the old monarchy, the German Right, resented this sudden burying of their traditions and considered the leaders who had signed the treaty to be 'November criminals', a phrase constantly spread about by Hitler.

This republic was no more than a 'flimsy fabric'. It could not hold the loyalty or the imagination of the people. A large element of the populace, especially from the disbanded armed forces, felt they had lost their purpose in life and had been betrayed yet again. These new nihilists embarked on a twenty-year dream of overthrowing the German Republic. The resulting void in German politics yawned ever wider, a void into which Hitler, from his base within a highly unstable Bavaria, could gain entry.

Hearing of the signing of the Treaty of Peace at Versailles, Marshal

Foch, who had refused to attend the event, observed: 'This is not Peace. It is an Armistice for twenty years.' With this observation, Foch had made an astonishingly accurate forecast of the date of the next German war.

Four decades later, in his book *The Age of Illusion* Ronald Blythe was to observe:

> It would have been better for mankind if the Treaty of Versailles hadn't been signed until 1925; it would have given the self-righteous time to repent, the professional haters to see their doctors or priests and the merciless time to realise that the cries of starving children would be almost certain to drown the satisfying sound of pips squeaking.

THE ABERMULE DISASTER, 1921 This accident revolved around a safety device patented in 1878 by Edward Tyer. It was designed for the protection of single-line sections. Formerly, the signalman would hand the unique staff to a driver at the start of the section, who handed it to the signalman at the other end. Tyer's system issued a tablet from an electric machine which was linked to a similar machine at the end of the section. Once a tablet, inscribed with the name of the section (which the driver was supposed to check), had been issued to a driver, both machines automatically locked until the tablet was replaced in one or other of the two machines. By the time Tyer died in 1912 the safety record of the system was unblemished. But the weak point in the chain was finally found...

The disaster at Abermule, a country station in Wales, between Montgomery and Newtown, is quite a tangled tale, so I shall simply list the circumstances and actions which combined to cause the accident.

The first adverse circumstance was that the tablet machine was not placed in the signal cabin, as it should have been, but in the station building.

The second circumstance was that although only the stationmaster and the signalman were allowed to work the machine, in practice it was being worked by anyone who happened to be there. On the day in question there were *four* employees of the Cambrian Railway who might have been party to the working of the electric tablet: signalman Jones; Lewis, the deputy stationmaster; Rodgers, a porter and Thompson, a boy who collected the tickets.

It was a late morning in January. Two trains from opposite directions were approaching Abermule station, where they would be able to pass each other: a southbound stopping train from Montgomery and a northbound express from Newtown. Each driver had the correct electric tablet for their section. But it was the porter, Rodgers, alone in the station building, who, by pressing the release on the tablet machine, had allowed the tablet to be given to the northbound driver at Newtown, now heading towards Abermule. Signalman Jones in his cabin knew nothing about it, nor did anyone else. From this point a curious sequence of events occurred:

1. At Abermule the boy Thompson sees the southbound train arrive and collects the Montgomery-Abermule tablet from the driver. He crosses the station to return the tablet to the machine, but meets Lewis the deputy stationmaster on the way, who asks about the northbound express. Inexplicably, for he knew nothing about it, he replies that it is still somewhere south of Newtown, giving Lewis the idea that it was running late. (But as we know, the express was already getting closer to Abermule.) Thompson then hands Lewis the tablet from the southbound train, without explanation, and disappears to collect tickets.

2. Lewis now assumes that Thompson has already returned the tablet to the machine and has drawn out the tablet for Abermule-Newtown. This he believes he now has in his hand. But he does not examine the inscription. He goes over to the driver of the

southbound train and, believing the express to have not yet reached Newtown, hands over the tablet – not to the driver, who is oiling below, but to the fireman.

3. Neither the fireman nor the driver examine the inscription, as required. It is of course the wrong tablet for that section. It is their death warrant. This handing over of the wrong tablet was also seen from a distance by Jones, Rodgers and Thompson who separately assumed everything was fine. None of them knew of the intervening steps in the deadly sequence.

As far as I can tell, at least *eight* assumptions were made during this chaotic sequence. In the head-on collision at speed about a mile down the line to Newtown, seventeen people were killed and thirty-six injured. Both electric tablets were found under the wreckage, confirming the error. How could both the stationmaster and the engine crew – whose lives depended on it – have become so casual about such a vital matter? The Tyer tablet machine had succeeded because the regulations and rules had been followed, but human indiscipline and a dangerous lack of communication eventually contrived to beat the system.

From then on the tablet handover was restricted to signalmen and drivers only, as originally intended.

GOOD ADVICE, 1923 A reader dizzy with the onset of his own hubris in this day and age might be calmed by this advice from John Buchan's *The Three Hostages*. It is offered by Sandy Arbuthnot, that arch-adventurer in all mysterious regions: 'A very wise man once said to me that you could often get success in this life – if you didn't want victory.'

INVENTION OF THE MODERN SLALOM RACE, 1924 As a daring and successful ski-mountaineer, Arnold Lunn devised a ski race that would test and improve a skier's skill and safety under the stress of High Alpine conditions. Although he named this race 'slalom' it was quite different from the race of that name already exported from Norway. Lunn's modern slalom used variable gates to create an unpredictable twisting race on natural snow. And he succeeded, for this race quickly caught on with ambitious skiers. Lunn had released the genie of Alpine racing from its bottle.

Those racers who tasted the speed and spirit of Lunn's slalom, and 'downhill' too, which he codified, did not necessarily see them as a way of acquiring High Alpine skills, as Lunn had assumed. They felt they had discovered a compelling and independent form of skiing. Downhill and slalom thus escaped from the orbit of mountain adventure.

The result was that racing came to be considered the highest criterion of skiing ability. It was a classic case of unintended consequences. Lunn admitted he had been naïve about this. But the two race disciplines he invented or codified were a great success and are essentially the same nearly a century later.

SIR GEORGE JUMPS TO A CONCLUSION, 1925 Sir George Sitwell was a restless, energetic man, quite eccentric, with many interests and enthusiasms, and not a few anxieties in the course of his life. He had purchased a castle in Tuscany before the war and in 1925 he and his wife took up permanent residence. His eldest son, Osbert, records in his autobiography that his father had developed an intense enthusiasm for a local pilgrimage route lauded in mediaeval romance.

Sir George's only friend in Italy was a Signor Bracciaforte, a charming antique dealer and artist. Together they would embark on 'antiquarian wild-goose chases' in an ancient motor car. A typical episode in this happier phase of Sir George's life occurred during a search for the site of the Castle of Ogher the Dane, one of the Twelve Paladins of Charlemagne and a ward of the fairy, Morgan le Fay.

Sir George had insisted that this wild-goose chase should include

Osbert and his brother Sacheverell, who advised Osbert that they should just sit back and 'something funny is sure to happen!'

Sir George now began to feel very confident that they were getting close to the site of the castle. But in a small hill town, the car broke down in the main square. Osbert observed that this piazza, with its shop windows hung with Bologna sausages, 'afforded a perfect background for old-fashioned pantomime action and humour'.

Signor Bracciaforte wandered off down an alley, in search of antiquities, but Sir George could think only of Ogher the Dane. He scanned the facades of the promising piazza. Suddenly he was ablaze with unusual excitement:

> 'But look over there! This must be the very place! That shop is called OGHERI! Probably its owners are actually descended from the Great Dane himself!! Fetch me my notebook at once – it's in my hat box – and I'll make a note of it!' At this moment, Bracciaforte, who had drifted back, and had heard what my father had said, remarked, 'But that not OGHERI, Sir George! That DROGHERIA! The first two letters and the last, they 'ave fallen themselves off: these little shop, they no money to repair.'

After that unwelcome clarification, Osbert Sitwell records that 'things went rather flat for a while...'

THE MURDER OF ROGER ACKROYD, 1926 The third detective story of Agatha Christie broke the convention, and the assumption of most readers, that the narrator cannot be the criminal himself. It set her career alight and few readers seem to have felt unduly led astray. Did the notion of the 'unreliable narrator' start with this publication?

G.K. CHESTERTON, 1927 The *Father Brown* stories were published between 1911 and 1936. They are partly a tribute to Conan Doyle and Baker

Street, for both Holmes and the priest had trained themselves to question assumptions. These examples mostly come from stories published in the mid-twenties.

A retired so-called 'admiral' has concocted a legend about his forbears' disastrous sea-going careers. He has used these to keep hold of the family estate by creating fatal 'accidents' at sea or in the adjacent Cornish estuary. Several relations have already been disposed of in this way, disguised as victims of the family legend. He has also claimed to have discovered the last eight Pacific Islands and his house is full of artefacts from this exploit, with which to delude his visitors. Into this peculiar environment a neighbouring friend of the 'admiral' casually invites Father Brown, who has already been told a great deal about the legend.

But Father Brown has over many years acquired an instinctive trick of analysing his own impressions, so that when he encounters a display of Pacific shells, exotic birds, a sixteenth-century chart with 'tritons and little ships dotted about a curly sea' and curious weapons, and is then waited upon by the admiral's two native servants dressed in yellow, he feels a first faint suspicion of this assemblage. He examines the map. It has in fact nothing to do with islands in the Pacific, it is just a chart of the local Cornish estuary. It was the context of the surrounding display which had conned previous visitors. *The Perishing of the Pendragons*, 1914.

An American plutocrat is found dead with an arrow piercing his neck. It is therefore assumed by others that he must have been shot from a distance. Father Brown is not so sure. An arrow can easily be used as a dagger, to stab the victim at close range. *The Arrow of Heaven,* 1926.

The Oracle of the Dog (1926) is Chesterton's salute to Conan Doyle's *Silver Blaze*. He considered that short story to be the most perfect detective story ever written. Chesterton's story could indeed be sub-titled 'The curious incident of the dog on the seashore'.

An inexplicable murder has taken place in the garden of a seaside country house. Various ideas are thrown around by the extended family and neighbours, but to no avail. Father Brown is told about it second-hand by a young friend who was present. A large black retriever, Nox, had been near the scene at the time of the murder. 'I always like a dog, as long as he isn't spelt backwards,' observes Father Brown. But as he hears all the circumstances, he becomes intensely cross with his friend, who has been making suggestions such as 'the dog knows something about it,' 'sometimes I think they know more than us…' and other half-baked opinions. His friend's easy assumption of dog superiority jars against the priest's logic.

The friend, Fiennes by name, goes on to tell how a stick had been thrown into the wavelets for Nox to retrieve. But he couldn't find it afloat and returns to the beach to bark loudly in complaint. This outburst of barking is interpreted as the dog's knowledge of the murder. But Father Brown suggests a simpler explanation: 'Never had such a thing happened before. Never had such an eminent and distinguished dog been so badly treated by a rotten old walking stick.'

Clearly the stick must have sunk, so it must have been made of something other than wood. Was it metallic, perhaps even a murder weapon? A swordstick comes to mind, and does indeed fit the method used to slaughter Colonel Druce in the summer-house. Father Brown concludes sadly that Fiennes has not treated the dog as a dog, but has been carried away by 'a lurid halo of dog superstitions'.

A survey by Father Brown of the shops and occupations of a village street rules out any suspicion that someone there had a role to play in the sudden disappearance of Sir Arthur Vaudrey. But after his body is found with throat cut on the riverbank just downstream from the village, Father Brown checks more thoroughly these shops and recalls that sometimes a tobacconist can also operate as a barber. The priest had initially made a category assumption that a tobacconist is only a tobacconist. *The Vanishing of Vaudrey,* 1927.

A long tiring journey brings Father Brown to a remote northern castle to deal with an issue in the Musgrave family. On entering the hall, he sees – but does not observe – the strikingly symmetrical display of the weaponry of centuries: two battle axes on either side of the fire-place, two round shields on opposite walls and a complete suit of fourteenth-century armour standing at one side of the hearth – but an empty space on the other. In his worn-out state Father Brown takes it for granted that there was only one suit of armour. Later the penny drops: it is highly likely that there was a second suit of armour, to fulfil the careful balance of the display. What, then, had happened to it? As we saw, a similar discovery is made in *The Valley of Fear* when Holmes finds one dumb-bell under a table in the study, but no sign of its partner. In due course both these absences lead to sinister findings and the subsequent solution. *The Worst Crime in the World,* 1927.

DR HERBERT SUMSION, 1928 Many assumptions are reasonably accurate, and may end well.

In 1928 Sir Herbert Brewer, Organist of Gloucester Cathedral, died unexpectedly a few months before the Three Choirs Festival which he was traditionally expected, as Organist, to direct and conduct. This year's programme included Verdi's *Requiem.*

Dr Herbert Sumsion, in his late twenties, was already Brewer's choice of successor. He was therefore invited to take up the position and its demanding role in the festival. He was released from a contract in the United States. Despite arriving only a short time before the festival, his appointment led to a great success.

In a concluding speech Sir Edward Elgar noted, in a famous pun: 'What, at the beginning of the week was *assumption,* has now become a certainty.'

THE 'CAMBRIDGE FIVE' From the warm-hearted collegiality of the Three Choirs Festival and the generous imagination of Chesterton, we shift to the sombre phenomenon of the recruitment of traitors at Cambridge University. This happened in the early 1930s. The 'Cambridge Five' – Philby, Maclean, Burgess, Blunt and Cairncross – were apparently motivated by ideological anti-capitalism and the experience of the Wall Street Crash. Whatever else they were in search of, it would have been a rather convenient assumption to believe, if they did, that Stalin's propaganda of a paradise of justice for worker and peasant reflected the truth. The fact was, though, that Stalin presided over one of the most brutal totalitarian regimes ever recorded. In 1932 some one million Russian peasants had died from famine in his so-called perfect society.

A middle-class craze for Soviet Russia, a blind and unquestioning assumption, was growing at this period, especially in academia. Whatever their other achievements, the visits of Sydney and Beatrice Webb to Russia in the thirties, and the book they published based on Soviet statistics, were ridiculed. The book – *Soviet Communism: a new civilisation?* – was described by A.J.P. Taylor as 'the most preposterous book ever written on Russia'.

THE MIRAGE OF BOA VISTA, 1933 The young Evelyn Waugh, a constant inquisitive traveller to remote places, tells us, in *Ninety-two Days*, of his journey from New Amsterdam southwards across the savannahs of British Guiana. His guide and companion was a voluble Creole, Mr Bain, Commissioner of the Takutu district. Information about routes had been elusive and unreliable, but Waugh's plan in general was to reach a tributary of the Amazon and to pass over into Brazil. After several weeks on the cattle trail, they reached a place called Kurupukari on the Essequibo river, a district rhapsodised by Mr Bain as eminently suitable for a literary man. Kurupukari was writ large on the map and had been talked about for the last week. Thus Waugh had gradually built up the place in his imagination to resemble a lake station in East Africa: a pier and offices, the Commissioner's residence, some shops and stores, a post office, a handful of native huts and a flagstaff. On arrival he was surprised to find a flagstaff lying on the grass, without a flag, and one single wooden house. Waugh had demonstrated the propensity of hopeful travellers to inflate and romanticise a destination lying ahead. But other assumptions lay in wait…

At this point Mr Bain had to withdraw his services as a guide, but not before raising the possibility of Waugh reaching the Rio Branco, in Brazil, by taking a canoe down the Takutu. Here, explained Mr Bain, lay Boa Vista, the most important town of the Amazonas after Manaus. No, he had never been there himself, but with flashing eyes and sweeping gestures he seemed to conjure up 'a place of peculiar glamour – dissipated and violent; a place where revolutions were plotted and political assassinations committed'. And beyond, down river, lay Manaus. Waugh's route into Brazil now seemed a little clearer.

During the thirst and discomfort of the southward journey Waugh had allowed the name 'Boa Vista' to take on an ever greater importance. 'Everybody… had spoken of it as a town of dazzling attraction.' Mr Daguar, a ranch manager, 'had extolled its modernity and luxury – electric light, cafés, fine buildings, women, politics, murders'. From Mr Bain he had learnt that fast motor launches plied constantly between there and Manaus. Thus Waugh had taken comfort in these seductive images, anticipating some respite from hardship at Boa Vista:

Shady boulevards; kiosks for flowers and cigars and illustrated papers; the hotel terrace and the cafés; the baroque church built by seventeenth century missionaries; the bastions of the old fort; the bandstand in the square, amidst fountains and flowering shrubs; the soft, slightly swaggering citizens, some uniformed and spurred; others with Southern elegance twirling little canes, bowing from the waist and raising boater hats, flicking with white gloves indiscernible particles of dust from their white linen spats; dark beauties languorous on balconies, or glancing over fans at the café tables.

On reaching Boa Vista it did not take long for this extravagant mirage to dissolve. His dizzy expectations were cruelly undermined, toppling sickeningly to the level of the dried mud of the main street, the one-storied mud houses and the apathetic yet hostile populace. Echoing the prone flagstaff at Kurupukari, 'the remains of an overhead electric cable hung loose from a row of crazy posts, or lay in coils and loops about the gutter'. No hotel, no motor launch, all a dream…

After this classic fate of the imaginative traveller, Waugh was unable to get any further into Brazil and returned through British Guiana by another way.

AN ABDICATION AND AN ASSUMPTION, 1936 One might think that a king could abdicate the throne and yet remain quietly and modestly within the United Kingdom. But this turned out not to be the case, and Edward VIII was required to relinquish other elements of his life beyond that of kingship itself.

The passing of His Majesty's Declaration of Abdication Act in 1936 was agreed by parliament and then required King Edward to give his own Assent to the act. This happened on 11 December. Immediately the throne passed to his brother Albert, who now became George VI.

Edward was given the title 'Duke of Windsor' by his brother. George had little faith in his character and this title ensured that Edward could not stand for election to the House of Commons or speak in the House of Lords. Any descendants of Edward were barred by the Abdication Act from the line of succession to the throne.

He had to leave the country forthwith, and fairly soon settled in France with Wallis Simpson, now his wife. During the war he served briefly as a major general in France. The couple next showed up in neutral Lisbon. The Duke was then obliged by Churchill, who had come to distrust his loyalty, to take up the Governorship of the Bahamas for the remainder of the war. Edward was not keen on this idea, but Churchill threatened him with a court martial if he did not return to British-owned territory.

As for the United Kingdom, he could only return at the invitation of his brother. These occasions were infrequent, mostly for attending funerals. Payments of his allowance were in the direct gift of the King, who made it clear that these would be suspended if he tried to return to the UK without permission. In the biography by Philip Ziegler we learn of Edward's comfortable assumption that after a few years exile in France he would be quietly allowed back to Britain. He told journalists that he wanted some sort of government job – and was available right now.

But nothing was ever offered.

WINSTON CHURCHILL IN THE THIRTIES These years were famously described by W.H. Auden in his poem *September 1st, 1939* as a 'low, dishonest decade'. The failure of any British prime minister of the thirties to grasp the threat of Hitler must make it one of the strangest and most dangerous periods of British history.

In a frank letter written in May 1932 to Lord Linlithgow, chairman of the select committee, Churchill shows his deep suspicion of assumption in its many forms, a suspicion acquired during an already long career. I quote its opening lines:

> I think we differ principally in this, that you assume that the future is a mere extension of the past, whereas I find history full of unexpected turns and retrogressions. The mild and vague liberalism of the early years of the twentieth century, the surge of fantastic hopes and illusions that followed the armistice of the Great War have already been superseded by a violent reaction against Parliamentary and

electioneering procedure and by the establishment of dictatorships real or veiled in almost every country...

In my view England is now beginning a new period of struggle and fighting for its life...

From the start of the thirties, Churchill had observed with curious gaze the 'Baldwin-MacDonald Regime', guided by those two leaders from different parties who were so remarkably sympathetic to each other:

Both men excelled in the art of minimising political issues, of frustrating large schemes of change, of depressing the national temperature, and reducing Parliament to a humdrum level. Their ideal of government appears to be well expressed by the noble lord in the Gilbert and Sullivan opera who 'did nothing in particular, but did it very well'.

It might, observed Churchill, have been desirable to treat John Bull as a person supremely in need of a rest cure after the First World War and its aftermath. Than Baldwin and MacDonald, 'no two nurses were better fitted to keep silence around a darkened room and protect the patient from anything in the nature of mental stress and strong emotion'. But Churchill pointed out that Britain was not an island a thousand miles off in the Atlantic Ocean, but a mere ten minutes by air from a turbulent Europe.

By 1932 Churchill saw how these two nurses of John Bull reacted to the 'jarring clang of external events' now breaking upon the sleepy scene. They received news of the sinister growth of Nazi power with incredulity. They retreated to a private world of self-delusion and wishful thinking. They assumed things would turn out all right, that the matter would just 'blow over'.

PERSUASION METHODS OF ADOLF HITLER In *Mein Kampf*, 1925, Hitler is very open about his discoveries of how to control the thoughts of the mass of the population. His aim was to create large simple assumptions in the public mind. These are the interesting chapters in what is generally considered a turgid work. From his robust experience of the political maelstrom of Munich in the 1920s, Hitler had drawn these lessons:

Speak to the masses.

All effective propaganda must be confined to a few bare necessities.

Constantly repeat your message.

When you lie, tell a big lie.

Never hesitate, never qualify, never concede; present everything as black or white.

Use vehemence, passion, fanaticism.

The spoken word is more powerful than the written.

Violence and terror have their own value and attraction.

Violence should be as visible as possible.

The best form of defence is attack.

THE PROPAGANDA OF DR GOEBBELS Joseph Goebbels had studied at several universities and had attempted to write for the theatre and cinema. Like Hitler, the aspiring artist, Goebbels had encountered only rejection. He undoubtedly had an artistic and performing temperament, but had become embittered.

Hitler first met him in 1926: a young Rhinelander now finding some success as a journalist and public speaker. Hitler appointed him as propaganda chief for the Nazis two years later. After Hitler's elevation to Chancellor,

Goebbels became the Minister of Public Enlightenment and Propaganda. Hitler had realised, from the success of British propaganda during the war, that it would be an absolutely crucial weapon for National Socialism.

When Horst Wessel, a young SA leader in Berlin, was shot by communists, Goebbels turned him into a martyred Nazi idealist. He was constantly brought to the public mind by the singing of the *Horst Wessel Lied.* It became the SA's marching song.

Goebbels was, in the phrase of Machiavelli, 'more feared than loved'. Yet there seems to have been a curious charm too. On his visit to Germany in 1938 Lord Halifax had expected to dislike Goebbels intensely, yet found to his surprise that he didn't.

Alan Bullock, in *Hitler, a Study in Tyranny,* summarises his talent thus:

> Goebbels, undersized, lame and much disliked for his malicious tongue, could rise only under the aegis of someone like Hitler, to whom he was useful for his abounding energy and fertility of ideas, apt at times to be too clever and to over-reach himself, but exploiting with brassy impudence every trick of propaganda.

Goebbels' approach was simple, totalitarian: like Hitler, he created vast simple assumptions in the mind of the German populace. Under the complete control of the media, the silencing of a free press and the constant repetition of only a few ideas, the German public found it hard or impossible to resist the popular distortions and lies he poured out. They had little or no alternative information. This was John Stuart Mill's 'assumption of infallibility' as deliberate policy.

Goebbels had worked out his principles of propaganda only too well: 'Propaganda should be popular, not intellectually pleasing. It is not the task of propaganda to discover intellectual truths.' Its popularity would help to spread it more widely.

The word 'propaganda' comes from the Italian word for propagation, notably the propagation of the Roman faith during the Counter Reformation. But Goebbels raised his propaganda to unrestrained levels of manipulation.

'The most effective form of persuasion is when you are not aware of being persuaded.' From this he moved easily to the idea that 'You cannot change someone's mind; you can only reinforce their existing belief or prejudices.' It seems therefore that Goebbels knew about Magruder's Principle, laid down by a senior Confederate commander in the American Civil War, John B. Magruder:

That it is easier to take advantage of the enemy's existing beliefs than to try to change them.

Goebbels also believed in the power of repetition: repetition led to a sense of normality and normality could perhaps become confused with the truth.

The vast machinery of Goebbels' propaganda reached everywhere by every means, including the most recent inventions, and through films and huge rallies. He himself made vigorous, incendiary speeches in punishing schedules all across Germany, though his style was more controlled than Hitler's. Alan Bullock reports that his speaking voice was considered 'beautiful'. The films I have seen of his speeches are certainly compelling; I was uncomfortably aware of his force.

He was ruthless against anyone who got in his way, exposing them to the brutality of the SA. He forbade newspapers from publishing obituary notices of those executed, thus encouraging rumours of even greater horrors. His ambitions for Hitler and the Nazi Party were extreme and clear-sighted: 'We shall go down in history as the greatest statesmen of all time, or as the greatest criminals.'

At this period, similar control of the media was being developed by authoritarian regimes in Russia and Italy. Goebbels' career ran parallel to the growth of the hidden persuasion created by the advertising and PR industries. Edward Bernays, the father of public relations, wrote his book *Propaganda* in 1928. Two famous dystopian novels, Huxley's *Brave New World* (1932) and Orwell's *Nineteen Eighty-four* (1949), demonstrate the further ingenuity by which ruthless dictatorial regimes control the thoughts of the populace.

HITLER'S 'FOOT IN THE DOOR': WINTER, 1933 The astonishing sudden rise of Adolf Hitler in the January of this fateful year was the result of Franz von Papen, a recent chancellor, and Alfred Hugenberg, leader of the German National Party, making an approach to Hitler – on behalf of the German Right. This led to a minority coalition government in the Reichstag, with Hitler elected as Chancellor, the extraordinary result of tortuous negotiations in a long, desperate search for a coalition that might eventually gain a parliamentary majority. The President, Paul von Hindenburg – the former Field Marshal, now in his eighties – was of course involved, being a close friend of von Papen, but remained deeply sceptical of Hitler.

Von Papen was an over-confident aristocrat of reactionary views, and a senior figure in the Roman Catholic Church. He now comforted himself that in the cabinet of this new coalition, the Nazis would be safely outnumbered by the Right by eight to three. But von Papen and Hugenberg had allowed Hitler to get his foot in the door on the strength of two disastrous assumptions, the enormity of which hit them only *after* Hitler's election.

We go back eight years. After being released from Landsberg prison in 1925, Hitler had re-founded his National Socialist Party. At Landsberg he had confided to a colleague that their policy would now have to be different: they would work within the constitution and law of Germany, in the Reichstag, rather than trying to take over the country by the usual means of an armed coup.

In the years that followed he was constantly pointing out the 'legality' of the party's approach. In Hitler's case, 'legality' could be a rather flexible term. He was perfectly capable of condoning the brutal actions of the party's paramilitary group, the SA. The Potempa murder was one that had to be tidied up, but rather openly. As we saw, one of Hitler's principles was that violence should be as visible as possible. An SA slogan ran: 'Possession of the streets is the key to power in the State.' But, officially, Hitler was always at pains to declare that the SA were to respect the law at all times.

By 1933 then, politicians, including von Papen and Hugenberg, were accustomed to see the Nazis – although they were alarming – apparently devoted to the idea of working within a framework of 'legality'. Thus von Papen and Hugenberg made their first assumption: that once Hitler and the Nazis had been brought into the machinery of government, they could be held in check, and be tamed by their own respect for 'legality'. Von Papen advised the President that this was the right course of action. But these leaders of the German Right had never really understood, had never carefully assessed, what Hitler and his vigorous right-hand man Hermann Göring really meant by 'legality'. They were very soon to learn. Over the next few weeks they had ringside seats at the relentless dismantling of their comforting illusions.

I summarise the flow of events:

30 January At the first cabinet Hitler states that if the Centre Party cannot be brought in to make a majority for the coalition, then there would have to be yet another general election.

February Hitler deliberately undermines his negotiations with the Centre Party representative, Monsignor Kaas. The Centre Party protest they have been misunderstood. But Hitler, as Chancellor, had immediately requested Hindenburg, the President, to sign a decree for the dissolution of parliament and had fixed the date of the election. It was now too late to reverse this stunning *fait accompli*. The Nazis are now on the inside of the government machine; at last, Hitler's revolution can charge blatantly into action.

3 February Joseph Goebbels writes in his diary: 'The struggle is a light one now, since we are able to employ all the means of the State. Radio and Press are at our disposal. We shall achieve a masterpiece of propaganda...'

20 February Göring speaks to the leading industrialists at his 'palace' in Berlin and openly tells them 'that this election will be the last for ten years, probably even for the next hundred years'.

The **second assumption** of von Papen and Hugenberg was that Hitler more or less shared their ideas of reform: to destroy the hated German (Weimar) Republic, restore the monarchy, put the working classes back in their place, to restore the old ruling class, and so on. But during the campaigning for this sudden election it dawned on them that Hitler had never had any policy or programme at all. He was only interested in power, by any means, with which to raise Germany to its rightful stature and at the same time to destroy Marxists, Jews and Slavs.

Campaigning in Munich, Hitler declares that 'programmes are of no avail, it is the human purpose which is decisive... the first point in our programme is: Away with all illusions!'

The 'legality' of the Nazi Party did not extend to campaigning behaviour. Hundreds were injured and fifty-one people killed by the interventions of the SA, the 'Brownshirts'. As Sir Alan Bullock puts it: 'This time the Nazis were inside the gate, and they did not mean to be robbed of power by any scruples about fair play and free speech.'

Further consequences

Now, with breathtaking speed, Göring showed his true colours. By a quirk of the dual government of Prussia within the Reich, Göring had been appointed *Prussian* Minister of the Interior, responsible for administering two-thirds of Germany, including the Prussian police force. Part of von Papen's assumption that he could keep the Nazis in check was that he himself, as *Reich* Minister of the Interior, could restrain Göring. But Göring completely ignored him, and immediately began a purge of state and police officials, replacing them with Nazi sympathisers and SA and SS leaders. He instituted a regime in which the police must show no mercy in dealing with enemies of the state: defined as communists and Marxists. Out of the ranks of the SA and the SS he instantly created an auxiliary police force of 50,000 who now represented the State. Thus all was perfectly 'legal' within the constitution as interpreted by Göring.

In late February the police raided the headquarters of the Communist Party and three days later the Reichstag was on fire.

Hitler had learnt, like Bismarck, to await events and exploit the opportunities they provided. Thus on 28 February, the day after the fire, the Chancellor signed a decree for the 'protection of the People and the State'. This terrible document overrode all the guarantees of individual liberty under the Weimar Republic, and authorised the full power of the Reich over the federal states. Such decisive, ruthless action had the effect of intimidating the populace, soon to take part in the election.

March Göring speaks at Frankfurt:

Certainly I shall use the power of the state and the police to the utmost, my dear Communists, so don't draw any false conclusions; but the struggle to the death, in which my fist shall grasp your necks, I shall lead with those down there – the Brownshirts.

In the election that followed this month of brutal campaign and dark intrigue, the other parties had languished, but the Nazis had risen to nearly 44 per cent of the vote, on a very high turn-out. But the nation had still not provided the outright majority Hitler needed. He had the solution: he simply proscribed the eighty-one Communist seats in the Reichstag. This left the Nazis with a clear majority, and with no further need for the

National Party's support. Von Papen and Hugenberg must have realised that Hitler was already beyond their control – after only one month.

The next use of 'legality' was to pass the openly dictatorial five clauses of the so-called Enabling Bill. As this was an alteration of the constitution, it required a two-thirds majority in parliament. Hitler negotiated politely with the National Party and the Centre Party, but in the minds of all these members was the threat of being arrested in accord with the terrifying decree of 28 February.

Two days before the vote on the Enabling Bill, an extraordinary state ceremony took place on 21 March in the Garrison Church of Potsdam, the royal town of the Hohenzollerns near Berlin. Religious services attended by senior Nazis had taken place nearby. Alan Bullock judged the ceremony in the Garrison Church, a baroque building beneath a noble spire, to have been a 'masterstroke of conciliation towards President Hindenburg, the Army and the National Party'. Its immediate purpose was to mark the start of the Third Reich and the opening of its first parliament. Its deeper purpose was to display Hitler firmly wedded to the traditions of the Hohenzollern monarchs. Frederick the Great, whose tomb lay in the crypt of the church, was the German leader most admired by the Führer. Frederick, too, had had no other policy than the attainment of power.

This ceremony was the apex of what was called 'The Day of Potsdam', a complete programme of propagandising events and symbolic moments, carefully staged by Hitler and Goebbels.

Hitler and Hindenburg walked side by side down the nave, towards the empty throne reserved for the former Kaiser (in permanent exile in the Netherlands). The former Crown Prince Wilhelm (supportive of Hitler) was seated behind in full dress uniform. Hindenburg and Hitler made speeches and then Hitler approached Hindenburg's chair and, bending low, shook the old Marshal's hand. But was this really a gesture of continuity, of respect for the House of Hohenzollern? That may have been the assumption, but in fact it was a polite dismissal of Hindenburg, and the generals and Herr Doktors that he particularly hated. As for the presence of the Crown Prince, Hitler had never had the slightest intention of reviving the monarchy.

The solemn reverent performance of Hitler himself and the care that seems to have been bestowed on the ceremony could not have been in greater contrast to the scene two days later. The first Reichstag of the Third Reich was held at the Kroll Opera House, its temporary home after the fire. The Enabling Bill was presented to a chamber not just filled with members, but crammed with intimidating Brownshirts. After a restrained speech from Hitler, he lost his temper when the lone voice of Otto Wels dared to oppose the bill. Hitler mounted the tribune a second time, brushing away von Papen, and delivered a brutal speech that clearly demonstrated his utter contempt for the parliament – a parliament that he would never need to consult again, for the Enabling Bill was passed by a majority of 441 to 94.

Thus in only *seven* weeks since joining the coalition Hitler had 'legally' established himself as the dictator of Germany. In contrast to the usual procedure, the Nazi revolution had been held back until they had gained full control of the machinery of the state. The speed at which this happened must have stunned von Papen and Hugenberg. The irony is that until Hitler 'got his foot in the door', the Nazi share of the national vote had been steadily waning in the previous elections.

Focusing on von Papen as the more prominent figure of the two, his two assumptions must rank as some of the most dangerous in world history. Naturally, we seek for an explanation. Here is not the place for moral judgments on this remarkable, many-sided man, for that has been done long ago. But those two assumptions, why did he make them? This is rather tricky ground. But here goes…

In Franz von Papen some powerful motives were mixed together:

– a genuine desire to revive the forces of the old Prussian political Right, and to restore them to their rightful place, after years of national indecision, 'the tragic incompatibility of German wishes', as A.J.P. Taylor puts it. To achieve this, the temptation to sup with the devil using a long spoon, as it were, and to manipulate Hitler to his own ends, even at the cost of consorting with the thugs of the SA, was too strong to resist.

– but other aspects were also too strong to resist. An unnamed cabinet colleague wrote of von Papen in 1934 that 'He found it intolerable not to be in the game, even if he did not like his fellow players.' At the Nuremberg Trials, Thomas Dodd, Counsel for the Prosecution, concluded in 1946 that 'despite his façade of independence von Papen was an ardent member of the [Nazi] conspiracy and, in spite of warnings and rebuffs, was unable to resist its fascination.' The lawyer assessed him as 'a wily one and very difficult to question… very ambitious… years of diplomatic deceit have given him excellent self-control. He admitted great responsibility for Hitler's rise to power and said he believed Hitler to be the greatest crook in history. An admission at last! But he was ever so vague as to when he first concluded that Hitler was a knave.'

His earlier career of diplomacy and espionage, and those years of 'diplomatic deceit' seem to have had a lot to do with it. Did he find it easy to deceive himself?

In fact he continued to work for Hitler in diplomatic roles (Austria, Turkey) until the end of the war, admitting to Sir David Maxwell-Fyfe at Nuremberg that 'My opinion about Hitler and his inner political significance was completely clear after the 30th June 1934 [the purge known as 'The Night of the Long Knives']. But, like all other human beings, I could assume that in the field of foreign politics at least he would be sensible…' Well, his faith in the value of his own assumptions seems to have been unshakeable.

In his final statement to the court he offered no admission of fault or naivety in the 1933 catastrophe. In the event, the Nuremberg Tribunal acquitted von Papen of any war crimes by a two-to-one majority, with the Soviet judge offering a strongly dissenting opinion.

A.J.P. Taylor, in *The Course of German History*, concluded:

> Von Papen's sublime self-confidence had already landed him in many disasters, but even he never made a more fantastic mistake than to suppose that Hitler's treachery and dishonesty, immutable as the laws of God, would be specially suspended for Franz von Papen.

THE BURNING OF THE REICHSTAG, 27 FEBRUARY 1933 Who started this notorious act of arson? While the fire was still spreading, a Dutch communist, van der Lubbe, was found in the deserted building (parliament being in recess) in suspicious circumstances. But Hermann Göring used the communist connection to arrest the leaders of the German Communist Party (KPD) and accuse them of the arson plot, with van der Lubbe as a mere pawn. The trial in Leipzig was promoted with all the power of Nazi publicity, but blew up in Göring's face, because the KPD leader Dimitrov defended himself persuasively. Neither could any link be proved between the Communist Party and van der Lubbe.

After this fiasco, van der Lubbe was beheaded at Leipzig.

But Göring's enthusiasm for attacking the communist leaders began to make many people think that it was the Nazis themselves who had started the fire, as a convenient pretext for damaging the communist cause, the hatred of Bolshevism being at the very core of Hitler's struggle. Circumstantial evidence was put forward that a team of SA men had been led into the Reichstag through an underground tunnel and set it alight. They had taken van der Lubbe along with them, who they claimed had been found firing other buildings, and left him in the Reichstag to be the dupe for the crime.

Thus in both versions there was no hard evidence, just accusation based on assumption. The case remained a mystery until 1955, when Fritz Tobias started an independent investigation. Tobias finally came down – like Ockham's Razor – on the explanation with the fewest assumptions: that van der Lubbe had simply started the fire as a protest. That is what he had admitted consistently ever since his arrest.

Alan Bullock considered that Herr Tobias may well have been right to go for the simplest explanation. But since then, there have been many further theories, tending to point the finger at the Nazi Party.

CHURCHILL, A VOICE IN THE WILDERNESS From 1933 Churchill intensified his attempts to awaken a complacent nation to the threat of Hitler, now inexplicably elevated to the Chancellorship of Germany and soon after, to a dictatorship able to ignore the German parliament.

Hitler had immediately shown his true colours politically; his foreign policy was revealed as a matter of power and will; his chief ambition, well-known to readers of *Mein Kampf*, was to abolish the Treaty of Versailles. Being himself Austrian, he aimed to enlarge the borders of Germany even beyond Bismarck's definition of 'Greater Germany', by taking in the German-speaking lands within the old Hapsburg Monarchy and territory far beyond, at the expense of the Slavic nations.

But Churchill found that he was, like John the Baptist, 'a voice crying in the wilderness'. Roy Jenkins in his biography of Churchill describes him as 'an alarm clock, but he was a rasping one, which made most listeners more anxious to turn it off than to respond to his summons'. Compared to Hitler's clarity of ambition, the United Kingdom and France only knew what they did *not* want – and they did not want a war. But Hitler seemed to have a considerable appetite for war, to judge from the large increases to the German military budget, made public in 1934.

In 1935 Stanley Baldwin, the Conservative Prime Minister, proposed a policy of sanctions against Mussolini and won a general election. It was probably assumed by parliament that the sanctions would have a rational basis and be effective; but it was only when Churchill uncovered the truth a few months later, that they were seen to be flawed – and parliament woefully ignorant. Churchill had discovered that Baldwin was disabled by his policy's three principles: that there would be sanctions; that sanctions meant war; that there must be no war. It was clearly impossible to comply with all three of these.

In the event, Mussolini stated that any sanctions that interfered with his occupation of Abyssinia would indeed be regarded as an act of war. The League of Nations bowed to this and no serious sanctions were applied to Mussolini's military adventure. Churchill accused the general policy at Geneva as being 'Sanctions with no teeth'. Thus the careless Baldwin had managed both to alienate Mussolini and to undermine the authority of the League of Nations. But never mind – he took very little interest in foreign affairs anyway. When they were discussed, he was known to say, 'Wake me up when that's finished.'

In that same vein, Churchill was now questioning the general belief that the 1918 Armistice – which meant a 'cessation of arms, or truce' – had somehow been magically transformed into peace. He therefore consciously opened himself up, as a constant foe of such assumptions, to the startling possibility that there was *still* a state of war: a war without fighting, engagement or death; a war on a map, on paper; and with the same antagonists facing each other as on 11 November 1918.

A FORTNIGHT AT A TIME WITH CHURCHILL, 1936–39 The stifling, exasperating atmosphere of complacency is described in Churchill's *Step by Step*. This book is a compilation of the fortnightly and widely syndicated newspaper articles he wrote leading up to 1939. Churchill is deeply frustrated at the lack of urgency to re-arm Britain's defences and to prepare for battle in the air. He was not yet able to wrench the controls from the timid ministers. *Step by Step* makes for vivid and painful reading. It is only too easy to imagine the growing dismay and horror felt by much of the British people, trapped by their own government's dereliction of duty.

After the Nazi seizure and occupation of Austria, Churchill noted that 'The scales of illusion have fallen from many eyes, especially in high quarters.' But this was now March 1938 and to Churchill it was heartbreaking that so much time and opportunity had already been squandered through this ignorance or misreading of Germany's intentions.

ASSUMPTIONS OF NEVILLE CHAMBERLAIN, 1938–40 By now it was harder to remain blinkered to the ambitions of the Nazis. But Edward Wood, Lord Halifax, the Foreign Secretary since February 1938, was worried that Neville Chamberlain, though energetic, alert and self-confident, nevertheless believed that personal contact would enable negotiation with the Nazi leaders. He was assuming they were 'normal statesmen'.

Halifax also noted how Chamberlain's government was still infected with the pacifism of the 1930s, seeming to exist in a world of 'strange, if respectable illusions', expressed in language such as 'collective security', 'general settlement', 'disarmament' and 'non-aggression pacts'.

But none of these concepts meant anything to Adolf Hitler, who had fought his way to power through a twenty-year struggle, and had made his long term ambitions for living space (*Lebensraum*) in the east abundantly clear. He had no time for the subtleties of diplomatic language; he only used plain, blunt or brutal language. He could, however, skilfully imitate and twist the ambiguous language of the League of Nations to his own advantage.

Chamberlain still seemed to have a blind spot about the real character of the Nazi leadership, even after he and Halifax had met Hitler and his ministers face to face. He was so sincerely keen, even desperate, to be the great peacemaker, to reach a settlement with Germany, that he left himself at risk of diplomatic blackmail, something that Hitler was not slow to appreciate. Churchill helplessly contrasted Chamberlains' 'addressing Herr Hitler through the language of sweet reasonableness' with his own knowledge that 'Hitler was more open to the language of the mailed fist'.

By late 1938, after Munich and the surrender of the Sudetenland to Germany, Halifax's loyalty to the naïve, inflexible Chamberlain was severely tested. He told Chamberlain that he must abandon appeasement of the Nazis. The name 'Halifax' today seems often linked with that dreaded word 'appeasement', but the Foreign Secretary had fought in the trenches of the First World War and had stated that he was prepared to fight another one: he could imagine much worse outcomes than war. His view seemed clear: Britain was powerless in 1938 to fight against Germany; the Nazis knew it, and she must therefore buy time in which to re-arm.

MI5 had now obtained information from Hitler's meetings with his staff. Their hostile intent was unmistakable. Sir Vernon Kell, the founder and long-standing director of MI5, was determined that Chamberlain should understand what was really going on, and what Hitler really thought of him. They gave the report to Halifax, who boldly underlined in red ink Hitler's insulting reference to Chamberlain as an *arschloch*. I don't think I need to translate. There were also jokes made by Hitler about Chamberlain's trademark umbrella, seen by Hitler as a symbol of feebleness and what he called 'umbrella-pacifism'.

It seems incredible, but by March 1939 some ministers of the Crown had found reasons for giving out optimistic forecasts of an imminent Golden Age for Europe, most of which was lapped up by the British press. Churchill though, was questioning the purpose of heavy movements of German munitions and supplies through Vienna and Munich.

The ordinary railway services are restricted while these great convoys pass. What is their destination? What is their purpose?

The German army is maintaining a far larger number of troops than even its own establishment requires. Many straws of technical information show the way that the wind is blowing.

A month later Hitler invaded Czechoslovakia, imposing an iron rule. Only at this point did Chamberlain abandon his policy of appeasement. If only he had paid more attention to *Mein Kampf*. That failure is surely an egregious example of George Orwell's warning: 'that to see what is in front of one's nose needs a constant struggle.'

Even so, it is curious that such a gifted scholar of history as Halifax – elected a Fellow of All Souls at the age of twenty-two – had seen 'no evidence' of the brewing of German mischief towards Czechoslovakia.

When Churchill took over from Chamberlain in May 1940 he retained Halifax as Foreign Secretary. But Halifax, driven almost to despair by the potential fate of his beloved East Riding, now harboured the idea or illusion that a settlement with Hitler might be possible. This was not really appeasement, but a reflection, as the historian Andrew Roberts points out, of his logical reasoning, in contrast to the stubborn, emotional and romantic mind of Churchill. Nevertheless, Churchill replaced him with Anthony Eden, who he understood better.

For Halifax, Churchill had found a more suitable role. He had also presented him with a great opportunity to redeem his reputation, tainted by his initial support for Chamberlain's futile negotiations with the Nazis. As British Ambassador in Washington he was charged with 'bringing the United States into the war'. In particular, he was to push for legislation in Congress that would allow Britain to purchase military equipment on credit. Halifax worked hard, visited every one of the fifty states and won the admiration and friendship of many Americans from all backgrounds.

A BATTLESHIP SUNK IN SCAPA FLOW, 1939 In the small hours of the calm autumn night of 14 October, a sudden dull thud was heard on board the

Royal Oak. Or could it have been a muffled explosion? The one explanation that did not occur to Admiral Balgrove, or to the captain, or to the other vigilant and experienced officers on board, was attack by a German U-boat. The general assumption was that the Flow was inaccessible to the enemy. Yet in several ways the security was known to be inadequate. For example, rusting old blockships no longer formed a proper underwater barrier across the southeast entrance to the ample harbour.

And that is exactly what had just happened, out there in the dark waters, where *Kapitänleutnant* Günther Prien had manoeuvered U-47 through Kirk Sound at high tide. It was a moonless night, but alternative illumination was provided by the aurora borealis. Prien's twisting, redoubling course across Scapa Flow had soon revealed the tall, crowded masts of the *Royal Oak,* which he had torpedoed straight away.

Investigations within the battleship were immediate. The main worry was of attack from the air, many of the crew taking up air-raid stations. The ship stayed in position. Some quarter of an hour later Prien doubled back to fire another salvo, for initially only one torpedo had hit the ship, the 'dull thud' heard earlier. Prien's second salvo hit the *Royal Oak* amidships, so comprehensively that the ship capsized and sank within two minutes. That was not enough time for those in the bowels of the ship to escape. 835 crew members died, from drowning or from other injuries.

There were two naval inquiries, but no blame was attached to any individual. Nor did the government wish to take that course. Yet there *had* been a group assumption, in a situation where the stakes were extremely high. Lord Chatfield, the Minister for the Co-ordination of Defence, speaking in the House of Lords in November, declared that 'the Admiralty has resolved to learn a bitter lesson – namely, that in this new war, with its many novel complications, nothing must be taken for granted.'

SCHARNHORST AND GNEISENAU: THE CHANNEL DASH, 1942 On the evening of 11 February, at 9:15pm, these two notorious Atlantic battle cruisers and the heavy cruiser, *Prinz Eugen*, with supporting destroyers and other vessels, escaped from Brest harbour in Brittany. This was done at the behest of Hitler himself, who remained obsessed with concentrating German warships up in Norway. They had been confined at Brest by the bombing attacks of the RAF for most of the year. So how had the warships managed to escape?

To avoid Allied coastal radar detecting the German squadron's departure, a deception had been created by General Martini, head of the Luftwaffe Signals Service. Over a two-week period, at the same time every evening – around the time the ships were intending to make their escape – the Allied coastal radar was jammed by the Germans. A jam would usually suggest some activity was afoot, but since nothing in fact happened it was assumed by the radar operators to be 'atmospherics'.

The Luftwaffe deceivers made small daily increases to the level of jamming. Such increases are hard to detect, even if the cumulative effect is large. The Allied operators became so used to the repetitive phenomenon that they did not notice how much stronger the 'spherics' had become. They did not react any differently on the night of the 11th when these powerful ships really were moving out to sea, and off and away round Finisterre. The incremental jamming was a classic case of 'conditioning' or 'desensitising' the enemy's reaction to information.

Thus the Allied coastal radar lines across the Channel had been unable to detect the squadron's passing. Fourteen hours elapsed before the squadron was spotted next morning way up the Channel.

Hitler himself had reckoned that this sudden appearance of the battle cruisers would be a shock, leaving the British unable to react quickly – and on this occasion he was right. This was one of the lowest points of morale in the war. The 'Channel Dash' appeared to a puzzled, unhappy British public to be an astonishing success for the Germans, but the two battle cruisers reached harbour heavily damaged by British air-laid mines. The *Gneisenau* played no further part in the war, and the *Scharnhorst* was out of action for six months. But as this information had been obtained by secret intelligence, it could not be made public at the time.

THE PATH TO MOSCOW III: WHAT DID HITLER LEARN FROM CHARLES XII AND BONAPARTE? Absolutely nothing, it seems. The military leaders of Germany had already underestimated the Red Army, being almost totally focused on closer military matters and afflicted with a dangerous conformity. But Hitler, spurred by his rapid victories in mainland Europe, had discovered that he was a military genius. He was now going for total master-race victory over Soviet Russia, and the eventual annihilation of nearly all Slavic peoples to make room for German living space. The plan also aimed to transport slave labour to Germany to help the war effort, and to secure Russian oil fields and supplies of grain. As these aims had become essential to Hitler's overall war strategy, he could not give them up. Nor had his colossal hubris abated with experience. He was even more certain of his imperial dreams and personal destiny.

Goebbels tried to moderate his Führer's ambitions with ideas of negotiating with the eastern nations, but to no avail. Thus the Russian campaign began in June 1941, delayed by some six weeks on account of a Balkan distraction. Despite many warnings about German troop movements, the Russian leadership was still taken by surprise. It was only twenty-two months since the Molotov-Ribbentrop Pact had been signed between them.

Hitler's staff had studied Napoleon's invasion of Russia, but Hitler had always found it difficult to take advice, and thus suffered even direr consequences than the Grand Army. Of course, Hitler was not personally leading his troops from the front, like Napoleon, but from the Wolfsschanze, the 'Wolf's Lair', a permanent HQ in the forests of East Prussia. He moved to other HQs further east, as needed. He was not seen much in Berlin.

Like his two predecessors, Hitler was expecting a fairly short campaign. It would be completed, he said, by spring 1942, allowing him to restart Operation Sea Lion, the invasion of Britain. His over-confidence against the Russians was based on assumptions about the low morale of their officer class, for the Red Army had been easily defeated during the Winter War in Finland. He also assumed that Russia was in a shaky state politically. He told General Jodl that 'We only have to kick in the door and the whole rotten structure will come crashing down.'

Believing that the Wehrmacht's three Army Groups would achieve their main aims well before the onset of the winter, the armies were not supplied with winter clothing or equipment. Their tanks had narrower tracks than those of the enemy, a disadvantage on snow.

As with Napoleon, we see that hubris and ambition are the real driving force, creating a state of mind where multiple assumptions are easily made and barely challenged. And this was the campaign in which Hitler assumed more and more power from the generals he had always resented.

Although the Eastern Front would stretch from the Arctic to the Black Sea, it was Moscow – not only the Soviet capital, but a centre of communications and arms production – that emerged as the most urgent target.

The campaign – Operation Barbarossa, involving 161 divisions, some three million strong – began well, and by 16 July they had reached, as had Charles XII and Napoleon, the city of Smolensk, little more than 200 miles from Moscow. But it was clear that however many Russian troops were taken prisoner, there were others to take their place. Then a difference of opinion arose between Hitler and his High Command: they favoured a straight attack on Moscow, while the Führer showed more interest in Leningrad to the north and the vast resources of Ukraine to the south. Hitler got his way, but he had wasted so much time that the move against Moscow did not start until 2 October. But the Ukraine campaign had gone well and Hitler was accordingly even more elated and convinced of his 'destiny'.

Unable to stick to a single objective, Hitler caused further delay by spreading out his forces. At least Napoleon had remained obsessed with the one 'decisive victory'. We are not surprised to learn that by October the autumn rains had reduced the Germans' route to a quagmire. Still farther they advanced into the depths of Russia, with winter ever nearer. General Guderian noted the first snowfalls on the night of 6 November. By 2 December an advance party claimed they could discern the spires of the Kremlin to the east.

Winter caused severe problems both to troops on the ground and to those in the air. Hitler's Directive 39 put the blame on the 'early winter', as Napoleon had done. Hitler refused to admit any responsibility or to change tactics, just repeating unconvincing stock phrases: the Russians were 'virtually' defeated, all forces had been 'wiped out', 'decimated' etc. Napoleon too had sent back similar fantastical messages about his progress.

But four days later, out of the blue, a massive counter-offensive by one hundred fresh Soviet divisions swept back the frozen, exhausted Germans and repelled them some 150 miles. The Battle of Moscow was lost – at an overall cost of 830,000 men.

By now all hope of a quick victory against the Soviet Union had vanished. But Hitler's one success here was to order the armies to stand firm – at risk of severe penalties – and he thus prevented a panic retreat. He would be ready to continue the campaign in the spring of 1942. This vast, unparalleled theatre of hostility and atrocity then continued right to the end of the war.

The path to Moscow, summary

It is uncanny how similar assumptions and errors are repeated in the three campaigns – Charles XII, Napoleon, Hitler. And in each case the loss of life and liberty of the soldiery are blamed on any forces or factors other than the commander himself.

Only Napoleon seems to have felt some responsibility for what happened and is known to have written many letters to the widows of his slain officers.

HUBRIS OF THE JAPANESE IN THE PACIFIC THEATRE: BATTLE OF THE CORAL SEA, 1942 Admiral Yamamoto, commander-in-chief of the Imperial Japanese Navy, had been at the battle of Tsushima as a junior officer. Since that critical victory in 1905, Japan had continued to evolve into a nation dominated by aggressive nationalism and military leadership. This had continued through the First World War and the 1920s and 30s. 'Divine Japan' had come to believe that their navy was invincible and their expansion into Asia their obvious destiny. They also felt a sense of racial superiority over other Asians, and the Chinese especially. As for the Western world, that was considered 'decadent'. The historian Sir Alistair Horne has described all this as 'a suicidally dangerous philosophy'. We see a nation in the grip of long-term hubris.

Some Japanese must have been aware of this, for in the 1930s hubris was termed *senshobyo*, meaning 'victory disease'. This term is now used, it seems, by the military historians of the US Army.

But Japanese actions became ever bolder and on 7 December 1941 their air force attacked Pearl Harbour in Hawaii with considerable success, though it did not amount to an annihilation.

Of this phase in Japanese imperial ambition Churchill commented:

> Japanese exultation was at its zenith. Pride in their martial triumphs and confidence in their leadership was strengthened by the conviction that the Western powers had not the will to fight to the death.

But by their astonishing hubris in attacking Pearl Harbour, the Japanese had brought the United States into the war.

Japanese ambition now extended over the western Pacific, bulging out to a line that would enclose such points as the Aleutian Islands, Midway Island, Samoa, New Caledonia and Port Moresby in New Guinea. This would further threaten Pearl Harbour and advance the envelopment of Australasia.

The skill and daring of their plans was not in doubt. Where they were less accurate, wrote Churchill, was in trying to understand the power of the United States. Their senior naval officers mistakenly assumed a low level of morale existed in the US Navy.

The expansion plan was soon put into action. Armed conflict with the United States was inevitable. But a decisive victory was badly needed by the Americans, at this dangerous stage in the Pacific theatre. Churchill tells us that he had always believed that the US Navy would regain the Pacific, his hopes based on careful calculation of the speed of construction of American and British warships. This majestic fact, he wrote, was soon crystallised into 'a brilliant and astonishing naval battle'.

In the first days of May 1942 a Japanese naval force, heading for Port Moresby, including two carriers and a light carrier, passed to the east of the Solomon Islands and entered the Coral Sea from the northeast. Prompt intelligence and code-breaking had already allowed US Admiral Nimitz to summon together as strong an American force as possible, two carriers and nine cruisers. For two tense days the rival forces were unaware of each other's position in the thousand miles of the Coral Sea, yet one evening were only seventy miles apart. Battle came the next day, a battle like no other: the first sea battle in which surface ships never exchanged fire and never caught sight of each other; all attack made remotely by the pilots of the carrier aircraft. By early afternoon the intense firing and dive-bombing was finished.

For the US Navy, the Battle of the Coral Sea was the much-longed-for first strategic defeat of Japanese expansion in the Pacific. The Japanese now withdrew their Port Moresby operation. The news blazed around the world, to the especial relief of Australia and New Zealand.

In fact the American toll of light damage was deceptive, for a few hours after the end of the battle the carrier *Lexington* had suffered an internal explosion and had to be sunk. But this news was kept back until after the next clash.

As for the Japanese, they had lost their light carrier and one of their carriers was severely damaged. But they put out a false report that the US Navy had come off much worse and had lost both their carriers. They seem to have believed their own propaganda, for apparently the decision to attack Midway Island was based on this report.

THE BATTLE OF MIDWAY, 1942 Only a month later a force of the Imperial Japanese Navy – including four of the carriers that had attacked Pearl Harbour – sailed discreetly across the higher latitudes of the Pacific. Their plan was to attack from the emptier north the US base on Midway Island, a thousand miles west of Pearl Harbour. Again the US intelligence was prompt and accurate, and the date and location of the attack was known. But Admiral Nagumo, in command of the critically important carrier group, wrote beforehand in his Estimate of the Situation that 'the enemy does not know our plans'.

As we repeatedly find, a state of hubris encourages the making of assumptions: somehow, the admiral was not expecting to find US carriers hundreds of miles north of Midway, an area of the ocean he assumed would be empty. 'It is not believed that the enemy has any powerful unit, with carriers as their nucleus, in the vicinity.'

On the morning of the first attack on Midway, Admiral Nagumo was surprised when the US carriers, which had indeed been biding their time to the north, pounced on his forces. In the clash that followed the Americans sustained the loss of most of their torpedo bombers, but their dive-bombers followed up and incapacitated three of Nagumo's carriers in about five minutes. After this astonishing blow, Nagumo was reported standing on deck in a rigid trance, before being transferred to another ship. His four flight decks had been unusually vulnerable and flammable because of the hurried refuelling and rearming of aircraft back from the first Midway raid. Thus the arrival of the dive-bomber group from the US carrier *Enterprise* might seem to exhibit brilliant timing, but is thought to have been accidental rather than planned.

The fierce sudden reversal of fortune suffered by the Japanese in the Coral Sea and at Midway was the *peripeteia* of their hubris. A year passes and the Japanese realise that they will never catch up with the phenomenal rate at which the US can turn out new warships and aircraft. At the end of this drama, three years after Midway, came the horror of Hiroshima and Nagasaki, a nemesis like no other, before or since.

The American experience of the Pacific theatre had shown that flexibility and learning from numerous mistakes is likely to outwit the rigidity often found, it would seem, in totalitarian commands.

THE FALL OF SINGAPORE, 1942 Beneath the complex details of this notorious disaster lay an assumption that Singapore Island had landward defences against attack from mainland Malaya. Churchill himself confesses that he was party to the delusion.

The steady, relentless Japanese advance southwards through Malaya was aiming at Singapore. In the event of a siege, Churchill counted on at least a two-month resistance. But on the morning of 16 January, three weeks before the actual fall, he received a painful surprise in a telegram from General Wavell: he reported that there were *no* permanent fortifications covering the northern side of the island west of the naval base. This astonished Churchill. And *nothing* had been done by any commander since the beginning of the war, or since the Japanese had overrun neighbouring Indo-China. And the commanders had never even *mentioned* the glaring weakness. When Churchill's numerous telegrams had suggested that a siege was likely, no one had responded that this was in fact impossible, because the island was defenceless along its northern shore.

Churchill did not attempt to excuse himself at this point: 'I ought to have known.' And his advisers should have known. He should have asked, and so on. He then explains why he had not asked: 'The possibility of

Singapore having no landward defences no more entered my mind than that of a battleship being launched without a bottom.'

The dilemma that now faced him was one of the most painful of the war. The subsequent controversy over the disaster still rumbles on today. But going back to Churchill's assumption – which was a venial sin, considering his distance from the evidence on the ground – it was a case of confusing the unlikely with the impossible. It was unlikely that Singapore had no landward defences, but it was not impossible. That the question had not 'entered the mind' of anyone on the ground in Singapore, is far more reprehensible, and far less comprehensible.

ANOTHER ANGLE ON HUBRIS: C.S. LEWIS, 1943 In *Mere Christianity* Lewis declares that 'Pride leads to every other vice; it is the most anti-God sin of all.' It is the opposite of humility.

D-DAY, 1944 Perhaps the finest and largest deception of all time, reinforcing assumptions already in the mind of the enemy, was devised for D-Day. This was a classic example of deception according to Magruder's Principle: that it is generally easier to take advantage of the enemy's existing beliefs than to try to change them. It was known that Hitler already believed that the re-invasion would be launched across the Straits of Dover, and that an earlier northern invasion would be made of Norway: 'the zone of destiny in this war' according to the Führer. Thus the Allies built their deception plan around those beliefs. It was also known, thanks to Admiral Dönitz, that once a notion had wedged itself in Hitler's mind, it was almost impossible to shake it loose.

The D-Day deception was so successful that Hitler and most of the German High Command firmly believed – even *after* the Normandy landings had begun – that the main invasion would come across the Straits of Dover. Any attack in Normandy would only amount to a diversionary tactic. Consequently, large German forces were tied up in the Pas de

Calais – and Norway – instead of defending the Normandy coast.

As with the Kaiser at the outbreak of the First World War, one wonders to what extent it was advisable for military staff to disagree with the Führer. Göring and Goebbels, the nearest in status, were well aware of how far they could go. Göring had confided to Sir Nevile Henderson that 'When a decision has to be taken, none of us count more than the stones on which we are standing. It is the Führer alone who decides.' So the gigantic assumption survived well in this airless atmosphere. The muffling of opinion and the resulting loss of truth seems to be a recurring weakness of totalitarian systems. It feeds the growth of hubris, and a comparison of the Hitler of *Mein Kampf* and that of *Hitler's Table Talk* compiled some twenty years later shows that his crude views on a thousand subjects had hardly shifted at all. His assumption of infallibility was set fast.

The D-Day deception scheme was ambitious, technical and determined – like Winston Churchill himself. It was indeed Churchill who, after Dunkirk, had immediately ordered preparations for a re-invasion of Europe, steered by him through the Committee of Special Means.

The deception operation leading up to D-Day was codenamed 'Bodyguard' (D-Day itself was Operation Overlord, the naval component was Operation Neptune). The whole business was done to a formidably high standard of thoroughness and security, a spectacular success.

Operation Bodyguard

A complete phantom army had been created in the south east of England, mainly in Kent, under the command of General Patton. It was known as FUSAG (First United States Army Group) and consisted of dummy military units, rubber aircraft, landing craft, tanks, and other convincing paraphernalia, to support the illusion that an attack would come over the Straits of Dover (Operation Fortitude South). Some of the army units were real, and went on to play a part in the actual invasion. The FUSAG phantom army was 'larger' than all the US forces used for D-Day. George

VI, Eisenhower and Montgomery were making appearances in conspicuous locations down there, for example at a huge dummy oil terminal near Dover, built by Shepperton Film Studios. The illusion was backed up by a network of double agents, who were an absolutely vital component of the operation. The Germans had a great respect for Patton, his skill and guile, and so assumed that he must be playing an important role, and that FUSAG would cross the channel from Kent to the Pas de Calais.

At the Tehran Conference in 1943, Stalin had spoken of Russia's own deception plans and wanted to co-ordinate them with D-Day preparations. Churchill approved this warmly and gained much appreciation from Stalin and his comrades with this reply:

> In wartime, truth is so precious that she should always be attended by a bodyguard of lies.

The Germans were to fall heavily for the multiple illusions of Operation Bodyguard.

At sea something similar was going on. Phantom naval exercises and movements were conjured up in the form of radio traffic, in the Channel and North Sea and also in the Firth of Clyde area. Some actual ships and aircraft were involved. Some of this deception was in support of the Norway 'invasion' (Operation Fortitude North). George VI had appeared at the Scapa Flow naval base in the Orkneys.

There were two assumptions which the Germans made without any help from the Allies: that their Atlantic Wall fortifications would deter attacks and that anyway the Allies would need to invade via a deep-water port. This would be found north of the Seine, because Lower Normandy lacked such ports. As for the Atlantic Wall, it was in poor condition and when Rommel visited, he realised he had been misled.

Closer to D-Day, another deception was launched: huge quantities of Map 51 were purchased from the Michelin company. This sheet covered the Pas de Calais. Orders were sent in from a wide variety of locations and countries, to expose this phenomenon as much as possible.

During the night of 6 June

Five precisely planned deception operations took place while the naval force, Operation Neptune, was heading across to Normandy. Here are four of them:

Operation **Mandrel** had aircraft constantly circling off the Hampshire and Dorset coasts. These interfered with German radar. The Sea Commandant in Normandy reported that his radar was faulty, but this did not arouse any suspicion that the jamming was to conceal the approaching invasion.

In Operation **Taxable**, sixteen Lancasters from the Dambuster Squadron dropped a chaff window (consisting of aluminium foil) over 325 square miles along the coast between Le Havre and Fécamp, well northeast of the D-Day beaches. Precision was of the essence in this highly technical flight. The chaff interfered with German radar and mimicked a naval convoy advancing towards them. Many German defensive positions along this stretch of coast were thereby deluded, and fired waves of artillery rounds into the stormy night. This was done three hours before the Normandy landings.

Likewise, Operation **Glimmer** simulated an invasion fleet heading from Kent to Boulogne. It used only navy launches and six Stirling bombers dropping chaff. Fake messages were broadcast from rehearsed scripts, easily intercepted by the enemy. These messages included samples of interference and static. In synchrony, Operation **Moonshine** used launches which towed radar-reflective barrage balloons with transponders. These distorted the signals received on German radar, so that what had seemed like a flotilla of six torpedo boats appeared as a large formation of planes and 10,000-ton ships. Loudspeakers on barges broadcast the sound of ships dropping anchor.

Thus the belief persisted that the Allies were attacking Upper Normandy and the Pas de Calais. It was not until nine in the evening of D-Day that Admiral Dönitz realised something of what was happening and ordered an all-out submarine attack on the real Allied invasion fleet. But by then 160,000 troops had crossed the English Channel and had breached the coastal fortifications.

The Germans did, it has since been discovered, know the weather forecast around D-Day. But this knowledge worked against them. The fact that the forecast was atrocious for 5 June and still rough for the 6th (to which D-Day was delayed) misled the High Command into assuming that the invasion would be postponed still further. They were so sure, that Rommel went home to Bavaria for his wife's birthday.

But why were the Germans confident that the rough weather would cause further postponement? Well, it seems that they had analysed a number of occasions when the Allies *had* postponed operations because of poor conditions and assumed that the same reaction would occur for D-Day. But the sample data they had used was tiny, and therefore highly unreliable. This trap is known as The Law of Small Numbers.

They certainly underestimated the determination of Eisenhower, who refused any further delay.

'OVER BY CHRISTMAS': ARNHEM, SEPTEMBER 1944 Field Marshal Montgomery, as he now was, no doubt riding high after D-Day and the push northeast, proposed a plan for avoiding the Siegfried Line by taking Rhine bridging points further north. The most northerly bridge was at Arnhem in the occupied Netherlands. Once over the Rhine, the forces would turn south to attack the Ruhr industrial region, leading to the final fall and surrender of Germany. Montgomery expected it would be 'over by Christmas'. The plan had been put together in only a couple of weeks, as the enemy forces there were growing day by day.

All this was odd, because Montgomery was known for his overcaution and for prioritising the safety of his soldiers' lives. And this plan relied on complex airborne action about which he knew very little. Had 'Monty' gone through some sort of change? The historian Sir Anthony Beevor reckons so, and points out that quite a few of the generals in that heady period seem to have been afflicted by some sort of hubris. After all, they had been drawn from relative obscurity into the limelight and were being treated like film stars. MacArthur, Patton and Clark (known as 'Marcus Aurelius Clarkus' for his identification with ancient Rome) were prime examples.

Montgomery had now allowed himself to aim for dramatic success at Arnhem and in the glorious dash to Berlin that should follow. He was thus rivalling the neighbouring campaigns of Patton and Omar Bradley, farther south on the Rhine. Although vital Allied action was still needed to clear German forces from the estuary of the Scheldt, thus opening Antwerp to the sea, Montgomery and Eisenhower both prioritised the Arnhem plan. (Monty did admit afterwards that he had underrated the value of opening the Scheldt.) His inability to listen to the opinions of others was noted at this time. Was it Asperger's Syndrome, as now seems likely, or increasing hubris?

There was some scepticism about the ambitious plan for Arnhem, now code-named Operation Market Garden. In particular, the intelligence officer assigned to the airborne forces, Brian Urquhart, had found evidence that the 2nd Panzer Corps was refitting close to the Allied dropping zone. But this discovery was not welcome at staff level and Urquhart was sent away. Somehow the operation all went ahead. Urquhart could only watch with dismay from the sidelines; the staff assumption of the inaccuracy of his intelligence moved ever closer to exploding.

The Arnhem failure was complex. Controversy still hangs around the tragedy, redeemed only by the courage of those who refused to give up the fight. Montgomery's reputation certainly suffered. But it wasn't all down to Monty: the American generals at that time had made a group assumption that the German army must be weak and close to internal collapse, as indicated by the Stauffenberg Plot to assassinate Hitler a few months earlier. But they had overlooked the German genius for recovery from impossible situations, and the German forces around the northern Rhine took them by surprise.

After a distinguished forty-year career in the birth of the United Nations, Urquhart was still haunted by his experience of Arnhem, in which he had learnt that being right after all did not make one popular. But he had gained an insight into the action of hubris and vanity in great enterprises, and began to fear risky assumptions:

> Before [Arnhem], I had been trusting and relatively optimistic, with a self-confidence that was sometimes excessive. After it, I doubted everything, tended to distrust my own as well as other people's judgement, and became deeply sceptical about the behaviour of leaders.

THE TWILIGHT OF DR GOEBBELS No details of the Holocaust were ever reported under the regime of Goebbels. Yet he cynically let the German press hint at what people already had some inkling of. Thus the German populace were made to feel somewhat complicit, though with little chance of being able to do anything about it.

Goebbels was one of the few people able to calm Hitler and get him to act rationally. After the Stauffenberg Plot of July 1944, which Hitler survived, he at last gave Goebbels – his *de facto* second in command – the powers to order a total mobilisation of ground forces. Goebbels had first pleaded for this over a year ago: 'It takes a bomb under his backside to make Hitler see reason.'

With the coming of the Anglo-American air bombing of German strategic cities such as Hamburg and Dresden (an industrial and railway nexus on the Elbe), Goebbels portrayed the bombings and fire-storms as

'Jewish terror'. He declared that global Jewry was manipulating the Allies to exact revenge for German crimes. Is this an example of the axiom that 'the bigger the lie the greater the chance of it being believed'? This idea had been recommended by Hitler in *Mein Kampf* and was also used by Goebbels throughout the war.

Goebbels became Hitler's closest and most valuable colleague and chose to die with him in the Berlin bunker. Not only a genius of propaganda to the end, he was inclined to self-dramatisation, wishing to perish in the flickering shadows of a perverse Twilight of the Gods, rather than submit to the tedious court-room fate that would follow.

On the day after Hitler's suicide, Goebbels shot his wife, Magda, and then himself. He had already killed their six children by poison. Most proponents of Nazi power turn out to have been evil and often banal. Joseph Goebbels was as evil as any, yet he was hardly 'banal'. As the self-conscious manipulator of the German mind, the hardest-working force in the Nazi elite, possessed of unmistakable, almost 'camp' bravado, I wonder if this strange personage still exerts a serpentine fascination and glamour over susceptible minds.

A DOUBLE VIEW OF GERMAN HISTORY 1945 provides a suitable moment to contemplate a long-standing false impression that may have been made about Germany, with its very long history and its tendency to extremes. A.J.P. Taylor's *The Course of German History*, written during the Second World War and published in 1945, seems to have filled a gap here. He explains how Germany had always shown two faces to Europe: one to the west and one to the east. To the west she had appeared to the French and the English as a barbarian state which had nevertheless been keen to learn from them and had excelled in arts and sciences.

To the east, however, she had shown a very different visage. Since the eleventh century there had been a continuous German thrust against the Slavic lands by military conquest of their vast sandy plains. These eventually formed the territory of an ever-expanding Prussia. Other Slav peoples had been the victims of German Crusaders, of the Teutonic Knights or of the German need for *lebensraum* or 'living space'. But this consistent thousand-year pattern of extermination does not seem to have registered much in the nations to Germany's west: 'No one can understand Germans who does not appreciate their determination to exterminate the East.' A.J.P. Taylor refers to the 'Cloud in the East' that had loomed over German history: 'This is the fear which underlies their ceaseless plans for aggression and mastery.'

In an interview, Sir Antony Beevor relates that Kaiser Wilhelm II had assumed that Russian POWs taken from the battlefield of Tannenberg in 1914 would be left to starve to death.

CHURCHILL'S SPEECH AT ZÜRICH, 1946 There is a strain of opinion that seems to assume that Churchill believed Britain should be a member of a United States of Europe, that he would have been horrified by Brexit, etc.

What really happened? In his famous address to the Swiss Technical University, Churchill certainly recommended the establishment of a 'United States of Europe'. This was not the first appearance of the phrase, as Jean Monnet had already published a book with that title in 1931. But the concept perhaps reached a wider audience through Churchill. Certainly he was one of its founders, and active in getting it up and running. Initially just France and Germany should form the institution, he declared, to be joined later by neighbouring European nations both great and small. Thus, 'Europe' would eventually take its place as one of the world's 'natural groupings'. There were already three of these, he stated: America, Russia (he hoped) and Britain and its Commonwealth.

Britain's role should therefore be limited to being 'friends and sponsors' of a United States of Europe. Thus, as Prime Minister in the 1950s, he decisively blocked all movement towards actual British membership of a USE. In a written response to the Schuman plan for a European coal and steel authority in 1951, Churchill made it clear that the UK should not forfeit its 'insular and Commonwealth character', nor submit itself to the rule of a federal government.

> It is only when plans for uniting Europe take a federal form that we ourselves cannot take part, because we cannot subordinate ourselves or the control of British policy to federal authorities.

A COLLECTION OF GENERALISATIONS, 1949 The American author and journalist James Thurber began to collect 'broad generalisations' and 'sweeping statements' heard mainly in New York City and its hinterland. This was because he had found the collecting of actual objects too much of a strain. For example, his collection of snowstorm paperweights had been diminished from seventeen to a mere four or five, by the wandering hands of house guests.

Thurber's overheard generalisations are inaccurate, exaggerated or plain crazy. I suspect that many of them were heard at the cocktail parties that feature quite frequently in his writing. In 1949 he shared his expanding collection with readers of the *New Yorker* and suggested that they could enjoy collecting them too. I suppose in 1949 you could still get away with his advice to listen especially to the conversation of women, 'whose average generalisation is from three to five times broader than a man's'.

Herewith some of the gems of his collection:

'There are no pianos in Japan.'
Thurber quickly finds that to be completely wrong.

'You never see foreigners fishing.'

'People who break into houses don't drink wine.'
Thurber rates this as fascinating but impossible to prove. It is 'a Comfortable Conclusion that may cost you a whole case of Château Lafite'.

'Gamblers hate women.'

'Sopranos drive men crazy.'

'Jewellers never go anywhere.'

'Intellectual women dress funny.'

'Sick people hear everything.'

Thurber's criteria for admittance into his collection are stringent. It is interesting to ponder his reasons for rejecting 'Nobody taps his fingers if he's all right' or 'Generals are afraid of their daughters.' The original article can be found in *Thurber Country*, 1953.

ASSUMPTION WITH A CAPITAL A: THE BLESSED VIRGIN MARY, 1950 This is a special use of the word. The Assumption is generally described as the elevation of the Virgin Mary to heaven; 'Assumption' as a physical and spiritual 'taking up' of the Virgin, by God, to heaven. 15 August has become its established feast day.

The event is not mentioned in the Gospels. The authority for it comes from other sources. In 1950 Pope Pius XII spoke *ex cathedra*, declaring an infallible definition of the Assumption of Mary as an article of faith of the Roman Catholic Church.

'HOME BY CHRISTMAS': GENERAL MACARTHUR, 1950 This cosy, irresistible assumption seems to recur quite frequently. It is the kiss of death in military matters. In this instance, during the Korean War, the great General MacArthur had just pulled off, against the odds, the brilliant success of landing troops at Inchon and recapturing Seoul. But he succumbed to hubris. He now visualised a speedy push in late November up to the Yalu River on the border with communist China. A defeat of North Korea would, he announced, soon be completed. Most of the troops would be 'home by Christmas'. At the same time he decided to reject the supply of intelligence from the CIA, relying instead on his internal team in Japan. It seems that this intelligence was biased towards the idea that the Chinese would be unlikely to attack.

But they did. 'We face an entirely new war,' admitted a shocked MacArthur – with the result that the Korean War continued, mostly in stalemate, until 1953.

'Home by Christmas' was first heard, it seems, at the outset of the First World War. Even the most respected generals – Montgomery, MacArthur – have somehow fallen for its charm.

THE PATH TO THE TREATY OF ROME, 1957 Here follows a very potted history, focusing only on the background and the theory of the first stage of the European project.

The story begins in the First World War, not after the Second as is sometimes assumed. Jean Monnet, later the accepted founder of 'Europe' as a political entity, became frustrated in his role as an organiser, in 1917, of the shipping of food and war materials to the Allies. What was needed, he reasoned, was a supranational body that could override the ideas of ship-owners or any national government. After the war he became a senior official in the League of Nations, but was again frustrated by what he called 'national egoism', which he saw not only as the source of the war but also a continuing risk. In 1931 he published *The United States of Europe,* in which he proposed a supranational government of technocrats and supporting lawyers, bent on pursuing uniformity and harmonisation. They would operate through four core institutions: Council, Commission, Assembly (Parliament) and Court with which we are now familiar. The first step was to build a customs union or 'common market', to be financed by a tariff on external trade. National governments were to be reduced to the status of local assemblies.

The Second World War and its aftermath hindered the progress of this idea. Monnet's plan to develop the European Coal and Steel Community into a political community was rejected by the French National Assembly. At this point, in 1955, he and his powerful allies (Spaak, Schuman) realised that it would only be possible to create a United States of Europe very gradually. Thus they would launch the first step, the European Economic Community, the 'common market', without revealing its ultimate purpose. From now on, many assumptions would arise to fill this vacuum of knowledge.

Although the ensuing Treaty of Rome, 1957, stated in its first line that the six signatory nations were 'determined to lay the foundations for *an ever closer union* [my italics] among the peoples of Europe', the rest of the treaty deals with economic matters only.

THE CUBAN CRISIS, 1962 In the summer of this year the CIA had observed a growing number of Soviet missiles on Cuba, but these had all been identified as surface-to-air missiles. These could not be used to attack the US, but were merely defensive. And the CIA seems to have been okay with that assumption.

By good fortune, though, in September the director of the CIA, John McCone, went on honeymoon to Cap Ferrat on the French Riviera. In this refreshing environment he found himself asking a very obvious question which somehow no CIA official, including himself, had yet asked. If these missiles were 'defensive', what exactly were they defending? Could it be that they were there to defend the *construction* of *offensive* missile sites? He sent a telegram to the President in which he insisted that the Russians were planning to bring ballistic missiles to Cuba and that the CIA should be more imaginative about Soviet weapons policy.

This theory was confirmed by aerial observation and the first intelligence reached the Kennedy White House on 16 October. A majority of the President's chief advisers were in favour of an air strike, but changed their minds on account of the sites not yet being operational. By October

Kennedy had imposed a blockade around the island to prevent Russian ships delivering more missiles. The crisis was yet to come…

It rather looks as if there had been a lack of systematic thinking by the CIA about the use of the word 'defensive'. Instead, as we saw, a rather simple assumption seems to have been made. How could that happen? Was it the result of stultifying bureaucratic procedures? Was it a case of Orwell's warning that 'to see what is beneath one's nose is a constant struggle'?

THE IMAGE OF PRESIDENT KENNEDY, 1961–63 The general public mostly assumed that John F. Kennedy was indeed the energetic, glamorous, healthy, youngest-ever President and unstoppable 'dream hero' that he appeared to be. This was the aim of the carefully managed image control of the presidential campaign. Yet the truth was somehow kept quiet until a historian, Robert Dallek, managed to examine his medical records. These revealed that he was racked with health problems and had spent more time in hospital and convalescing than the length of his presidency, nearly three years. He had been read the last rites three times before he was thirty-five. He suffered from Addison's Disease and painful spinal damage and was taking several drugs on a daily basis even during the Cuban Missile Crisis. His image was illusory, his reputation not so clear with the passing years; yet his overcoming those chronic health problems could in itself be considered heroic.

ROBERT FOGEL, A PIONEER OF DATA-LED HISTORY, 1964 Robert Fogel (born in New York of Russian-Jewish immigrants in 1926) became aware, after the war, that much of US history consisted of conventional wisdom or comfortable assumptions. He felt these could be challenged through the use of detailed historical data of all kinds. He was the first to use new high-speed computers for this task. This combination of 'what if?' scenarios and data mining he called Cliometrics, after the Greek Muse of history.

His first investigation was published in 1964: *Railroads and American Economic Growth*. Until then, senior economists had assumed that the growth of the US railway system was a primary driver of the nineteenth-century economic boom. But Fogel concluded that railroads had contributed only an extra 2.7 per cent of growth. This revision of such a fundamental period of US history brought Fogel some fame, and controversy.

His next investigation, published ten years later, was far more controversial: *The Economics of American Negro Slavery*. Through a detailed assessment of the living and working conditions of slaves in the South he was able to challenge the general assumption that slave owners had treated their workforce badly. He showed that they were aware of the value of their human assets and looked after their well-being, as a farmer cares for the condition of his livestock. Fogel showed that they had, on the whole, better conditions than manual workers in the North. He and his co-author Stanley Engerman found that they had to justify their conclusions to those convinced of the utter venality of slave-owners. In fact Fogel was himself married to an African-American, but did not enlist this fact when defending his methods and findings.

In a long career, including a Nobel Prize in 1993, Fogel constantly drew attention to this idea: that you cannot understand current problems without a correct account of the past. This calls to mind the words of Edmund Burke when he declared that 'Those who don't know history are condemned to repeat it.' With the backing of Fogel's data, those that *do know* history may gain greater authority for their policies.

A later investigation by Fogel challenged the notions of the English economist Malthus about the self-limitation of population. Using data such as pensions, tax, public health, genealogical records and bodily height, Fogel was able to prove a link between health and economic growth. For example, he found that a third of per capita economic growth in Great Britain from 1790 to 1980 resulted from improved nutrition.

A SCHOOL PRIZE At the end of the Easter term at my school, it was announced that, in order to win a long-standing Literature Prize, an essay of a certain length should be submitted at the start of the following term. The subject was to be chosen from a list of British authors of the twentieth century. While frantically finishing my own entry (on Evelyn Waugh) as the summer term began, I happened to pass down the corridor where the list of approved authors had been displayed. In fact it was still there. I had of course assumed that Waugh was on this list – how could he not be? I thought I might as well see which other authors I could have chosen to write about… Iris Murdoch, Graham Greene, D.H. Lawrence… But, oh dear, NO mention of Evelyn Waugh, would you believe it!

I decided to submit my essay anyway. A week or so later I glanced at the headmaster's noticeboard. I was astonished to learn that I had won the prize. For a brief ridiculous moment I wondered if I should 'do the decent thing' and alert the judges to the conditions of entry. But, I soon reasoned, *they too* must have assumed that Waugh would be on that list. How could he not be?

I chose a splendid volume on English cathedral architecture.

THE *TORREY CANYON*, 18 MARCH 1967: THE FIRST SUPER-TANKER DISASTER
Several human errors lay behind this unnecessary accident. I found the story of Captain Rugiati difficult to tell. The many published accounts vary considerably in their details. From studying several that seemed more authoritative, this may be the gist of what happened.

Captain Rugiati, the master of the *Torrey Canyon*, one of the largest tankers in the world at that time, carrying 119,000 tons of crude oil from the Persian Gulf, was under pressure. His employers had impressed upon him the importance of reaching Milford Haven in Wales as soon as possible, before tidal fluctuation would prevent the entry of such a large ship for several days.

The scheduled route for the tanker was to pass to the west of the Isles of Scilly. Rugiati accordingly set a course of eighteen degrees before retiring for the night. But at 6:30am he was informed by the chief officer that the ship had been forced off this course (by the east-flowing Rennell Current), and they were now passing the islands on their eastern side. Thus in navigational terms Rugiati had already made a huge assumption about his course, by not knowing of the deflecting current.

He decided to continue with this course, which was – whether intended or not – a short-cut to Milford Haven. But he did not have a copy of the British Admiralty's *Channel Pilot* and was not familiar with the area. He therefore had no choice but to hope for the best, that it would be a straightforward passage with no problems – such as fishing boats blocking his way, for example…

That sunny morning in March the weather was calm.

Rugiati was now in the wide sea area between the Isles of Scilly and Land's End. But he was now planning to take a course through a *narrow* channel to the *west* of a notorious reef known as the Seven Stones. That was an odd decision in itself for such a large vessel, 300m long. It was a thousand pities that he had no copy of the *Channel Pilot* on board, for it specifically warns against large vessels going west of the Seven Stones. On the eastern side of the Stones, the twelve miles of open sea to Land's End was the obvious and recommended route. Another reason to stay east of the Seven Stones was the constant breeze from the northwest, which would steadily push the supertanker back towards the lethal hazard. His 'decision' was so little based on evidence that it must be counted a dangerous assumption, or even a complete absence of thought.

Further confusion undermined this final and fatal phase, an error in the design of the steering gear. The lever that selects the mode of steering stood to one side of the helmsman, and could easily be overlooked. That lever could be set at 'manual', 'autopilot' or 'control'. The latter two settings disabled any attempt at manual steering.

Rugiati now decided the moment had come to turn the *Torrey Canyon* towards the western channel. The Seven Stones were directly ahead and not so distant. But at 8:30am he became aware of French fishing boats and submerged nets blocking his intended turn. He therefore delayed. By 8:40 he was aware that he was only some three miles from the southernmost Stone. But – incredibly – instead of going with the wind to the open sea, he *still* persisted in trying to get across to the western channel. He ordered the instruction 'Hard to port'. The helmsman turned the wheel assuming it was in manual mode, but unbeknownst to him, it was set at 'autopilot'. Why the ship was not responding, no one seemed to know. The autopilot continued to direct the tanker to the reef. Farcical scenes of panic now took over. An emergency telephone call was answered by the kitchen staff. Eventually the helmsman managed to regain control and steered the ship round by ten degrees. It was too late. The *Torrey Canyon* foundered and broke open on Pollard's Rock.

When Rugiati was asked at the inquiry why he had not taken the eastward escape route, he gave the breath-taking answer that 'It never entered my mind'. The Liberian Commission of Inquiry blamed the disaster solely on the negligence of the captain.

THE UNITED KINGDOM JOINS THE EUROPEAN PROJECT, 1973–75 In 1973 the Conservative government of Edward Heath took the nation into the common market, or European Economic Community. The Prime Minister insisted that there was no risk to the integrity of UK sovereignty. There seems to have been a widespread agreement or assumption that he was right. There was no referendum, but a bill in favour of joining was passed in the House by a clear majority of MPs.

In 1975 the new Labour government held a referendum on whether to continue in the EEC. I remember very clearly how Enoch Powell – a modern Laocoon – in the eloquent accent of the Black Country, spoke out loud and clear, insisting that the United Kingdom's sovereignty was indeed at risk. He read out that first line of the Treaty of Rome – perhaps not the reading matter of most of the electorate – and appealed to them to reflect very seriously before the vote. 'It's not an economic project, it's a *political* project.' To no avail, for the trend towards a shiny-and-new Europe held firm. In the referendum there was a clear majority in favour of staying in.

That earlier assumption of 1973 could not be shifted. But Powell did not blame the British public. He had come to realise that British people simply could not believe that the UK could ever lose its independent nationhood – by treaty, law and bureaucracy, and 'without a shot being fired'.

CHESAPEAKE BAY COLLISION, 1978   On a dark October night a US Coastguard cutter, *Cuyahoga*, was heading north up the bay. Commander Robinson identified by its lights a distant approaching vessel as a fishing boat. He expected it would turn west into the Potomac, as would the cutter. He confirmed this on radar, though only cursorily. But his identification was badly wrong, for the vessel was in fact a large coal freighter heading out of the bay for Argentina.

Robinson now began the turn to the west, thus putting his cutter in danger of a meeting and possible collision with the freighter. But at no point was bridge-to-bridge radio used to confirm each ship's intentions, only blasts of the horn.

The cutter was on training duty and the crew was a mixture of regular seamen and officer candidates. Several of the candidates had observed the lights of the freighter and had concerns about the course of the *Cuyahoga*, but were either suddenly distracted by other matters or told that the commander already knew about it. The regular crew were also distracted by their additional role of training. Thus an assumption seems to have spread that the commander must have had a good reason to order the turn – and they left it at that.

Robinson finally realised the danger. The cutter was sharply reversed, only to be smashed by the bow of the freighter and to be violently broken up and sunk in two minutes. Eleven died, eighteen survived.

There must often be situations in groups when something looks to be going wrong but, for various reasons, juniors or bystanders fail to find their dissenting voice and become party to a dangerous assumption that whoever's in charge is probably getting it right.

THE HITLER DIARIES, 1983 The German magazine *Stern* was offering the British press the chance to examine the sixty 'diaries' of Adolf Hitler, with a view to selling the publication rights. The historian Hugh Trevor-Roper, one of the greatest authorities on the Nazis, was consulted by *The Times*, owned by Rupert Murdoch. Trevor-Roper went over to Zürich and examined the 'diaries' in safe custody. He assumed that they were genuine, asking himself who would have created sixty fake diaries when six would have been enough? However, some of Murdoch's senior staff recalled nearly falling for some 'diaries' of Mussolini ten years previously. They urged caution. To no avail, for Murdoch had complete trust in the historian and gave the green light for their serialisation. But this had just been switched to *The Sunday Times*, also owned by Murdoch.

But now, Trevor-Roper, after meeting the essential German link-man in the transaction, began to have serious doubts about their authenticity. Yet by the evening of 23 April he had still not shared this change of mind directly with the editor of *The Sunday Times*, Frank Giles. Why not? Well, he seems to have assumed that the editor of *The Times*, for whom he *had* been working, would have passed on his revised opinion.

But that information had *not* been passed on. On the Saturday night the presses were rolling and during the celebratory drinks at the office, Frank Giles phoned Trevor-Roper to share congratulations. But the celebrators detected a sudden change in Giles's voice. The office went silent. 'Well, naturally, Hugh, one has doubts... but I take it that these doubts aren't strong enough to make you do a complete 180-degree turn?

Oh. Oh, I see. You *are* doing a 180-degree turn.'

Rupert Murdoch was informed of the bungle, but ordered the print-run to go ahead.

Frank Giles claimed that he had been steam-rollered by the proprietor. His journalistic career was effectively over from then. Already he and Murdoch had not seen eye to eye about the role of editor. Two weeks later the German government declared that the diaries were forged. *The Sunday Times* had serious egg on its face. Rupert Murdoch in due course admitted it was one of his worst misjudgements, that he would 'have to live with'.

Trevor-Roper apologised, and felt very damaged by the incident. Later he was able to see it as more farce than tragedy.

THE REITH LECTURES, 1985: TOO MUCH POLITICS? Many in the political world seem to assume that prosperity flows easily from the fountain pen of politicians or that the nation can be quickly changed for the better by the passing of a bill. Those in government want to be seen to be 'doing something'. But do they check the impact of their plans enough? It certainly takes effort to run all the imaginable scenarios. Often they fall victim to the law of unintended consequences. Rather than 'doing something', might it be more productive to allow others better qualified to do these sorts of things, unimpeded by extra taxation and intervention?

An example of government not doing too much, with great success, had occurred in Hong Kong. John Cowperthwaite became financial secretary of the colony in 1961. He did not believe in big government and intervention. He refused to collect vast quantities of statistics about the colony, reckoning that they only encouraged more intervention and meddling.

Not all his superiors agreed. But taxes stayed low, red tape was minimal, restrictions on business light – and the economy boomed. By 1971 he had transformed the place out of recognition. The law of unintended consequences had been given less material to work with.

Samuel Johnson had believed that the sadness of earthly life cannot be solved by politicians; those that try may do more harm than good:

Boswell: 'So sir, you laugh at schemes of political improvement.'
Johnson: 'Why, sir, most schemes of political improvement are very laughable things.'

Thus I was intrigued to learn of the work of David Henderson, a British economist endowed with the robust clarity of mind of a Yorkshireman. He had built up considerable experience of working in the government, at the World Bank and as an academic. He used the Reith Lectures in 1985 as a platform against the kind of 'bigger government' assumption we began with. He sharply criticised 'the lazy DIY economics of policymakers who fail to think through the likely consequences of their interventions'. Too often these interventions acquire a soap-opera kind of simplification which leads to wrong conclusions and further unintended consequences. He gave as examples the joint project with the French to build Concorde and the Central Electricity Generating Board's investment in the gas-cooled reactor, 'the most wasteful such project ever undertaken'.

In the 1990s he took aim at the interventions being made into business, in the shape of 'corporate citizenship', 'stakeholders' and various environmental and social aims. He accused their promoters of a basic failure to understand why capitalism works. These interventionists assumed they were on the high moral ground in including ever-wider welfare as part of a company's work, but the result was that costs and prices rose and employees were distracted from attending to the firm's real business: making money for shareholders. These shareholders were perfectly capable of making charitable decisions themselves. The interventionists and meddlers undermined the very source that would be expected to provide funds for welfare; they were killing the goose that laid the golden egg.

AFTER THE TREATY OF ROME, 1957–1997 From the day of the Treaty, a subtle
and relentless process, that Louis XIV, Colbert or Napoleon might have
admired, began to work ratchet-like upon the member nations. Ever more
powers were gradually conceded by treaty to the same four institutions
of Monnet's original plan. These were all based in Francophone cities:
Brussels, Luxembourg and Strasbourg. The most sacred principle,
an article of faith at the heart of the Brussels creed of uniformity and
harmonisation, stated that the *acquis communautaire* – now amounting
to some 190,000 pages of legislation acquired by the EU from member
states – could never be reversed.

Then, at the time of the Maastricht Treaty in 1992 the European
Economic Community became simply the European Community, in open
confirmation of its underlying political purpose. In the following year
it renamed itself the European Union. The great assumption up to this
point had been that the so-called 'common market' was just an economic
arrangement, and would remain as such for the UK.

Then, by the Amsterdam Treaty of 1997, the so-called precautionary
principle was incorporated into EU law. It holds that if there is no
evidence of something, the worst should be assumed, an extreme form of
risk-averse policy, and not encouraging of business and innovation. This
was seen, for example, in the banning of genetically modified crops, the
shutting down, in Germany, of nuclear plants after Fukushima, and in
2021 with the excessive suspicion and denigration of vital vaccines.

MARINE SAFETY, 1996 A report by Dr Anita Rothblum of the United States
Coastguard's Research and Development team throws light on all sorts
of errors, including assumptions, and the context in which they occur.
Dr Rothblum had been puzzled to find that modern ship systems were
technologically advanced and highly reliable, but that the casualty rate in
the maritime industry remained high. Why was this? Because the maritime
system is much more dependent on its people than on its technology. For

example, over a seventeen-year period, 86 per cent of tanker accidents were caused by human error and a similarly high percentage in other categories such as collisions and fires.

In her research, Dr Rothblum realised that most accidents are not the result of a single error, but by a cluster or chain of errors. But remove just one of those errors from the cluster or chain and the accident would not have happened. Thus, she suggests, even the most trivial errors should be avoided so as to reduce the likelihood of accidents that are certainly *not* trivial.

We've already encountered the multiple errors of the two maritime accidents that she gives as examples in her report: the *Torrey Canyon* disaster and the night collision on Chesapeake Bay.

A 1995 report by the US Coastguard – *Prevention through People* – ranks in order of danger the human problems encountered in the maritime industry.

1. Fatigue.

2. Inadequate communication.

3. Inadequate knowledge both in general and of own ship's system.

4. Poor design of automation.

5. Decisions based on inadequate information.

All of these failings could lead to the making of assumptions, especially 2 and 5.

DANIEL KAHNEMAN: *THINKING, FAST AND SLOW*, 2011 Based on research and experiments in psychology with the help of his former colleague, Amos Tversky, this book by Daniel Kahneman must play a vital part in this history. It also extends the recent Spinoza-inspired work of the American psychologist, Daniel Gilbert.

In fact, Kahneman seems to reserve the term 'assumption' for working assumptions, which are made consciously. But he very much does go into the question of how intuitive thinking can cause error and considers this a vital, recurring question. Whereas Spinoza had termed intuitive thinking 'belief', and Bain used 'belief' or 'assumption', Kahneman uses the phrase 'jumping to conclusions'. He reminds us of Danny Kaye's remark about a difficult woman of his acquaintance: 'her favourite position is beside herself and her favourite sport is jumping to conclusions.' As we've seen, there are many synonyms for the word 'assumption'. Kahneman's choice is perhaps the most vivid.

As I mentioned earlier, this phrase – 'jumping to conclusions' – implies both speed of thought and that there is a gap of some kind in the process. Kahneman considers it to be an apt description of what he calls 'System One', the first 'half' of human thinking, the 'Fast' thinking of the book's title. Kahneman recognises System One as 'the hero of this book'. The second half is System Two. We all of us have these two sides to our mind. These terms were already being widely used by psychologists, at least since 2000, but Kahneman tells us that 'he goes further than most in this book, which you can read as a psychodrama with two characters'.

I now attempt to paraphrase Kahneman's understanding of what he calls 'System One'. I highlight in bold its essential characteristics. Indeed he has found it useful to personify System One as a heroic character, with recognisable strengths and weaknesses. This character springs into action whenever we meet a new situation, whether it be a person, threat, environment, surprise, any new stimulus: the list is endless. System One then **automatically** attempts to believe the situation and to build a plausible understanding. It works **unconsciously**. Spinoza had described 'belief as 'automatic, effortless and passive' some three centuries earlier.

If System One becomes uncertain, it will **gamble** on the answer, which will be influenced mostly by recent events and the current context. But the uncertainty was never conscious. System One is **unavoidable**, it cannot be switched off. It is **gullible**. It is **vulnerable** to the 'halo effect' which exaggerates the emotional coherence of an idea, thus tending to simplify reality.

All the above functions feed into what System One is best at: building the best possible 'story', but without allowing for missing evidence or troubling to search for it in the memory. It seems to be more important to build a coherent and consistent story, than for the story to be complete. Mankind yearns to find patterns, explanations. An instant example! While writing this book I was living in close proximity to a lively mountain beck in Cumberland. Each evening, though it was winter, I had the garden door ajar so as to enjoy the complex repetitive sound of the playful water. After a while I heard people talking outside and went to investigate, as the village was especially empty in the winter of 2021. Nobody there! After a few of these fruitless searches I realised that my System One had searched for pattern, for explanation, for a story, however simple – and after a while had found voices in the pattern of the water. It happened most evenings, if the water level was lively enough.

As System One builds its story it also **suppresses** doubt and ambiguity. Kahneman has an acronym for the story-building role of System One: WYSIATI – What You See Is All There Is. WYSIATI allows us quickly to accept a statement or story as true. Thus we can think fast through a complex situation, even if we don't have all the information. More information would likely spoil the story. Yet, for us, this may also be the point of maximum danger!

The building of a coherent story is probably the same as Spinoza's 'belief', which then allows further assessment. Assumption is bound to play a part, and may turn out later to be false. But that's a price mostly worth paying, because without some assumption, the belief would build more slowly and less clearly.

The **speed** of System One is a vital characteristic. Its thinking is not a linear process; rather, it is a sudden cascade of information which is simultaneously being reorganised. The speed of System One strongly suggests that it evolved to provide a continuous assessment of the dangers and uncertainties faced by earlier mankind, from the ancient savannah of East Africa to the cities and societies of the Mediterranean and the East, for example.

Sir Francis Bacon seems, in retrospect, to have been well aware of what Kahneman calls 'System One', to judge from his Aphorisms 45–48 in the *Novum Organum*.

Assumptions and risk My paraphrasing finished, it's important to emphasise that the assumption-making of System One is mainly a good thing! It is an evolutionary ability of our mind under any kind of pressure. Most of the time these quite accurate assumptions work well, and therefore may never need to come to our attention. It is the false assumptions that we get to know about, sooner or later.

Since they are made in the twinkling of an eye, unconsciously, how can we learn to recognise what is going on? Well, it may just help if we know that a distinct mechanism for jumping to conclusions *does exist*. Also, by being familiar with the many varieties of assumption and related words and expressions (listed in this book), we might better recognise such moments.

Then there are circumstances which increase the risk of making assumptions of the less accurate type, that is, 'false'. When we are under stress or in a hurry; when timid or shy; when embarrassment looms; or from being in a group mindset. Winston Churchill, a sworn foe of assumption, was suspicious of 'mental inertia, an August holiday mood and a refusal to confront facts with a steady eye'.

In a familiar, predictable situation, making assumptions may be fairly safe; but in an unfamiliar situation, or when time is running out, and especially when the stakes are high, it can be positively dangerous.

Since I met Kahneman's character, 'System One', I am more aware of my own instant assessments, and with a bit of luck and a following wind, I may be able to slow down my thoughts… to double-check… to say 'hang on a moment…' (That should take us to the territory of System Two, of which more later.)

I am also more aware of periods when ideas or solutions to existing problems start popping out of the blue. It feels as if System One is still at work. Fresh air seems to be useful here.

But I don't think we can ascribe assumptions entirely to System One. There are many more complex assumptions, as we've seen in these pages, which evolve more gradually and involve more people, even whole societies. The action of System One, perhaps millions of System Ones in loose co-ordination of thinking, must surely play some part, though.

Memory Experience suggests that our memories can be reshaped. For example I have often noticed that, returning to a place previously visited, and which has made an impression, I now find that an important element is missing or has changed its position or has changed in some other rather haunting way. By this means I've created a very fine but non-existent square in Paris. In the old town of Geneva my memory shifted a restaurant from one side of a street to the other, quite a common experience, I imagine.

How does this happen? Here is Arnold Lunn, at the end of a long January ski-tour in the Bernese Oberland:

> But the serene sunlight of the heights still lingered in our minds. We clung to the day that was dying, as if loth to cross the frontier which divides vision from retrospect, things seen to things remembered. Meanwhile memory was already busying herself with her task of selection, choosing that which was to be secured against the rust of time…

'Memory… already busying herself': does that sound like the quick automatic action of System One? Does that mean that memory can evolve as a kind of unstable assumption about the past? Is the search for a coherent story still going on, even in memory?

A brief look at System Two When one becomes painfully aware that an assumption is exploding, or slowly crumbling in the light of later evidence, System Two is required. This is the 'hang on a moment' type of thinking, when we recognise, reflect, modify or even reject a false assumption. 'Unbelieve' was Spinoza's term.

But the process is very different to System One. It is not automatic, so the conscious mind must initiate the thinking. This is the 'thinking slow' of the book's title. System Two can be lazy, for it requires mental and perhaps moral effort. System Two is in charge of doubting and unbelieving. Sir Francis Bacon calls it 'weighing and considering'. It is also often engaged on other matters. Kahneman has run experiments that show that when we are otherwise engaged, we are more prone to believe anything else that arises.

The two Systems in practice Over longer periods of time one can imagine that the alternating interaction of both systems may yield valuable knowledge.

System Two lets us think in a considered, more rational and wider way. 'Reason works best in a blend which includes not just logic but experience, evidence, judgement, subtlety of thought and sensitivity to ambiguity.' Julian Baggini, *A History of Truth*.

MISCELLANY OF ASSUMPTIONS ENCOUNTERED IN THE LAST TWO DECADES

I collected these examples from newspapers, journals and other sources and from my own experience.

USEFUL ADVICE I don't know how long this neat little mantra has been going around. I came across it when I worked as a management consultant: 'Don't ass-u-me – it will make an ass of you and me.'

ISSUES IN AMBRIDGE I stopped listening to *The Archers* about ten years ago, after half a lifetime of catching it now and then. But remarks like this were easily made: 'Oh, sorry Jill – I assumed you were happy with that…'

In one episode Linda Snell and another stalwart of Ambridge – I think it was Jim – were examining a projected road scheme. It contained a list of councillors and other members of the official body involved. All very nice. But, asked Linda, was that a *complete* list? Well, no, it was not, and therefore the villagers might be at a disadvantage as objectors. Jim then questioned the statistics of a traffic flow survey and it turned out that there was no source for the figures. Thus the risk of making two assumptions was detected by two local people, who had perhaps acquired a sceptical cast of mind from previous experience.

FATAL ASSUMPTION WITHIN A FAMILY An assumption can certainly have fatal consequences for individuals and families. The following recent true story, reported in an English broadsheet, is simple and painful. A fourteen-year-old boy with an interest in computer games had met up online with a young man of nineteen. His parents met this youth and after discovering that he was 'anti-government, anti-church, anti-everything' they banned their son from communicating with him. They reported his location to the police. The policewoman who took the call was 'detached', according to the boy's mother. But when they heard nothing back, 'we assumed the young man didn't pose the threat we feared.' That was how it was reported in the broadsheet.

Sometime later the boy went to visit a 'schoolfriend', but in fact travelled to the suspicious address, where he was fatally stabbed in the neck. Those are the bare facts. Was one simple assumption all it took to allow a family tragedy? In such a painful context I naturally hesitate to ask – but one must – why didn't they check the matter with the so-far non-communicating police?

Assumptions about trivial matters are likely to be made without causing much damage; but where the stakes are higher, the greater must be the need to question any assumption that has been made – and to act.

PARTY WALL PROBLEM New neighbours had moved into the next-door house of the London terrace in which we lived at the time. After a while some building work was heard. By the Saturday afternoon tremendous thumpings were shaking the party wall and the sound of falling debris was beyond a joke. I went outside and peered through their open front door. In the dusty half-light I discerned the figure of a 'mad axeman' knocking the bejasus out of various beams and walls. I immediately phoned the borough planning department. The officer I spoke to briskly assumed it was nothing of significance and did not wish to investigate. Eventually I persuaded him to visit and see for himself.

Later that afternoon he called me: 'Thank you so much for insisting that I make a visit; I have put an immediate stop-order on the work.'

Things were duly sorted out over the next few weeks and harmony was more or less restored.

'WHEN THEY DIDN'T CALL BACK...' This phrase seems to be a common indicator that an assumption has ended badly. This brief tale was the subject of a letter to a broadsheet in 2019. It concerned a prestigious

Michelin-starred restaurant in West London.

A customer had booked a table for dinner for himself, his wife and five guests. Not long after, his wife was taken ill. He contacted the restaurant to cancel, at what was short notice. The restaurant pointed out that there was a cancellation fee of £125 per person, but said they would try to sell the bookings to others. 'When they didn't call back we assumed that they had sold the other bookings.' The generous host then decided to book his guests into a cheaper restaurant. But the first restaurant had *not* managed to sell the old bookings and thus cancellation fees amounting to £875 still had to be paid. A pricey assumption for most of us. Surely, when people don't call back as expected, one should investigate…

MARRIAGE AND RELATIONSHIP Studies in the United States have shown that between 73 and 90 per cent of the population believe that there is a soulmate 'out there' waiting for them. This seems to be a common belief in the UK too. But this unrealistic expectation or romantic idyll can be risky, as further research has shown that marriages made under this illusion more easily collapse, with the participants perhaps moving on to the next illusion. By contrast, it seems that less romantic marriages, in which both partners realise that the relationship must be nourished and actively worked at, are the ones that last longer and are more satisfying.

HOMEOPATHY There appear to be two basic assumptions in homeopathy: 'Like cures like': for example, onions as a cure for the tearful eyes of hay fever, or coffee as a cure for insomnia; secondly, 'Less is more' which promotes extreme dilution of the remedy. Their perhaps appealing symmetry does not make them logical and they have never been proven clinically. They are unwarranted assumptions.

In 2017 the NHS banned the funding of homeopathic cures. In November 2019 the director of the NHS, Simon Stevens, attacked the Society of Homeopaths and recommended their exclusion from the

NHS register of medical organisations. In particular he pointed out their dangerous opposition to vaccination.

Debate about the subject seems to muddle up scientifically proven botanical medicines with homeopathic remedies. But the real distinction of homeopathy lies in *how* its remedies are applied. It was devised in 1796 by Samuel Hahnemann in an era before the discovery of bacteria and viruses. It has long been considered by the mainstream medical community to be quackery and pseudoscience. Although the remedies themselves are harmless, the accompanying undermining of mainstream medicine is dangerous to people who are ill.

HEALTH SCREENING The political pressure on the NHS in recent years has been to push for 'early diagnosis', especially of dementia. It sounds so plausible and sensible to try to 'catch it early'. It is only too easy to take for granted that this is a good thing.

But once put into practice the whole screening operation becomes too complicated and the results have been very disappointing and often unclear. People who visit their doctor find they are being screened for other illnesses they were never aware of. People who are well become 'patients' and may be sent for tests that are unnecessary, unreliable and even dangerous. Many senior practitioners do not recommend screening, nor the five-year health checks for those over forty.

Without going into detail about the paradoxes, distortions and complications that arise through screening, this seems to be a classic case of political initiative making unwarranted assumptions that run far ahead of any evidence. Is it another example of 'too much politics'?

SAD MOMENT ON A NORTHERN FELLSIDE Winding my way up a Lakeland fell a few summers ago I was witness to a painful scene. A young couple, having parked below, exploded into a loud and protracted disagreement about how far to climb up the rather steep hillside. She had perhaps expected a quick burst of fresh air, prior to arriving at the village and perhaps working out a plan over coffee. But her companion was thrusting upwards with all the pent-up vigour of an office worker who has long dreamed of a Cumberland fellside on a fresh sunny morning.

I could readily sympathise with both points of view. I thought of traversing to them and somehow defusing their quarrel. It was horrid to think that their special day out had so soon deteriorated. Arnold Lunn, the great pioneer of mountain life, was of the view that 'To be grumpy on a mountainside is an unforgivable sin'. But by now they were too much vertically apart. Later they seemed to be reunited, in place if not in mind.

Perhaps their individual expectations about the day had differed, undiscussed until too late. I hope they were soon reconciled, by a conversation in which their assumptions about the day were gently resolved.

AN AVALANCHE IN SCOTLAND As the nineteenth-century pioneers in the Alps found, the wilder districts of the world are places where assumptions are inevitable. Even within the smaller scale of the English Lake District, its fells devoid of signposts, it is remarkably easy to set off on a path that appears to lead to your chosen route, only to find further up that it has very different ideas. And British mountain country in winter can be very easily underestimated.

The accident below, in which four of a small group of winter mountain walkers lost their lives, was headlined by a broadsheet as being 'just unlucky'. The victims had been swept down for some thousand feet.

We learn that the walkers were descending from a north-facing ridge into a corrie just before two o'clock in the afternoon. They were thus in the classical location for snow to be transformed by wind into wind-slab, that is, on the leeside of a ridge, on steep ground. And they were very close to the 2–3pm danger window for avalanche, well-recognised in the Alpine world. Wind-slab avalanches are often set off by skiers in the Alps, from the weight of the skier breaking the hard slab of wind-blown snow and releasing fragmented slab downwards. But if you are wearing walking boots, there may be an even greater risk of breaking the slab, the person's weight being focused on a smaller surface area.

A member of the local rescue service suggested that the avalanche was probably triggered by the walkers themselves. He used the term 'a raft of snow'. Both these observations suggest a wind-slab avalanche, a well-known phenomenon in the Alpine world and no doubt in the wind-lashed Scottish Highlands too.

Thus the route and the timing were stacked against this group. We also learn that the avalanche risk given out by the Scottish Avalanche Information Service was rated at 3 out of 5, meaning 'considerable'. They specifically mentioned the presence of wind-slab below north-facing ridges.

These relevant facts are in opposition to that glaring and dangerous assumption, namely, that this accident was 'just unlucky'. That is fatalistic, as if the considerable present-day knowledge of snow and avalanche, first studied systematically over a hundred years ago, had no part to play. Such a headline suggests that nothing can be foreseen and avoided, it's just a matter of luck. Of course, risk cannot be wholly eliminated by snow and avalanche craft, but it can certainly be mitigated, as generations of mountaineers and ski-mountaineers have learnt. Of the other broadsheet reports, one highlighted the avalanche forecast and quoted the chief officer of the Scottish Mountaineering Council recommending that visitors should check forecasts and assess the risk; another quoted a chief inspector of Police Scotland on the importance of using the website of the SAIS. Of course, in the immediate aftermath of such an event, the reporting will focus on the human tragedy and detailed analysis will come only in time, though I have been unable to find any retrospective opinion.

As for other assumptions that may be made in the winter mountains, several types can be suspected when a group is involved. For example, a group may come to trust a leader with whom they have been safe in the past, leading to complacency or an uncritical frame of mind. Or an individual member of the group may assume that others have already weighed up the risks sufficiently. If a date has been fixed in advance and members have travelled some distance to form the group, as happened in the case above, it may be too disappointing to change the plan in favour of caution. Or perhaps there is no leader, and individuals may be unwilling to point out dangers of which they have an inkling – but no systematic knowledge. A more outspoken member may scorn the doubts of others.

But this is merely to scratch the surface of a complex situation.

AN ILLUSION OF RISING GROUND All who walk on the hills will have learnt the hard way that a slope, seen from its starting point below, has a seductive inbuilt deception: that it is not so steep, really, and may even look quite welcoming. This assumption is gradually dispersed during the climb, but by then you've put too much effort into the project and don't want to waste it – I think this is called the 'sunk-cost fallacy' – and so one just keeps at it. An undignified scramble at the top may await you, deceived yet again! But at least this deception helps us to get going in the first place.

This happens partly because from below you can only see limited surfaces of the slope. There can be much hidden ground, 'dead ground' to the military, caused by uneven terrain. It also happens because the top to bottom dimension of the hillside is squeezed into a narrow angle of vision when you are at the foot of the hill.

This is why holiday photos of apparently impressive mountains are usually disappointing. To convey the mountain at its most imposing, I've found from experiment that you need to be at an opposite point at more than half the height of the subject mountain. That mountain now soars up to a more impressive grandeur because of the larger angle of vision you have gained.

AN ILLUSION IN SKIING Descending a ski run often involves approaching a steeper section. All that can be seen is the snow horizon. The mind, lacking any evidence of what lies beyond, seems automatically to treat this approaching drop as 'the end of the world'. But the expected horrifying plunge generally turns out to be only a few degrees steeper... though I have known exceptions to this rule, much to the amusement of friends who witnessed the spectacular and chaotic results of my flight through the air.

THE QUALIFIED PILOT ASSUMPTION I've heard several versions of this story, including one from an RAF pilot. Perhaps such tall stories get spread as a useful myth.

A cameraman dashes to the local airfield – this is in the United States – where he had been told that a plane awaited him. He needed to take some aerial shots of raging forest fires. As he parked, a plane was revving up outside the hangar. He hurled on his kit, jumped aboard and shouted to the pilot 'Let's go!' Somewhat unsteadily they rumbled onto the runway and took off. 'Now make some low passes over that hillside; I've got to get some close-ups of the fires back to the office fast,' said our impulsive hero. After a moment of silence, the man with the joystick in his hand stuttered, 'So I guess you're not my instructor?'

THE KITTIHAWK EXCHANGE A British aircraft museum made a transaction in 2015 in which they apparently handed over to Egypt, through a restoration company in Essex, a Spitfire of considerable value. This was done in return for the salvage of a Kittyhawk P40. This fighter aircraft had crashed in the Egyptian desert during the Second World War.

The museum seem to have made an optimistic assumption that this would be a straightforward matter, for the Spitfire was transferred to the restoration company *before* the salvaging operation in Egypt was complete. The risk of legal and bureaucratic delays and blockages, such as are not uncommonly encountered in foreign countries, let alone in a turbulent country such as Egypt at that time, seems not have counted for much.

In the event, the retrieved Kittyhawk got as far as El Alamein in a container, where it was impounded behind a wall of impenetrable bureaucracy, coincident with the overthrow of President Mubarak. After a few more years the Kittyhawk was found on display (still legally belonging to Egypt) at the El Alamein Military Museum near Alexandria, in a gruesome 'restoration' that has left British aircraft historians quivering. As for the Spitfire handed over to Egypt, the restoration company has since gone into receivership and, as of 2018, the whereabouts of the Spitfire is apparently not known.

PATRIOTISM Is there now a commonly held assumption in some circles that nationalism and patriotism are more or less the same thing? And equally embarrassing? But there is a distinct difference between them, made very clear by George Orwell: 'Nationalism is inseparable from the desire for power. Patriotism is of its nature defensive, both militarily and culturally.' And I would humbly suggest that patriotic feeling about one's own country can furnish us with sympathy for the patriotic feelings held in other countries. Nationalism, though, is associated with the more extreme ends of the political scale, fascism and communism, and has no interest in the nurturing of sympathy for anywhere else. Charles de Gaulle expressed the difference as 'Patriotism is when love of your own people comes first: nationalism, when hate for people other than your own comes first.'

Does a related assumption lurk in the oft-quoted words of Dr Johnson: 'Patriotism is the last refuge of the scoundrel.' This was specifically addressed to William Pitt the Elder, whom Johnson considered was guilty of a false patriotism. But has his remark also been taken to mean that patriotism is itself scoundrel-ish? This was certainly not Johnson's view.

THE EUROPEAN UNION The most significant and controversial change since the turn of the century has been, probably, the development of the Euro, in force from 2002. In an article for *The Times* in 2013, Gavin Hewitt identified the underlying dangerous assumption: that Germany would be less dominant once the Deutschmark was taken away. But the Deutschmark had actually helped to keep Germany balanced, through a flexible exchange rate. But once all states used the Euro and were unable to use the balancing mechanism of setting their own exchange rates and interest rates, Germany's strength became even more clear! 'The currency that was intended to bind Germany into Europe has ended up with the coronation of Germany as the dominant power.' Too much faith was put only in the currency, ignoring the deeper reality of the German work ethic and German technological success.

Meanwhile, Monnet's original idea from 1917 has been developing for over a century. But things have now overreached so far that EU officials no longer bother to hide the imminence of the United States of Europe. Centralisation of financial policies is ever closer, exploiting the crises of the Euro in Mediterranean Europe.

We have seen or heard the President of the European Commission, Jean-Claude Juncker, now retired, asserting with horror how the flames of national resentment have flared up in some countries of the EU. But he seems to assume that these flames can be doused with even more EU centralisation, when it is the reduction of democracy in a more centralised EU that has caused the problem in the first place.

Having in 1957 started the EU juggernaut on its relentless forward path, was there any instruction about how to stop it? I didn't find any in the Treaty of Rome. As Rory Sutherland has expressed the problem in a recent *Spectator*: the EU had the same problem as the Archduke Franz Ferdinand's motor car: it was very difficult to put it in reverse.

More and more Brussels!
A particularly notable part of the mechanism is the use of crises within the EU. The founders expected these, but realised that the subsequent treaties could be used to draw even more power from the member states to the federal centre. And there certainly have been some very useful crises in recent years. This gradual relentless process is known as 'treaty creep'. At the time of writing, the latest crisis has formed around the distribution of vaccines.

This whole project seems to have exploited the obscurity and impenetrability of complex institutions. It has created a hopeless atmosphere in which one can only cling to probably unreliable assumptions. And the mind-numbing dullness of the subject – I am astonished, dear reader, that you have not yet nodded off with Euroboredom – repels the investigation of all but the most determined observers, such as Daniel Hannan, Christopher Booker, Richard North and others.

Peace…
An oft-heard assumption is that the European project is the source of peace in post-War Europe. Yes, gradual co-operative steps were taken by some nations, but these are dwarfed by far greater initiatives. The Allied victory in 1945 and the demilitarisation of Germany happened twelve years ahead of the Treaty of Rome. By then it was the Soviet Union, not Germany, that had become the potential aggressor, held in check by the signature of the United States on the North Atlantic Treaty, 4 April 1949. Then there was the vast support of the 'Marshall Plan' (The OEEC) set up by the American General, George Marshall, which allowed the gradual return of prosperity to the European nations. Without the Marshall Plan, noted Churchill, the seeds of communism might have grown at a deadly pace amongst post-war misery and ruin.

The historian Antony Beevor refers to this EU-as-the-source-of-peace assumption as one of the fattest *canards* ever reared in Brussels.

RICHARD III AND THE MYSTERY OF THE TWO PRINCES Richard's remains were discovered by Philippa Langley, of the Richard III Society, in 2012 at the site of the Greyfriars monastery in Leicester. The King had been removed there after the Battle of Bosworth. But until the time and place of the fate of the two princes is determined, the reputation of Richard cannot be reclaimed. The Richard III Society has now launched a second venture: The Missing Princes Project. The society is clearly and squarely presenting this research as a battle for the proven truth. It hopes thereby to prevail over conventional wisdom, based only on the flimsy foundations of hearsay, rumour and political propaganda. The society is the foe of a tyrannical and remarkably long-standing assumption.

The society has categorised the project as a 'cold case' investigation, which will follow the principles and techniques of modern policing. This will include ABC methodology:

Accept nothing. **B**elieve nobody. **C**hallenge everything.

They are thus furthering the work of previous researchers and in particular the work of Alan Grant, the bedridden Scotland Yard man in Josephine Tey's unputdownable detective novel of 1951, *The Daughter of Time* ('Truth is the daughter of time', Sir Francis Bacon). In their reading list the Society recommends this novel as a 'very accessible' introduction to the mystery.

In the words of the Patron, the present Duke of Gloucester, 'the society derives from the belief that the truth is more powerful than lies; a faith that even after all these centuries the truth is important.'

ARE 'WORKING ASSUMPTIONS' DANGEROUS? In 2016 The World Bank's chief economist, Paul Romer, published *The Trouble with Macro-economics*. He makes a strongly worded case, but at the heart of his criticism lurks a quagmire of working assumptions. These are the ones that are made consciously.

The World Bank man declares that for thirty years, macro-economics – the study of large-scale growth and decline, boom and bust – has gone backwards. The practitioners have pretended to base their conclusions on revered authority, deep theory, a pretence of knowledge and theoretical deduction. But this hides the fact that they are still relying on assumptions behind those theories, 'working assumptions' hidden away from view.

Reading the review of Romer's book I encountered a dubious quarter of the financial world where these obscure assumptions are muddying the macro-economic argument: high-handed assumptions; naked assumptions (but clothed in fine theoretical robes); flat assumptions; shallow assumptions; questionable assumptions; arbitrary assumptions (particularly nasty, it seems); unappealing assumptions. Romer declares that between the quaking morass of these assumptions and the shiny new proofs of macro-economics there is enough mathematical 'blah, blah, blah' to hide the assumptions' sinister role.

Traditionally, a working assumption would be labelled by mathematicians, philosophers, and other researchers as 'A priori', meaning 'assumed without investigation'.

GUILTY UNTIL PROVED INNOCENT – BISHOP GEORGE BELL In 2015, fifty-seven years after George Bell's death, his former diocese announced that Bell had sexually abused a child between 1949 and 1953. They had paid compensation to the complainant.

The salient fact about this case is the shocking reversal of the usual legal position. In English law there is a presumption of innocence until proved guilty. But the diocese, backed by the Church of England, made an assumption that Bell was guilty. There has been no due legal process, only an internal investigation. There has been no proven verdict of guilt of sexual abuse, only what they called 'the balance of probability'. Only the complainant's untested testimony was used to decide the case. No legal advocate for the deceased bishop was brought in.

All this was greeted with so much anger that the Archbishop of Canterbury agreed to an independent inquiry. The Carlile Inquiry concluded in October 2017 that the process used to investigate the claim had been worthless. In November the Church announced that publication of the inquiry's report would be delayed by a few months. In the end the Church accepted the report, but still refused Bishop Bell the presumption of innocence. The Archbishop then declared that a 'significant cloud is left over his name'. For this he has been heavily criticised by senior lawyers and historians involved in the case or who are concerned at the rejection of the presumption of innocence. There have been calls for his resignation from within and outside the Church. As of May 2021 the situation remains unchanged.

It seems that the Church of England has put itself in the classic situation identified by John Stuart Mill. By rejecting due legal process, it has silenced or ignored any differing opinion, seeming to justify this action by the depth of immorality of the alleged crime. It has undertaken to decide the question for others. The Church has therefore made an assumption of infallibility. We may recall that John Stuart Mill's three examples of this stance made victims of Socrates, Christ himself and the early Christians under Marcus Aurelius.

ASSUMPTIONS IN THE BOEING 737 MAX DISASTERS, 2018–19 In order to give greater power to the 'new generation' of the 737, larger engines were needed. They had to be placed further forward from the wing and higher from the ground. But this arrangement increased aerodynamically the likelihood of a stall. I cannot find out *how much* greater the risk was, but to encumber an aircraft destined for large production with a greater risk of stalling seems questionable.

In the ensuing scandal many dangerous assumptions and errors were found to have been made, but here I focus only on what seem most fundamental.

To lower the risk of stalling, a new software system, MCAS, added discreetly, would automatically force the nose of the plane down by adjustment of the tail stabiliser or 'trim'. The system would know of the stall danger from sensors that measure the angle at which the aircraft is rising relative to the oncoming airflow. This is termed the 'Angle of Attack' (AoA). If the AoA reaches 15 degrees there is risk of stalling; at 18 to 20 degrees it is classed as dangerous.

Usual practice is to have two or three sensors. Sensors may give different data, and are known to have deviated by 20 degrees. With three sensors there is the chance of a two to one verdict, if one sensor is faulty. With two sensors you know there is a difference of data, but not which one is at fault. But on the new version, the 737 MAX, Boeing decided that, even if only one of the sensors was functioning, the MCAS could still accept the data.

But a lot can go wrong with these sensors, which are vulnerably exposed on the fuselage: icing-up, bird strikes, unintentional damage during maintenance, damage from passenger ramps, or they may just be plain faulty. Boeing's decision meant that if one lone sensor erroneously reports an imminent risk of stall, the nose of the plane will be pushed down and a level flight could become a descent, or even a dive if the over-riding of the pilots' decisions persists.

In the light of this, to rely on one sensor to measure the AoA seems to be either an astonishing assumption of reliability – or the deliberate taking of a known high risk. And this, in an industry wedded to checklists and the avoidance of assumption-making.

A related assumption was made by Boeing that the pilots did not need to know about the MCAS system, it would just operate 'in the background'. According to the *Report of the House Committee on*

Transportation, March 2020, 'Boeing… assumed that pilots, who were unaware of the system's existence in most cases, would be able to mitigate any malfunction.' The report also tells us that Boeing failed to classify MCAS as a 'safety-critical system', which would have led to greater scrutiny during the 737 MAX's certification.

The maiden flight of the 737 MAX had been in January 2016. Soon there were reports of mysterious Aircraft Nose Down (AND) alerts from pilots of the aircraft, and also in the simulators. In October 2018 a Lion Air 737 MAX arrived at Jakarta by night from Bali, reporting a traumatic event for passengers in which the aircraft had flown 'like a roller-coaster'. The next morning, twelve minutes after take-off, this aircraft dived into the Java Sea. Yet there was no immediate investigation into the MCAS system, despite a warning from the Federal Aviation Authority that 'it posed an unacceptably high risk of catastrophic failure'. In March 2019 an Ethiopian Airlines 737 MAX dived to the ground at 700mph, six minutes after taking off from Addis Ababa. 346 people died in these two catastrophes, in which there were no survivors.

Simulation videos of the cockpit problems faced by the pilots of those two aircraft are unpleasantly gripping. On both flights, even while still on the take-off runway, the pilots received faulty, contradictory data, including data about the AoA. Finally there was a chilling sequence of AND alerts, alternating with Aircraft Nose Up commands from the pilot, producing the roller-coaster effect. Eventually the ANDs succeeded in forcing each plane into a fatal steep dive.

Boeing's reputation and share price have suffered severely. A 'culture' of concealment has been uncovered. In November 2020 the Federal Aviation Authority finally gave the green light – after twenty months – for the 737 MAX to resume commercial flights. After a criminal investigation by the US Justice Department, an agreement was reached in January 2021 by which Boeing would pay compensation of over two and half billion dollars. Boeing employees were also accused of choosing the path of profit over candour by concealing material information from the FAA. The overall cost to Boeing of the grounding of the 737 MAX was estimated at over eighteen billion dollars.

PART TWO

NON-CHRONOLOGICAL

1. ASSUMPTIONS FROM MISLEADING LANGUAGE It is surprising how assumptions can lurk within phrases and even in single words.

– Does the word 'fracking' sound rather aggressive, provocative and even slightly obscene? Might one assume it was something rather nasty? It might be natural to feel a bias or prejudice against it, whatever it meant. In fact it derives from 'hydraulic fracturing', invented in 1947. Perhaps 'hydraulic gas release' (HGR) would have been less controversial, and a lot less trouble to the industry.

– 'Off the table!' In the debates over Brexit, certain politicians and pundits were often heard to demand that a 'no-deal Brexit must be taken off the table!' But that it could be taken off the table, was a false assumption. A no-deal Brexit was never 'on the table' in the first place; it was just the automatic non-negotiable result of not being able to make a deal with the EU. What those politicians and pundits really meant, I suppose, was that 'we must have a deal whatever the cost.'

– From my early schooldays *Our Island Story* was considered a respectable introduction to British history. The author was H.E. Marshall, an authoritative, balanced, reassuring sort of name, perhaps. I don't think at the time that we were biased, God forbid, against women writers – I had already admired Dorothy L. Sayers, Richmal Crompton and many others – yet it was still a bit of a surprise, many years later, when H.E. Marshall turned out to be a woman. I wonder if it was her initials that led us to think otherwise?

– The word 'economy' is nowadays taken to mean the system of money, but in fact derives from Greek, meaning 'The management of a family; the government of a household' (Dr Johnson's Dictionary). This became particularly relevant during the recent Coronavirus pandemic, for a division was made between our health and the economy, though they are both interlocking and essential elements in the management of our society.

– 'Getting away from it all'. This common expression may easily lead to the classic mistake of moving to the deep country or a remote island, only to find that an isolated life will make you, some of the time, at least, even more dependent on your neighbours and small local community. The choice and privacy of an English suburb may then be seen in a new light.

– We shouldn't assume that a crisis is an entirely bad thing. The word comes from the Greek 'krisis', which means 'a decisive moment, especially in the progress of a disease'. Thus crises, like every cloud, may have something of a silver lining, an opportunity for constructive recovery. We may recall the words of a former mayor of Chicago, Rahm Emmanuel: 'Never let a good crisis go to waste.'

– I described a publishing intervention in the case of Darwin's *Origin of Species*, back in 1859. Quite recently I noticed a striking repetition. Listening to an interview with the Darwinian geneticist Richard Dawkins, I was astonished to hear him casually mention that the title of his book *The Selfish Gene* wasn't his own idea – but that of the publisher. Well, no individual gene is capable of being selfish, as it lacks consciousness. And the mechanism is so much more complex than that. Dawkins' conception was, in my humble opinion, simplified in a similar way to that of Darwin's. And yet he seemed quite happy about it.

– Can an assumption be made from a misleading use of metaphor? Yes.

Public Concern at Work is an organisation aiming to obtain complete protection for whistleblowers. But the journalist Charles Moore points out that the metaphor 'whistleblower' is misleading here. The word comes from the action of the referee in football, who works to a code of rules and regulations. (Before that, it described the way British police alerted the public to crime or disorder.)

An assumption is thus formed that a whistleblower in a company is acting correctly and fairly. But a whistleblower is not a referee, but a player, a person with a stake in the organisation, a participant with no obligation to be fair or accurate. Moore concludes that the matter is a moral problem far more complex than PCW seems to think.

However, I have learnt that in the NHS there are staff employed officially as 'whistleblowers'. Are they genuine referees?

– 'Accident of birth'. This phrase may be heard around any new arrival in royal and aristocratic circles or other distinguished families. Well, there is certainly a birth – but where is the 'accident'? This phrase seems to be based on a bizarre assumption that births are taking place in some kind of giant casino whirling with roulette wheels and that thousands of babies are going to be randomly allotted to various families, just as the silver roulette ball rolls randomly into a numbered slot.

But that is not what happens. A baby can only appear in the 'slot', as it were, of its own family; there is nothing accidental about its appearance there. It is no accident that Prince George, for example, is the son of Prince William and the Duchess of Cambridge. How could George have appeared in any other family, carrying as he does the amalgamated genetic code of his parents? The phrase has come into being, perhaps, to make any birth into high station seem somehow unfair, just a matter of luck.

2. **HUBRIS IN LARGE ORGANISATIONS** The historian A.J.P. Taylor famously observed that a typical Englishman, up to 1914, might only have

encountered the state through policemen and the Post Office. After each of the world wars the spending of the UK government rose by some 10 per cent, as the role of the state enlarged itself, notably through the welfare state, and in the control of industrial policy.

Is it now the case that government agencies, the public sector, big finance, companies, the media, etc are playing a closer role in our lives? But such larger entities may be fertile ground in which assumptions can grow, especially where there is poor communication and a lack of discussion. Hubris at the top can further exacerbate these unhappy situations.

In the business world of today this dangerous state of mind is becoming better-known. (In the USA and Japan it is known as 'Victory Disease'.) CEOs that become known for their 'star' or 'celebrity' quality are in fact courting disaster. Thus Kevin Sharer, a former boss of Amgen, kept a painting of General Custer in his office specifically as a warning against hubris.

A chief deluded by grandeur is at risk of assuming that the success of the company is mostly down to himself. This may lead to self-promotion, demands for extravagant rewards, the publishing of a premature autobiography or appearance on the cover of business magazines. He may then make mistakes such as over-controlling the company, inhibiting criticism, and making distorted decisions through a loss of perspective.

Hubris might occur as a temporary over-confidence. It can also be a personality disorder consisting of a syndrome of symptoms that may persist beyond the appointment.

In the twenty-first century, I'm afraid that the hubris of Fred Goodwin is one of the more notorious examples, and surprising – for who would be less likely to succumb to the blandishments of hubris than the sober Scottish accountant? He is reported to have been egotistical and bullying, but was given the helm at the Royal Bank of Scotland in 2000. It appears that he was an awkward communicator and obsessed with detail beyond his remit. He micromanaged the building of a new head office, including the redesign of the company's Christmas card.

The bank had just acquired NatWest, a much larger bank, and Goodwin's challenge was to integrate it with RBS. Unfortunately he succeeded, received a knighthood, and the seeds of hubris were thoroughly sown. Hubris reached its highest point in 2007, when Goodwin and his board outbid Barclays to buy ABN Amro. I recall that this transaction allowed RBS to claim that it was now the fourth largest bank in the world! This was surely an example of something being 'too good to be true'.

In fact RBS was already heavy with toxic sub-prime loans; by purchasing ABN without full investigation they soon acquired a great deal more. As in the classical Greek form of hubris, Goodwin's complacency and illusion was fully endorsed by a chorus of the RBS board. Had they all swallowed that prophecy of Thomas the Rhymer about the capitals of Britain? 'York was, London is, Edinburgh shall be, the biggest and bonniest of the three…'

Thus there seems to have been collective hubris as well as individual. The turning point, or *peripeteia*, may have been 7 October 2008 while Goodwin was making a speech in London. The share price of RBS was plunging, its access to funding was frozen and the Chancellor of the Exchequer was called in to take the reins. A gigantic taxpayer-funded rescue of the bank soon followed.

The righteous indignation of Nemesis was clear to see: Goodwin's pension was halved, his knighthood was withdrawn and he became enemy number one in the tabloid press. Shunned by Edinburgh society, he nevertheless avoided the jail sentence and confiscation that his critics called for, because – as Martin van der Weyer in his *Spectator* column observed: 'Risk-taking with the full support of your board of directors is not a criminal offence.'

In February 2020 the name 'Royal Bank of Scotland' was abandoned and the bank reverted to the name NatWest.

3. **FREE SPEECH IN UNIVERSITIES** A report into groupthink in academia was drawn up in 2016 by the Adam Smith Institute. In the academic

world, it pointed out, the proportion of liberal or left-leaning lecturers has been steadily rising since the 1960s, particularly in the social sciences, humanities and the arts. 'Social settings characterised by too little diversity of viewpoint are liable to become afflicted by "groupthink".' The report defines this as 'a dysfunctional atmosphere where key assumptions go unquestioned, dissenting opinions are neutralised and favoured beliefs are sacrosanct.' The likely consequences are:

- systematic biases in scholarship
- defunding of academic research by right-of-centre governments
- curtailment of free speech on university campuses.

'Curtailment of free speech' seems to threaten the whole concept of a university as a place in which the flow of ideas and debate can flourish. The word 'university' comes from the Latin word *universus* meaning 'combined into one'. In the words of John Henry Newman, the university 'is a place where inquiry is pushed forward... and error exposed by the collision of mind with mind, and knowledge with knowledge.' The stagnant alternative is expressed by the American journalist Walter Lippman: 'Where all think alike, no one thinks very much.'

'Groupthink' is in itself a sort of assumption of simplicity in a community of comforting conformity, a view that the world is much simpler than portrayed by others and should not be polluted by alternative views. Groupthink has thus been described as 'a dangerous unanimity'.

Some universities in the UK have seen extraordinary changes. Visiting speakers report that audiences are clearly shocked to come across views that do not fit the groupthink in which they have been immersed. This has been supported by such procedures as: insulating students from any view that might make them 'uncomfortable'; 'trigger warnings' attached to online articles or lectures; and the banning or 'no-platforming' of visiting speakers, even if they have been invited by other students. Areas of the campus are being designated and disinfected as 'safe spaces'. Libraries and reading lists may be sanitised against alternative views.

A foetid, narrow, intolerant environment does not encourage clarity and openness of reasoning. Worse, it has been suggested by Douglas Murray that the pressure to appear to comply with thoughts you don't share is mentally deranging.

Those who silence the chance for others to hear alternative opinions were considered by John Stuart Mill, as seen earlier, to be making 'an assumption of infallibility'. If, he says, our opinions are not 'fully, frequently, and fearlessly discussed' they are 'held as a dead dogma, not a living truth'. And have these universities turned their back on Voltaire's breadth of vision, when he declared 'I disapprove of what you say, but I shall defend to the death your right to say it.' Churchill had a particularly practical view:

Free speech carries with it the evil of all foolish, unpleasant and venomous things that are said, but on the whole we would rather lump them than do away with it.

From the outside it is difficult to measure how widely or deeply this intolerance of opinion has spread within academia, but it has certainly been frequently reported in the British press. For example, in November 2020 a survey made for ADF (Alliance Defending Freedom) International showed that 27 per cent of students had actively hidden their opinions, including political views, when they were at odds with those of tutors. A further 40 per cent withheld opinions on ethical or religious matters for fear of reactions. Toby Young, founder of the Free Speech Union, has claimed being inundated with requests for help from students: 'They thought they'd applied for a university, but they've ended up in a Maoist re-education camp.'

A recent letter to a broadsheet by an alumnus of Cambridge University refers to 'a sinister wave of political correctness' to which the university has surrendered. He recalls the greater diversity of opinion and tolerance during his own three years there. He wonders if he will continue to make donations to his old college unless they can explain 'what they are going to do about removing this PC cancer before it destroys the university's ethos'. He concludes by hoping 'that all Cambridge donors and alumni, *of any political stripe*, [my italics] will do the same. We must save Cambridge.'

The phrase 'political correctness' has had a varied history. Apparently it first surfaced within Germany in the 1930s, as a way of judging the degree to which an individual conformed to the Nazi concept of Aryan racial purity. Its origins are therefore totalitarian. The phrase itself suggests intolerance, that debate is not invited, that an unseen judge knows best. Its re-appearance in America in the late 1980s was in the context of using language to protect groups perceived to be disadvantaged. It now seems to have enlarged its brief, attacking those who are perceived *not* to be disadvantaged. It's as if the fruits of liberal society are being turned into its foundations, on four pillars of 'rights': women's, gay, race and trans.

Could it be that the virus of silenced opinion may thrive in the hothouse of university, but die away in the more realistic and varied opinions found in the day-to-day world? Not any longer it would seem. A dangerous school of thought has established something known as 'Theory', consisting of 'post-modern' principles such as the impossibility of knowledge and the structure of power. It seems that these ideas have begun to escape from the orbit of academia and are now classed as 'applied post-modernism'. This seeks by practical local disruptions to undermine the thought and confidence of wider society.

What can be done?
The University of Buckingham has set up, in the words of its Vice-Chancellor Sir Anthony Seldon, 'an institute to challenge conventional wisdom whenever it raises its head most unjustifiably and dangerously'. Opinion would not be silenced, though the proposed institute would not

allow the promotion of hatred and violence to qualify as 'opinion'. John Stuart Mill himself was clear, as we saw, about the difference between liberty of Thought and liberty of Action. Liberty of Action must to some degree be constrained by any society for its own protection from harm. Even free speech must reach its limits, as famously expressed by Justice Oliver Wendell Holmes: 'Free speech would not protect a man falsely shouting Fire! in a theatre and causing a panic.'

Meanwhile, in early December 2020 the senior members of Cambridge University voted down, by a ratio of four to one, some amendments proposed by the university. The members considered that the amendments would compromise academic independence and undermine free speech: in particular, the amendment that academics should show 'respect' to the opinions of others.

There at last seems to be the beginning of a reaction against groupthink and political correctness.

4. THE VOCABULARY OF ASSUMPTION

A. Nouns and verbs that are synonyms or near-synonyms of 'assumption' or 'to assume'. This list is by no means cast in stone. It is more 'work in progress'.

acceptance	credulity
acquiescence	faith
all right on the night	fallacy
article of faith	foregone conclusion
belief	generalisation
castles in the air, in Spain	hypothesis
conceit	imagination
conjecture	impression
conventional wisdom	intuition

jump to conclusion

leap in the dark

leap of faith

preconception

prejudice

presumption

received wisdom

self-deception

self-delusion

snap judgement

speculation

supposition

sweeping statement

take as gospel

take as read

take for granted

take to mean

take up

theory

wishful thinking

B. Other words and phrases that may suggest a risk of assumption:

apocryphal (doubtful
  authenticity)

benefit of the doubt

best of intentions

bias

canard (a false report)

careless

cherished opinion

cognitive illusion

comfortable

commonplace

conclusion

confidence

consensus

deception, deceptive

deem

destiny

doubtless

dream

elephant in the room

euphemism

expecting

*fable convenue (*convenient
  fiction*)*

fait accompli (all done and
  dusted)

false narrative

falsehood

fancy

fantasy

feel

fingers crossed

first impression

good intentions (paving the
  road to hell…)

gospel truth

gossip
guarantee
guess, rough guess,
   guesstimate, informed guess
gullible
gut feeling
head in the sand
hearsay
hope for the best
hubris
hunch
hypnotic
idée fixe
ignorant
ill thought out
illusion
infallible
insensibly
intuitive
it is written
it'll blow over
it's in a good cause
it's fate
legendary
mantra
mirage
misleading
misplaced confidence
mistake
myth
narrative

neglect
no doubt…
obvious
opinion
optimism
orthodox
over by Christmas
over-confidence
overlook
parrot-talk
perception
platitude
predisposition
premise
pride
point of view
postulate
reputedly
rose-tinted
sleepwalk
supine
surmise
surprise
suspect
thoughtless
too good to be true
uncritical acceptance
unquestioningly
unrealistic
viewy

C. Types of assumption

agreeable assumption	high-handed
arbitrary	hubristic
blind	ignorant
bold	ill-informed
brave	implausible
breathtaking	impulsive
careless	incorrect
casual	inexplicable
category	instinctive
cherished	insulting
comfortable	irresponsible
complacent	long-standing
convenient	ludicrous
conventional	misleading
dangerous	mistaken
disastrous	naïve
dubious	oft-heard
easy	optimistic
expensive	outdated
extravagant	over-confident
fatal	persisting
general	popular
glaring	proverbial
glib	questionable
gross	rash
groundless	reckless
group	romantic
haughty	scandalous
heroic	seductive

simple

speculative

strange

superficial

sweeping

tragic

unavoidable

unchallenged

underlying

unexamined

uninformed

unjustified

unquestioned

unspoken

untested

unwarranted

unvoiced

vacuous

vast

widespread

wishful

worrying

TO SUMMARISE

THE PROBLEM Dear Reader, Having made this long journey through the stories, episodes, crises and other examples, I hope I've been able to show you that the false assumption – in its various types and guises – remains a persisting danger in human life. Maybe some of the examples have helped in a practical way? We have seen that false assumption can have personal consequences for individuals, cause difficulties or disaster for organisations, or change the course of history. 'Unintended consequences' often follow.

Assumptions can be:

- held by society as a whole.
- made within the state, the government, the military, etc.
- made within the professions, in business, in institutions, etc.
- made within families, small groups, clubs, etc.
- made by the individual.

As individuals, most of us live our daily lives in a flowing stream of background assumptions: the sun shall rise, tides shall ebb and flow, the Martians have not invaded in the night, our health shall persist, the train will arrive on time, the farm can pay its way, etc. It is simply impractical to be always checking such things. We have to get out and about, we cannot play too safe, we cannot cower behind the sofa. There are many fields of life where progress could not be made without some risk of making assumptions.

But which assumptions we can safely leave to themselves and which we should question is less clear. It must be a matter for our judgement. Should we examine more carefully that arrangement, that intriguing story, that person's reliability, that information, that transaction, etc? I can still hear the advice of my stepfather: 'Yes, well, let's just double-check that...' His caution went hand in hand with his career as a marine insurance lawyer in the City of London, where professionals aim to work in an assumption-free zone, I am told.

SOME SOLUTIONS It's worth knowing the many words and phrases, already listed, which can give a warning that an assumption may be in the air. I have used the synonyms of 'assumption' freely, as it is useful to recognise the many guises by which we can get caught out. It does seem that the term 'assumption' itself has only been in wide English use since some time in the nineteenth century; but it is now the most commonly used term.

Then we have those great foes of assumption who have led us to higher clearer ground, culminating in the fascinating and useful insights of Daniel Kahneman. And I highly recommend you take a look at his *Thinking, Fast and Slow.*

To reiterate what I wrote at that point, it may be not just helpful, but almost a human duty, to be aware that a distinct mechanism *does exist* for making rapid assessments, that we do have 'a machine for jumping to conclusions', as Kahneman puts it. He is not of course describing the mechanism in terms of neuroscience, but as a useful personification of a part of the mind, known as System One. The more we get to know the characteristics of System One, the more likely we are to recognise its action. Then perhaps we can slow down our thoughts, ask a question, double-check, exclaim 'hang-on-a-moment!' In other words, to think more like System Two, the other character of Kahneman's book.

But suppose we did manage to remove false assumptions from our lives – wouldn't it take away the element of surprise? Wouldn't everything end up being tiresomely predictable? No. Daniel Kahneman is not optimistic about humanity's prospect of controlling the false assumption problem.

Of all the reasons for making assumptions, a lack of communication seems to bear a heavy share of the blame. Not communicating, not conversing, not asking enough questions may be ways of avoiding effort, or of leading a quieter life, or coping with shyness or embarrassment at a particular moment. But giving in to those weaknesses should probably be resisted. Open communication, sensitive conversation, meticulous listening and the asking of careful questions, as recommended by Socrates, shall, I submit, give us at least a better chance in the endless battle against assumption.

SOURCES AND FURTHER READING

Abrutat, David *Vanguard,* 2019

Adam Smith Institute *Report on Groupthink in Academia,* 2016

Andrew, Christopher *A History of MI5,* 2009

Asprey, Robert *The Rise and Fall of Napoleon*, 2000

Baggini, Julian *A Short History of Truth,* 2017

de Beer, Sir Gavin *Alps and Elephants,* 1955

Birkenhead, Earl of *Life of Lord Halifax,* 1965

Blythe, Ronald *The Age of Illusion; England, 1919–1940,* 1963

Booker, Christopher and Richard North *The Great Deception,* 2005

Bullock, Alan *Hitler, a Study in Tyranny,* 1952

Bury, J.B. *The Idea of Progress,* 1920

Bryant, Sir Arthur *The Story of England*, 1953

Carrica, Loren *Peter the Great vs Charles XII of Sweden* University of Nebraska, 2017

Churchill, Winston *The World Crisis,* five volumes, 1923–1931

Churchill, Winston *Step by Step, 1936–1939,* 1939

Churchill, Winston *The Second World War*, six volumes, 1948–54

Clarke, I.F. *Voices Prophesying War,* 1966

FAS Army Intelligence *Field Manual 90, Battlefield Deception Fundamentals*, www.fas.org

Gibb, A.D. *With Winston Churchill at the Front,* 1924

Gibbon, Edward *The History of the Decline and Fall of the Roman Empire,*
1776–1789

Gilbert, Daniel 'How mental systems believe', in *American Psychology,* 1991

Hitler, Adolf *Mein Kampf,* 1925

Horne, Alistair *Hubris: The Tragedy of War in the Twentieth Century,* 2015

Howard, Sir Michael *Strategic Deception in World War Two,* 1990

Jenkins, Roy *Churchill,* 2002

Johnson, Samuel *The Vanity of Human Wishes,* 1749

Joll, James *The Origins of the First World War,* 1984

Kahneman, Daniel *Thinking, Fast and Slow,* 2011

Keegan, Sir John *The First World War,* 1998

Livy *History of Rome* 27–9 BC

Lunn, Sir Arnold *A Century of Mountaineering,* 1957

Lyons, Adam *The 1711 Expedition to Quebec,* 2013

Martin, Iain *Making it Happen,* 2013 (RBS collapse)

Nicolay, John and John Hay *Abraham Lincoln, a History,* 1886–1890

Nicolson, Sir Harold *The Age of Reason,* 1960

Petrov, Richard *The Black Tide,* 1968

Piccolomini, Aeneas Sylvius, Pope Pius II *Memoirs of a Renaissance Pope,*
1960

Pliny the Elder *Natural History,* AD 77

Pliny the Younger *Letters,* AD 97–109

Prebble, John *The High Girders,* 1956

RAF Historical Society *Breakout of the Scharnhorst and Gneisenau from
Brest* Journal 50

Report of the House Committee on Transportation *Boeing 737 MAX,*
2020

Roberts, Andrew *Churchill, Walking with Destiny,* 2018

Rolt, L.T.C. *Red for Danger,* 1955

Sitwell, Sir Osbert *Laughter in the Next Room,* 1949

Spinoza, Baruch *Ethics,* 1677

Strauss, David *The Life of Jesus Critically Examined,* 1835, 1846 in English

Thurber, James *What a Lovely Generalisation!* in *Thurber Country,* 1953

Tyndall, John *The Glaciers of the Alps,* 1861

Voltaire *Charles XII of Sweden,* 1731

Voltaire *The Age of Louis XIV,* 1751

Waugh, Evelyn *Ninety-two Days,* 1934

Whymper, Edward *Scrambles amongst the Alps,* 1871

Williams, Glyn *Voyages of Delusion,* 2002

Wilson, Craig *The Impact of the Torrey Canyon Disaster,* University of Montana, 1971